Scripture's Doctrine
and Theology's Bible

Scripture's Doctrine and Theology's Bible

How the NEW TESTAMENT Shapes Christian Dogmatics

Edited by

Markus Bockmuehl
and Alan J. Torrance

B)
Baker Academic
a division of Baker Publishing Group
Grand Rapids, Michigan

© 2008 by Markus Bockmuehl and Alan J. Torrance

Published by Baker Academic
a division of Baker Publishing Group
P.O. Box 6287, Grand Rapids, MI 49516-6287
www.bakeracademic.com

Printed in the United States of America

Library of Congress Cataloging-in-Publication Data
Scripture's doctrine and theology's Bible : how the New Testament shapes Christian dogmatics / edited by Markus Bockmuehl and Alan J. Torrance.
       p.   cm.
     Includes bibliographical references (p.   ) and indexes.
     ISBN 978-0-8010-3601-9 (pbk.)
       1. Theology, Doctrinal—Congresses. 2. Bible. N.T.—Theology—Congresses. 3. Bible. N.T.—Evidences, authority, etc.—Congresses. I. Bockmuehl, Markus N. A. II. Torrance, Alan J.
     BT78.S37 2008
     230'.0415—dc22   2008028126

In keeping with biblical principles of creation stewardship, Baker Publishing Group advocates the responsible use of our natural resources. As a member of the Green Press Initiative, our company uses recycled paper when possible. The text paper of this book is comprised of 30% post-consumer waste.

green press INITIATIVE

Contents

Introduction

MARKUS BOCKMUEHL

Recent years have witnessed the rapid proliferation of biblical scholarship engaged in what is called *theological interpretation*. This scholarly movement is now busy servicing a monograph series, a new journal, a major dictionary, and two commentary series,[1] not to mention numerous papers and seminars on the international conference and lecture circuit. It undoubtedly expresses a long-overdue reaction against the modernist critical excesses of twentieth-century professional guilds: poking and dissecting the biblical text on "educational" or "scientific" pretexts before publishing the carcass of "assured results," Gunther von Hagens–like, "plastinated" in contrived pseudo-lifelike positions that tended to bear little demonstrable relation to the human struggles and stories with God that actually animated these bodies and that alone can account for what they were and are.

But granted that such reductionism is intellectually and spiritually impoverished, what exactly is this newly popular phenomenon called *theological interpretation*? Is it, as the adjectival construct suggests, mainly a particular flavor or style of engaging in a familiar and self-evident task of interpreting (*interpret* is a notably transitive verb, of which Scripture remains grammatically, and one suspects hermeneutically, the object upon which one operates)? If so, is theological interpretation in that sense rather like "Cajun cooking" or

1. Studies in Theological Interpretation (Baker Academic, 2006–); *Journal of Theological Interpretation* (2007–); Kevin J. Vanhoozer, ed., *Dictionary for Theological Interpretation of the Bible* (London: SPK; Grand Rapids: Baker Academic, 2005); Brazos Theological Commentary on the Bible (Brazos Press, 2005–); The Two Horizons New Testament Commentary (Eerdmans, 2005–).

"retro design"? Alternatively, is there perhaps some sense in which the living and lived word of Scripture shapes both exegesis and theology reciprocally, and in which dogmatics articulately engages and in turn illuminates the hearing of that word?

Conceived as a contribution to the wider discussion and clarification of these questions, the present book gathers together revised papers originally presented in a unique series of seminars on the New Testament's relationship to systematic theology. Leading biblical and systematic theologians from Europe and North America came to the University of St. Andrews in the spring of 2007 to shine a probing searchlight from a variety of perspectives on a single focused question: "To what extent, and on what grounds, does the New Testament shape and prescribe Christian theology?" The serial effect of these encounters was little short of electrifying, and the resulting stimulus to debate made it clear that we should seek to make this exercise available to a wider audience.

For this publication, the contributions have been grouped into three topical sections, with the authors' expertise and reflection on the seminar's debate intended to engage both biblical and dogmatic disciplines.

Part 1, "Scripture's Doctrine," explores the question of how the Bible, and the New Testament in particular, may be understood to exert pressure on particular aspects of Christian doctrine and praxis. The contributors approach this problem from a variety of fresh and unfamiliar angles.

J. Ross Wagner's essay raises the question of how the two-testament nature of the Bible exercises its influence on Christian doctrine, given that the New Testament authors, most of the church fathers, and the Eastern churches to this day read the Greek rather than the Hebrew as the normative Old Testament of their Christian Bible. As Wagner rightly points out, the implications for Christian theology are not often taken on board. In dialogue with the work of Brevard Childs, he argues that the Septuagint highlights for theology the importance of the unfinished "search" for the Christian Bible, not least because it extends key canonical trajectories that arise from the final form of the canonical text.

Markus Bockmuehl examines the topical and heavily debated question of the New Testament foundations of ecclesiology. He takes as his starting point a debate about the New Testament's vision of the church, held nearly half a century ago between Ernst Käsemann and Raymond Brown, two giants of exegetical scholarship. It is soon evident that simple accounts of the church's unity swiftly run aground, both exegetically and indeed ecclesiologically, on the diversity of viewpoints represented within the New Testament. Nevertheless, and for all the hermeneutical potential of a conflictual or polemical reading of the New Testament's diversity, a certain ecclesial convergence can be shown to cluster around a number of key convictions, including the apostolicity (and, indeed, dominical sanction) of the church and its incorporation into the biblical story of Israel.

Walter Moberly, an Old Testament scholar, intriguingly takes as his focus the doctrinal application of the Fourth Gospel's emphasis on the exclusiveness of Christ to a contested topic in the contemporary church: the problem of interfaith dialogue, especially that between Jews and Christians. Calling into question casual assumptions about worship of "the same God" along with convenient evasions of the theological force of John 14:6 (and related passages), he demonstrates that exegetical attention to the place of this text in the Gospel compels a doctrinal appreciation for the "definitive content" of Jesus' self-giving love for others. At the same time, that content holds in tension both the particular and the universal; it is a mystery that always surpasses its particular (ecclesial) manifestations, being best captured in the historic trinitarian and incarnational doctrines. As such, it demands both doctrinal conviction and epistemological humility in interfaith dialogue.

Finally, taking the writings of the apostle Paul as his cue, N. T. Wright brings to bear his twin roles as bishop and scholar to ask how the biblical text can be encountered as challenging and life-giving word, addressing us and contributing to the formulation of creedal faith. It does so, he argues, above all in its narrative function, so that doctrine, as specially exemplified in the creeds, is best understood as "portable story"—not as an abstract checklist but as expressive of the narrative of the New Testament as a whole, indeed of the overall story of Israel. The place where Scripture most properly functions in that way is the worshiping congregation's central participation in the Eucharist; and it is this latter "portable story" that ought to shape not just academic debate but also the contemporary expressions of the church's corporate life.

Part 2 turns from the analysis of the Bible's own doctrine-evoking witness to a critical reflection on how some of the most influential theologians of the last hundred years have been shaped and engaged by what they encountered in the New Testament.

Chronologically, we move to contemporary theology from several leading twentieth-century theologians and theological movements that attempted not only to respond to advances in modern critical scholarship but also to break deliberately with the intellectual heritage of nineteenth-century liberal idealism in order to return to a more radical engagement with the Bible (a radicalness conceived, to be sure, in very different terms).

Engaging one of the most influential liberal theological and philosophical thinkers of the first half of the last century, James Carleton Paget analyzes Albert Schweitzer's (1875–1965) seemingly strict historical and antidoctrinal engagement with Jesus (and Paul). This study demonstrates that despite his assertions of disdain for ecclesial and creedal dogma of all kinds, Schweitzer shows a surprisingly personal and "mystical" fascination with the character (the "will") of Jesus. This engendered in him a fervent philosophical and theological advocacy of the ongoing importance of the person of Jesus (and Paul, as a thinker) for the present—a "Christology" rather higher, perhaps, than he himself allowed.

A very different reaction to nineteenth-century liberalism is encountered in the work of Schweitzer's younger contemporary Karl Barth (1886–1968). Jan Muis examines Scripture's role for doctrine and tradition in the work of Barth as well as of Friedrich Mildenberger (b. 1929), perhaps the German systematician most directly concerned with "biblical dogmatics" in the generation after Barth. Barth engages with Scripture extensively but uses it indirectly as a witness to God's self-revelation rather than as directly prescriptive for Christian doctrine. For Mildenberger, by contrast, there can in fact be no adequate God-talk at all without and apart from the biblical text (interpreted in keeping with confessions of the early church, the Reformation, and Barmen), which describes the events in which God is either present or absent. Dogmatics, for him, is reflection on biblical texts in their diversity; biblical texts are not foundations or guidelines for doctrinal answers but rather are the answers themselves. Neither author, in Muis's view, provides a consistent application of his stated principles: there is in fact more biblical heteronomy in Barth and more dogmatic structure in Mildenberger than either explicitly allows. Scripture is, in that sense, *indirectly* prescriptive for doctrine, while a biblically founded exegesis of the New Testament texts will, in all their diversity, bring into focus the living Jesus Christ.

John Webster's chapter provides a powerful exposé of one of the most fruitful and prolific theological writers of our own day. Rowan Williams (b. 1950) is not only Anglicanism's most senior bishop but also one of the English-speaking world's most influential theologians. Revelation, for him, is the community's temporal transfiguration through the appropriation of the infinitely resourceful Christ, whose relation with the Father reaches out to us in human time. Scripture serves as a sign of this new, living postresurrection relationship, spelling out imaginative patterns of Jesus as both alive to God and present with us. These "fugal" patterns of theology appear, however, on a wider, aggressively political canvas of conflict, suppression, and exclusion in which Scripture—along with its authors and readers—is complicit. Although sympathetic to these concerns, Webster asks if Williams's account in the end underplays the possibilities of divine intentionality behind the canon, of attending to the perfection of the ascended Jesus in the exercise of his royal and prophetic offices, and of the Christian specificity of scriptural interpretation.

After three chapters on the New Testament's authority for theologies in the Protestant tradition, Benedict Viviano offers a fourth on the normativity of Scripture and tradition in the last century of Roman Catholic theology. Beginning with M.-J. Lagrange's pioneering work in the face of Pope Pius X's resistance, Viviano traces the Catholic recovery of literary and historical sensitivity to the biblical text in the 1943 encyclical *Divino Afflante Spiritu* to its reception in subsequent debate about the relationship between Scripture and tradition. Particular reference is made here to the controversy surrounding the dogma of the assumption of Mary and to the work of J. R. Geiselmann. The Second Vatican Council's landmark statement *Dei Verbum* issued significant clarifications about the relationship of Scripture and tradition, biblical inerrancy in matters of salvation, and the reliability of the Gospels. Viviano concludes his survey with considerations of the Pontifical Biblical Commission's recent work and of the profound impact of the revised liturgical lectionary.

Part 3 moves from analysis to the more synthetic question of how in practice we are to envisage the New Testament's normative function for Christian theology and ethics.

Alan J. Torrance begins by drawing attention to the important problem of methodological slippage in much New Testament study of even mildly confessional bent: supposedly historical and descriptive treatments of Christian origins remarkably often move in a concluding flourish from second-order, phenomenological talk *about* early Christian God-talk to first-order, normative God-talk without stopping to acknowledge the hermeneutical sleight of hand. After examining some of the philosophical issues at stake, Torrance draws on Athanasius and Kierkegaard in developing the proposition that the exegetical move to valid God-talk requires a hermeneutical fusion of (not two, but) three horizons involving Scripture, the contemporary reader, and the ecclesial mind—conceived in irreducibly trinitarian and incarnational terms.

Oliver O'Donovan turns next to the timely but ticklish question of Scripture's authority in moral theology. Scripture is divinely set apart (hence "sanctified," in John Webster's usage) for its task as an integral part of God's self-attestation in the election of Israel and redemption of the world, the parts to be understood in relation both to the particularity and to the whole. Yet in contrast to Karl Barth's notion of the immediacy of the divine command, O'Donovan recognizes the need for biblical categories and analogies in order to be able to understand our own practical situation vis-à-vis the scriptural command, which by itself may often be quite bare. Thoughtful and faithful obedience, therefore, will express the mind-renewing "rational worship" of Romans 12:2.

Taking a similar focus on the problem of scriptural normativity in Christian moral theology, Bernd Wannenwetsch follows O'Donovan's programmatic chapter by posing the more specific question of what formal and methodological perspectives the New Testament itself envisages and exemplifies in Christian moral teaching. He argues that one can discern a circular hermeneutic of moral and spiritual perception, discernment, judgment, and giving of account. Drawing on key texts including Romans 12:1–2, Philippians 1:9, and the parable of the good Samaritan (Luke 10), he shows this sequence of moral reasoning to be deeply engrained in the New Testament witness.

Our volume concludes, as the St. Andrews seminar series did, with a wide-ranging and synthetic statement from Kevin J. Vanhoozer. Whereas C. H. Dodd recognized in the sermons of the book of Acts an apostolic *kerygma* shared with Paul and the Gospels, Vanhoozer employs the wider-ranging and more inclusive term of the New Testament's apostolic *discourse*. Biblical and dogmatic theology are here engaged neither as separate enterprises nor on a one-way conveyor belt but rather in a *pas de deux* that has both parties alternately leading and following in a common engagement with the human and the divine discourse. The church-building task of understanding the normativity of this apostolic discourse is to engage the many diverse parts of a whole, like the rooms in the heavenly mansion.

As editors and contributors alike, we are only too aware that what we offer here is eclectic, partial, and limited. It is an album of views through the shared window around which we happen to have gathered in our 2007 seminar—a window, one might say using a familiar St. Andrews image, with a view on the grippingly evocative ruins of a once-cherished cathedral. If that image appears in some circles as emblematic of much of the church's life in the contemporary West,[2] it arguably also captures something of the state of biblical studies and dogmatics today. There are, of course, signs of renewed activity, perhaps even of new life, not least in the "theological interpretation" enterprises cited above. But there also remains a powerful impression of theological subdisciplines fractured in their internal discourse and fraught in their intellectual relations with each other.[3]

If, then, our shared window shows diverse views of a ruined cathedral, it offers at the same time signs of promise, not only in being shared between us but also in revealing certain common impulses of investigation. These include, above all, the sense of growing urgency for each of our subdisciplines to account for its work in heedfulness of the concerns and questions of the other. To be intellectually and theologically viable, the "portability" of doctrines, creeds, and practices will necessarily be a function of their rootedness in the concrete particularity of the scriptural texts. More simply put, to the extent that theologians are not answerable to a biblical account of doctrine, their work is no longer based on Christianity's historic creeds and confessions. But conversely, no exegetical or historical engagement with that biblical address can do justice even to itself, let alone to the object of those texts, without a conscious recognition of how the critical analysis of any one part relates to the equally concrete reality of the whole. Similarly, the very methods and strategies of the biblical scholar's questioning inevitably presuppose a more

2. See, for example, Radner 2004; Reno 2002.
3. For an analysis of the aporetic state of New Testament studies and suggestions for the possible recovery of a common conversation, see Bockmuehl 2006.

self-involving and theologically vested set of aims and categories than most critics are generally prepared to acknowledge.

The way forward, we are united in believing, lies in the critical rediscovery of an old friendship: the ecclesial *pas de deux* of exegesis with theology, of Scripture with the Christian tradition of confession and discipleship. It is that critical task which the following chapters seek, severally and as a whole, both to commend and to exemplify.

In preparing this book for the press, I have benefited greatly from the unwavering support of my fellow editor and the contributors. Others who made this book better than it could otherwise have been include enthusiastic seminar participants and postgraduate respondents to each of our speakers; my doctoral student David Lincicum generously and astutely assisted the task of editorial proofreading. To them all, and to the visionary Jim Kinney and his colleagues at Baker Academic, heartfelt thanks are due.

PART 1

Scripture's Doctrine

1

The Septuagint and the "Search for the Christian Bible"

J. ROSS WAGNER

IN MEMORIAM BREVARD CHILDS (1923–2007)

Any attempt to elucidate how the two Testaments of the Christian Bible, individually and together, testify to the redeeming work of the Triune God must sooner or later address the question of the authority of the Septuagint as a witness to the biblical text and thus as a resource for doing Christian theology.[1] The question persists because, as Brevard Childs has observed, "the exact nature of the Christian Bible both in respect to its scope and text remains undecided up to this day."[2] Consequently, though it is often ignored, the complex problem of the Septuagint as Christian Scripture cannot simply be sidestepped by Christian theology. As Childs demonstrates through a masterful survey of the history of interpretation of Isaiah, a characteristic

---

1. In this essay the term *Old Greek* is reserved for the putative original translation of a particular book. The term *Septuagint* is employed in two ways: first, to refer to the broad stream of transmission of the Old Greek text, including efforts to revise the Old Greek to bring it into closer conformity to a Hebrew exemplar; second, to refer more generally to the books that are eventually collected (though never in a single standardized form) as the Greek Bible.

2. Childs 1992: 63.

feature of the church's theological reading of Scripture in every age has been thoughtful engagement with the hermeneutical problem posed by the diverse transmission of the two-testament biblical canon, "a struggle for understanding" that wrestles vigorously with "the textual tension between the Hebrew and Greek."[3] This "*search* for the Christian Bible" is, he argues, "constitutive for Christian faith" and, as such, "constitutive of the theological task."[4] That so few biblical scholars and theologians in our period of church history actually grapple with the question of the Septuagint has less to do with ignorance of the hermeneutical problem, I would venture, than with the fact that few of us are trained for a serious engagement with these Greek texts. As Hans Hübner wryly observes, the translation of the Seventy has become for most Western Christians a "book with seven seals."[5]

Following Childs, I propose locating the question of the authority of the Septuagint in Christian theology squarely in the context of the *search* for the Christian Bible. As the church seeks rightly to hear and obediently to conform its life to God's salvific address spoken through the two-testament Christian Bible, how are we to grapple with what Childs has described as "the textual tension between the Hebrew and the Greek"?[6]

The Search for "the Septuagint"

In taking up this question, we must first of all clear away some misconceptions and lay the groundwork for the constructive proposal that will follow. Christopher Seitz rightly observes that the problem of the Septuagint has at times been framed in quite simplistic and misleading terms, as if the church stood between a supposedly monolithic "Greek Bible" and a similarly petrified "Hebrew Bible" and had to choose one to the exclusion of the other.[7] The reality, as scholars representing a variety of viewpoints have increasingly recognized, is far more complex:

3. Childs 2004: 313. A case in point is the sharp disagreement between Augustine and Jerome over the latter's decision to base his Latin translation on a Hebrew text rather than on the Septuagint. Yet even as he vigorously defended the Septuagint as inspired Scripture, Augustine (*De civitate Dei* 18.42–44) continued to affirm the authority of the Hebrew text. And Jerome, for his part, when commenting on Isaiah, interprets the Septuagint alongside the Hebrew. (On Jerome's theologically sophisticated handling of the important differences between the Masoretic Text and the Septuagint at Isa. 6:9–10, see Childs 2004: 94.)

4. Childs 1992: 67–68 (italics in original).

5. Hübner 1990: 1.62.

6. I offer my sincere thanks to the members of the joint Biblical/Systematic Theology Seminar at the University of St. Andrews, and especially to Professor Markus Bockmuehl and to my respondents, Daniel Driver and David Lincicum, for stimulating discussion that has pressed me to sharpen my thinking at a number of points. However, much as I might wish to shift the blame, I alone am responsible for any deficiencies that remain in the argument that follows.

7. Seitz 2001: 90–96.

1. There existed in the Hellenistic and Roman periods no single "Septuagint" canon or text. Apart from the books of the Pentateuch, which may have been translated in roughly the same period (though by different translators), the books commonly grouped under the label "Septuagint" were translated (and in a few cases composed) at various times and in different locations by a variety of translators using a range of approaches to their task. Any standardization of the collection is a rather late achievement. The earliest codices (fourth to fifth centuries and later) vary both in which books are included in the Old Testament and in what order they are arranged.[8]

Similarly, witnesses to the textual tradition of the Septuagint exhibit a significant degree of diversity in their readings. This is attributable not simply to the normal vagaries of textual transmission in antiquity but also to a number of additional factors, including ongoing sporadic revisions, almost from the very beginning, intended to bring the Old Greek closer to a Hebrew form of the text;[9] the text-critical labors of Origen in the third century, which resulted in a mixture of Old Greek with later revisions and translations of Scripture; and still later recensional work on the Greek text attributed by Jerome to Lucian and Hesychius.[10] An examination of explicit quotations in the New Testament uncovers citations that reproduce the Old Greek nearly verbatim as well as those that reflect a Septuagint text previously revised toward a Hebrew exemplar.[11] A smaller number of citations apparently draw on otherwise unknown Greek translations.[12] There is, then, for early Christian writers no single "Septuagint" text. Rather, the New Testament witnesses to a certain diversity and fluidity of the biblical text in Greek, including a persistent tendency, already underway well before the rise of Christianity, to bring the Greek text into closer conformity to a (proto-Masoretic) Hebrew text.[13]

2. It would be wrong to suppose that "the Septuagint" represents an alternative tradition disconnected from—and, indeed, in competition with—the Hebrew Scriptures. As already mentioned, from the very beginning the Greek text was to one degree or another subjected to revision on the basis of Hebrew exemplars; in other words, as Robert Hanhart observes, it was from

8. See Swete 1900: 197–230.

9. See further Hanhart 1984 (reprinted in Hanhart 1999: 194–213); 2002.

10. Evidence for a "Hesychian" recension continues to be debated. On the history of the origin and transmission of the Greek versions, see Fernández Marcos 2001.

11. See, for example, for Paul, Koch 1986; for 1 Peter, Jobes 2006; for Matthew, Menken 2004.

12. For example, Isa. 6:10 in John 12:39–41; cf. Mark 8:17–21; Rom. 11:7–8. See the detailed treatment of these texts in Menken 1988; Wagner 2002: 246–51.

13. At the same time, the degree of fluidity in the Greek text should not be exaggerated. Paul's citations from Psalms, and to a lesser extent those from Isaiah, attest the continuing survival in the middle of the first century of what is essentially the Old Greek text of these books. See Silva 2001; on the text of Old Greek Isaiah in Paul, see Wilk 2006; cf. Wagner 2002: 24n86.

the beginning treated as a "copy" of an "original" text.[14] This attitude did not prevail at all times and in all places, as the *Letter of Aristeas* and Philo's account of the divinely inspired translation of the Pentateuch attest.[15] But even in the *Letter of Aristeas*, which seeks to legitimate the Septuagint as Scripture in its own right, the authority of the Greek Pentateuch rests on its being an accurate representation of its Hebrew *Vorlage*, the impeccable character of which is guaranteed by its having been sent from Jerusalem by the high priest himself. Hanhart comments, "As a translation of already canonized writings, the LXX translation itself has canonical significance both for Judaism and for the Christian church. It derives this significance, however, only from the strength of the canonical authority of its Hebrew original."[16]

Of course, in practical terms, Greek-speaking Jews and Christians often lacked the linguistic resources to make comparisons directly with Hebrew texts, and for all intents and purposes the Greek text that they heard in worship *was* Scripture. Nevertheless, the close connection of the Greek text to the Hebrew was often recognized even where the Greek was regarded as a sacred text in its own right. I have already mentioned the use of revised Septuagint texts by New Testament writers. In the case of Paul, at least, one may suggest with some confidence that the apostle's occasional citation of a revised manuscript of Isaiah reflects his deliberate selection of one form of the text from among a number of different versions known to him.[17] Among the church fathers, Origen by no means stands alone in his recognition that the Septuagint is a translation and that understanding of the biblical text may be enhanced by reference to other Greek versions, if not, ideally, to the Hebrew itself.[18] In his commentary on Isaiah, for example, Theodoret turns regularly to Aquila or another of the later translators to help elucidate a passage that is obscure in the

14. See Hanhart 2002: 5–9.

15. The *Letter of Aristeas* may plausibly be read, at least in part, as a defense of "the Septuagint" against those revisers who sought to conform the translation more closely to a proto-Masoretic form of the text (Müller 1996: 46–58). Philo's account of the translation portrays the translators as inspired prophets. On Philo and on later elaborations of the miraculous nature of the translation, see Müller 1996: 61–64, 68–97.

16. Hanhart 2002: 5. According to Emanuel Tov (2005: 385), increasing discomfort with the Septuagint in rabbinic circles stemmed from "the growing recognition that the content of the Septuagint version differed from the Hebrew text that was in use in Palestine in the last centuries BCE and the first centuries CE." Rabbinic sources evince positive attitudes toward the Septuagint (e.g., *m. Megillah* 1:8, where Greek is said to be the only other language in which the Torah may be written; *b. Megillah* 9a, which presents the translators as infused with divine wisdom) together with criticisms of the translators' divergences from the Hebrew text (*b. Megillah* 9a–b). As Martin Hengel (2002: 44) observes, the harshest polemics appear rather late (*Soferim* 1:6–7; *Sefer Torah* 1:8; *Megillat Ta'anit Batra* 21).

17. See Hengel 2002: 108 (contra Koch 1986: 81); cf. Wagner 2002: 22n82.

18. "The church fathers presumed the authority of the Septuagint, but they did not confuse authority with clarity. Some Greek words posed problems, and recourse to the Hebrew held out hope of shedding light on difficult words" (O'Keefe and Reno 2005: 50).

Septuagint or to add a further layer of meaning to the biblical text.[19] Eusebius not infrequently offers interpretations both of the Septuagint and of another version (such as Symmachus) without, apparently, feeling it necessary to prefer one to the other.[20] Similarly, Christian manuscripts of the Septuagint betray the interest of scribes and scholars in the Hebrew text behind the translation, as seen for example, in the inclusion of marginal references to other versions (and even to "the Hebrew") or in the attempt to mark instances where κύριος represents the Hebrew name for God, "ΠΙΠΙ (= יהוה)."[21]

3. Despite the truism that every translation is an interpretation, the Septuagint, on the whole, renders the Hebrew in a fairly conservative manner. Anneli Aejmelaeus quite rightly observes that a theology of the Septuagint in the sense of "a comprehensive presentation of the religious and theological content of the Septuagint . . . would actually be for the most part identical with a theology of the [Hebrew] Old Testament."[22] It was once (and in some quarters still is) thought appropriate to speak of a characteristic "Septuagint piety."[23] However, because the Septuagint is a translation, rather than an original composition, discovering the distinctive theology of a Septuagint book is an endeavor fraught with considerable conceptual and practical challenges. The clearest evidence of a translator's own distinctive theological outlook is to be found in instances where one can be reasonably sure that the translator's rendering does not reflect a variant Hebrew *Vorlage* or does not simply result from his default method of translating. Such clear cases of deliberate exegesis by the Septuagint translators, however, are rather more difficult to identify than is often supposed.[24]

Moreover, in this bright post-Hengel epoch one can no longer posit a clear and strict separation between "Judaism" and "Hellenism," or between Palestine and the Diaspora, or between Hebrew/Aramaic-speaking and Greek-speaking Judaisms (or Christianities, for that matter).[25] Where the Septuagint does offer evidence of interpretive traditions that go beyond what is found in

19. For example, at Isa. 8:15 Theodoret adduces the readings of Symmachus and Aquila in order to clarify the meaning of the Septuagint (Theodoret, *Commentary on Isaiah* on Isa. 8:15 [= Guinot 1980: 310]).

20. See, for example, Eusebius's comments on Isa. 8:11–13 (Eusebius, *Commentary on Isaiah* on Isa. 8:11–13 [= Ziegler 1975: 58]).

21. See Swete 1900: 39–40n4; Metzger 1981: 33–35.

22. Aejmelaeus 2006b: 23 (my translation); cf. Childs (1979: 664): "When viewed in the light of the entire canonical process, the formal differences between the two Bibles—text, scope, order—appear as minor variations within the one unified body of sacred tradition."

23. See Bertram 1961. Recent advocates of such a concept include Hans Hübner (1990: 1.61–62) and, in more nuanced form, Joachim Schaper (2006: 379–80). For objections to Bertram's views, see van der Kooij 1997: 9–10.

24. See further Aejmelaeus 2006b; Aejmelaeus forthcoming; Boyd-Taylor 2006; Pietersma 2006; Wagner 2007. A more optimistic perspective is offered by Rösel 2006.

25. Hengel (2002) continues to emphasize these points in his recent work on the Septuagint.

the Masoretic Text, in some cases these traditions find clear parallels in other Jewish texts written in Hebrew, Aramaic, or Greek.[26] Even at a point where the influence of the Septuagint on the development of Hellenistic Judaism appears to be both unmistakable and of great significance for early Christian theology—the rendering of the Tetragrammaton by the Greek word κύριος—the Septuagint depends on and remains connected to Hebrew/Aramaic-speaking Jewish tradition.[27]

This is not to downplay the significance of the Septuagint for the development of Hellenistic Jewish thought. Neither would I wish to deny the importance of the translation of Israel's Scriptures into Greek for the spread of Judaism among pagan sympathizers and proselytes,[28] nor to maintain that the reception of these Greek Scriptures by the early church had only a negligible influence on the development of early Christian practice and belief.[29] It is necessary, however, to insist that the historical picture is far more complex than is often recognized in debates over "the Hebrew" versus "the Greek" text and canon. One cannot neatly separate Greek-speaking Judaism from other Hebrew/Aramaic-speaking Judaisms of the Hellenistic period. It is dangerously reductionistic thinking to imagine that the early church faced a clear and decisive choice between the supposed universalism of a Hellenistic-Jewish "Septuagint piety" and the alleged narrow particularism of a (Pharisaic-rabbinic) Judaism rooted in the Hebrew Bible.[30]

4. Finally, regarding the tension between a wider "Septuagint canon" and the narrower canon of the Masoretic Text, it is crucial to emphasize that although the outer limits of the canon remain somewhat nebulous in the early Christian

26. For example, according to Schaper (2006: 376), the Isaiah Targum often "makes more explicit" an interpretive tradition "already present in the Septuagint." Tov (2005: 391, 388) claims that although the Septuagint evinces "only a thin layer of Jewish exegesis," it "shows more links with rabbinic interpretations than the other Greek versions."

27. See Hanhart 2002: 7–8. Compare the early use of Aramaic מרא in devotional address to Jesus (1 Cor. 16:22). See further Fitzmyer 1979.

28. As Hübner 1990: 1.57, 64 rightly emphasizes.

29. Quite the opposite is the case with regard to, for example, Paul's appropriation of Isaiah. See Wagner 2002; Wilk 1998.

30. This way of stating the matter is hardly a caricature of the issue as it has sometimes been framed in the scholarly literature. Dominique Barthélemy (1978: 138), for example, speaks of the Septuagint as an "attempt to enter into dialogue with Hellenism" and claims that "the church is the inheritor of the great openness towards the nations that the Septuagint was" (I owe the reference and translation to Barr 1999: 577). Such a characterization of the Septuagint requires considerable nuancing, to say the least. The Greek version of Isaiah, for instance, often appears far less universalistic in outlook than does its Hebrew counterpart: "It is often with respect to Hebrew Isaiah's most generous statements to and about the nations that the [Greek] translator shows a reluctance that at points comes close to hostility" (Baer 2001: 199). A striking example is the rendering of Old Greek Isa. 19:24–25. In the Masoretic Text the oracle speaks of God's redemption of Assyria and Egypt, but the Old Greek restricts the promise of salvation to the Jewish Diaspora in these lands.

period, the New Testament authors appeal through their citations and retellings of the biblical narratives to a core set of Scriptures that includes a majority of the books of the present Hebrew canon. If *Enoch* is invoked as Scripture (Jude 14), it is the only example of a book outside the Hebrew canon being cited as such in the New Testament. The numerous New Testament echoes (varying widely in volume) of books such as Wisdom of Solomon or Sirach certainly are significant for understanding the development of New Testament theology, but they function on a different level, rhetorically and theologically, from that of the explicit citations. Similarly, although the church has never come to a consensus on the precise limits of the canon, there remains an undeniable core that decisively shapes the contours of mainstream Christian practice and belief. Despite their often sharp disagreements concerning the shape and function of the canon, both Brevard Childs and James Barr agree that this canonical core has been far more determinative of orthodox Christian faith and life than any of the writings lying close to the periphery of the tradition.[31]

The Place of the Septuagint in the Search for the Christian Bible

Recalling Childs's observation that "the exact nature of the Christian Bible both in respect to its scope and text remains undecided to this day,"[32] we return to the question with which we began: How, in the theological task of wrestling with Scripture in all its complexity—in our "search for the Christian Bible"—are we to hear the Septuagint as Christian Scripture?

Childs, in *Biblical Theology of the Old and New Testaments*, charts a promising course through these murky waters. He depicts the search for the Christian Bible as a dialectic between Word and Tradition—between the Old Testament in its most pristine, Hebrew, form and the church's early and widespread practice of receiving the Old Testament in its most expansive, Greek, form.[33] Moving "from the outer parameters of tradition to the inner parameters of Word,"[34] the interpreter works "theologically within the narrower and wider forms of the canon in search for both the truth and the catholicity of the biblical witness to the church and the world."[35] This search for the witness of

31. Childs 1992: 66–68; Barr 1999: 572–76.

32. Childs 1992: 63.

33. Childs 1992: 64–68. Childs bases his argument for the status of the Septuagint not only on the New Testament use of the Septuagint but also on the argument from catholicity—that is, the reception of the Septuagint by the most ancient Christian congregations.

34. Childs 1992: 68.

35. Childs 1992: 67. The position that Childs stakes out here is more complex and sophisticated than his earlier statement in Childs 1979: 659–71. For an illuminating analysis of the evolution of Childs's views, see the forthcoming doctoral dissertation by Daniel Driver (University of St. Andrews, 2008), provisionally entitled "Brevard Childs: On the Logic of Scripture's Textual Authority in the Mystery of Christ."

the Old Testament, interestingly, corresponds closely to Childs's description of New Testament textual criticism from a canonical perspective.[36] Here, "the *search* for the best canonical text within the circle established by the church's tradition takes place within the context of the multiple textual options which have actually been used in the church."[37] New Testament textual criticism is thus "a *continuing search* in discerning the best received text which moves from the outer parameters of the common church tradition found in the *textus receptus* to the inner judgment respecting its purity."[38] It would appear, then, that the extent to which the Septuagint speaks as Christian Scripture must be determined in the same manner as the Word of God is apprehended in the voice of the Hebrew text or in the New Testament: "The complete canon of the Christian church . . . sets for the community of faith the proper theological context in which we stand, but it also remains continually the object of critical theological scrutiny subordinate to its subject matter who is Jesus Christ."[39]

As I read Childs, it seems clear that the theological task that he describes as "the search for the Christian Bible" requires full consideration of the Septuagint as part of the "complete canon of the Christian church," even though it may be thought in some respects to lie at "the outer parameters of tradition."[40] But how is this to be carried out in practice? Childs sketches a model of theological interpretation comprising three discrete stages: (1) discerning the witness of the Old Testament itself; (2) examining the New Testament in its own integrity as a witness that largely transforms the Old Testament; (3) "hearing the whole of Christian Scripture in light of the full reality of God in Jesus Christ."[41] Due to its considerable influence on the New Testament, the Septuagint obviously requires careful attention in the second stage of Childs's program. But in the context of the search for the Christian Bible (not simply New Testament), the Septuagint is also pertinent to the first task of discerning the witness of the Old Testament itself. It figures as well in the final step of Childs's program, in which the interpreter seeks to hear the Old Testament and the New Testament in concert as distinct, and yet complementary, witnesses. We will consider each of these stages briefly.

36. Childs 1985: 518–30.
37. Childs 1985: 529 (italics added).
38. Childs 1985: 529 (italics added). The context makes it clear that by "purity" Childs means "the truest witness to the gospel": "The process of seeking to discern the truest witness to the gospel from within the church's multiple traditions functions to remind the interpreter of the canonical corpus that the element of theological interpretation is not only constitutive of the church's scriptures in general, but has also entered into the textual dimensions of the tradition as well" (Childs 1985: 529).
39. Childs 1992: 67–68.
40. Similarly Seitz (2006: 96): "Following Augustine, a canonical approach will acknowledge the Holy Spirit's activity in both Hebrew and Greek canons, which guide and constrain the Church's reflection and confession."
41. Childs 1992: 87.

1. As the earliest commentary on the Hebrew text, the Septuagint certainly provides a valuable resource for interpreting the per se witness of the Old Testament. But apart from its pride of place in the *Wirkungsgeschichte* of the Hebrew Bible, the Septuagint also demands consideration in the search for the final form of the canonical (Christian) text. This is so, first, in cases where the Septuagint translates a Hebrew *Vorlage* different from the Masoretic Text. At times, the Septuagint may provide evidence of a stage of the Hebrew text earlier than that of the final form preserved in the Masoretic Text, as in 1 Samuel 17–18 or the book of Jeremiah. Alternatively, the Septuagint may reflect an edition of the Hebrew text later than the Masoretic Text, as in 1 Samuel 1–2. In the case of Daniel 4–6, the Septuagint and the Masoretic Text apparently offer two different versions of a common earlier edition that no longer survives.[42] Even if the form attested in the Septuagint were not ultimately to be accepted (a matter that cannot be decided on a priori grounds), the Septuagint offers crucial evidence for tracing the traditioning process that culminated in the final form of the canonical text.[43] The search for the Christian Bible therefore must seek to discern whether the form preserved in the Septuagint or the form preserved in the Masoretic Text, or perhaps both, represents "Israel's witness to God and his Messiah."[44]

But the Septuagint is also relevant to the search for the final form of a biblical book in those cases where the Greek translators themselves extend theological trajectories that are inscribed in the final form of the Hebrew text. One thinks of, for example, Joachim Schaper's identification (following William Horbury) of a robust "messianic intertextuality" in Old Greek Isaiah or his arguments concerning the heightening of eschatological and messianic expectations in the Old Greek Psalter.[45] Apart from the obvious relevance of the Septuagint shape of these books for the question of the reception of the Old Testament in the New, Childs's notion of the search for the Christian Bible requires that one consider the claims of the Greek version in determining the canonical form of a book in the context of the church's Bible. The greater part of this task remains to be done. Recent attention to the formation of the book of Psalms, for example, has stimulated fruitful reflection on the theological significance of the shape of the Masoretic Text Psalter. However, the question of the shape of the Septuagint Psalter and the "pressure" exerted by *its* final form on the

---

42. Examples from Ulrich 1992 (reprinted in Ulrich 1999: 51–78). Ulrich (1999: 73) emphasizes that in these instances "the creative, secondary editorial work was already done at the Hebrew (or, for Daniel, Aramaic) level within the Jewish community." See further Schenker 2003.

43. See Childs 1979: 95.

44. The phrase is one definition Childs gives of what he means by the per se witness of the Old Testament (Childs 1992: 722); cf. "Israel's voice of direct discourse proclaiming the promise" (Childs 1992: 722).

45. Schaper 1995; 2006. Cf. Gzella 2002.

contours of the biblical witness[46] has not yet been adequately addressed in the search for the canonical shape of the Christian Psalter.[47] Although it is by no means clear that one will always, or ever, decide in favor of the Septuagint form as the truest representative of the witness of the Old Testament to the Triune God, it belongs to the church's theological task to struggle with the question.

2. For the theological task of hearing the New Testament witness, especially to the extent that it is appropriate to characterize that witness as "a transformed Old Testament,"[48] the relevance of the Septuagint hardly requires further comment. It should be emphasized, however, that the influence of the Septuagint extends beyond explicit citations to more allusive modes of intertextuality.[49] In addition, the language of the Septuagint (whether the Septuagint is the source of new senses for particular Greek words or a witness to usages already current in Hellenistic Jewish communities)[50] has shaped, in varying degrees, the language of the New Testament writers. Though investigation of linguistic influence calls for considerable methodological sophistication, such research is essential to the task of delineating the full extent to which the Old Testament is taken up and transformed in the New Testament.[51] Tuning our ears to the rhythms and cadences of the Septuagint is a necessary exercise in gaining the reader competence that the New Testament expects of its implied audience.[52]

3. When one finally takes up the challenge of the synthetic task, that of hearing the witness of the Old and New Testaments together "in the light of the full reality of God in Jesus Christ" through a process of figural reading,[53] the Septuagint once again deserves serious attention. Certainly in the history of the church's wrestling with the scriptural text, the Septuagint has played an important role in such figural interpretation of the Old Testament, and this history ought to shape the contemporary church's readings in significant ways.[54]

---

46. "When the early church spoke of the coercion or pressure exerted by the biblical text on the reader, it was a formulation grounded on the conviction that the written Word possessed a voice constantly empowered by God's Spirit" (Childs 2004: 296). On the importance of pneumatology for an account of the "sanctification" of the Septuagint, and thus of its theological authority, see the concluding section of this essay.

47. The impressive commentary by Frank-Lothar Hossfeld and Erich Zenger (2005) devotes an unusual amount of attention to the Septuagint under the rubric of reception history, but the authors do not raise the question of the significance of the Septuagint for discerning the shape of the Psalter.

48. Childs 1992: 721. Cf. Hübner 1990: 1.67.

49. See especially the now classic study Hays 1989.

50. For the latter, see Aejmelaeus 2006a.

51. Jobes and Silva 2000: 258–72.

52. On becoming the sort of readers implicitly addressed by the New Testament texts, see Bockmuehl 2006.

53. Childs 1992: 87. See further Wilken 1997.

54. How the modern church may critically appropriate the best insights from its long tradition of theological interpretation is thoughtfully explored in Davis and Hays 2003.

And, to the extent that our theological task is not simply to reproduce the interpretations of the past but rather to listen attentively to the divine speech addressed to us here and now through the text of Scripture, we ourselves will have to grapple anew with the Septuagint as a resource for discerning the witness of the two-testament Christian Bible to the Triune God.[55]

If I have understood Childs rightly, in each of these three stages it is only by actually engaging in the interpretive task that one is able to discern in what ways and to what extent the Septuagint embodies the witness of the Old Testament to the reality of the Triune God that is the subject matter of the Bible. This search for the Christian Bible is not an optional pursuit; it is intrinsic to the theological interpretation of Scripture. At the conclusion of his wide-ranging study of the church's "struggle to understand Isaiah as Christian Scripture," Childs identifies a number of "basic features of enduring theological concern" that have shaped Christian exegesis through the ages.[56] Among these is an unwavering "commitment to the canonical coherence of scripture's twofold witness"[57] that compels sustained attention to "the hermeneutical problem raised by the textual tension between the Hebrew and Greek."[58] If our interpretations are to bear the "family resemblance" of the Christian exegetical tradition, we too must be willing to wrestle seriously with the Septuagint in the search for the Christian Bible.[59]

The Septuagint and the "Sanctification" of Scripture

I suggest, finally, that John Webster's dogmatic category of the "sanctification" of Holy Scripture specifies how the Septuagint—this variegated collection of translations and revisions of the Old Testament in Greek—may, within the church's ongoing search for the Christian Bible, legitimately be recognized as a norm for Christian faith and practice. As Webster defines it, "'Holy Scripture' is a shorthand term for the nature and function of the biblical writings in a set of communicative acts that stretch from God's merciful self-manifestation to the obedient hearing of the community of faith."[60] In this gracious act of

---

55. This, of course, is what many Eastern Christians continue to do today as they read and hear the Greek text of the Old Testament as Holy Scripture. How renewed attentiveness to the Septuagint by Western Christians may reshape our reading of the Christian Bible and enrich our understanding and articulation of Christian doctrine is a question that can be answered only as we in the West begin to engage these texts once again.

56. Childs 2004: 299–324.

57. Childs 2004: 312.

58. Childs 2004: 313.

59. Efforts currently underway to produce reliable and accessible translations of the Septuagint in several modern languages thus hold promise for the church as well as the academy (Harl 1986–; Kraus and Karrer forthcoming; Pietersma and Wright 2007).

60. Webster 2003: 5.

redemptive self-communication, God speaks in and through texts that at the same time remain very much human artifacts. The "sanctification" of Scripture refers to the Spirit's "election and overseeing of the entire historical course of the creaturely reality so that it becomes a creature which may serve the purposes of God."[61] "Because sanctification does not diminish creatureliness," Webster argues, "the texts' place in the divine economy does not entail their withdrawal from the realm of human processes. It is *as*—not *despite*—the creaturely realities that they are that they serve God."[62]

The concept of sanctification is crucial for any account of the Christian Bible that takes seriously both its normative role as Holy Scripture and the complexities of its text and canon, including the tensions between its Greek and Hebrew forms. As Webster explains,

> The Spirit's relation to the text broadens out into the Spirit's activity in the life of the people of God which forms the environment within which the text takes shape and serves the divine self-presence. Sanctification can thus properly be extended to the processes of the production of the text—not simply authorship (as, so often, in older theories of inspiration) but also the complex histories of pre-literary and literary tradition, redaction and compilation. It will, likewise, be extended to the post-history of the text, most particularly to canonisation (understood as the church's Spirit-produced acknowledgement of the testimony of Scripture) and to interpretation (understood as Spirit-illumined repentant and faithful attention to the presence of God).[63]

Webster's appeal to God's gracious and sovereign superintendence of Holy Scripture "from pre-textual tradition to interpretation"[64] bears close affinities, of course, to the theological justifications offered by Origen and Augustine for the role of the Septuagint as a norm for Christian practice and belief.[65] It is because of the sanctifying work of the Spirit in the translation, canonization, and reception of the Christian Bible that we are enabled to hear in the Septuagint, too, "the terrifying mercy of God's address."[66]

---

61. Webster 2003: 26.
62. Webster 2003: 27–28.
63. Webster 2003: 29–30.
64. Webster 2003: 26.
65. Origen, *Epistula ad Africanum*; Augustine, *De civitate Dei* 15.14; 18.42–44. On Origen's *Epistula ad Africanum*, see Hanhart 2002: 9–11.
66. Webster 2003: 41.

2

Is There a New Testament Doctrine of the Church?

Markus Bockmuehl

"The Church" is once again a lively and contested topic for theological discussion, and in biblical studies there is today plenty of talk about "ecclesial readings" of the Bible, about "interpreting communities," and simply about "the church."[1] But it is not always easy to know what this church is about, whether it has any concrete visible form or substance, what notion it conveys of historic continuity, of unity and diversity, inside and outside, whether it has identifiable forms of worship and orders of ministry or not. It sometimes seems a case of *L'église, c'est moi*—the church is anyone who shares sensible views and practices like mine. That should not perhaps surprise us, but it is an important caveat when we consider a range of topics from "ecclesial interpretation" to New Testament views of the church.

From a contemporary perspective, there is no doubt that we are at a very difficult moment in the life of the churches. Quite apart from the cultural challenges emanating from the post-Christian West, there has long been a

1. Early parts of this material were presented at the CTI Pastor-Theologian Conference in Sedona, AZ (June 2006). I am grateful for comments received from the conference participants on that occasion, from members of the 2007 St. Andrews seminar that gave rise to this book, and from Richard C. Beaton.

seemingly fatal contradiction between the Christ as the one Savior and Lord whom Christians confess and the fractured multiplicity of the churches in which they do so. Yet even as late as a decade ago it seemed that signs of spring might be brightening ecumenical dialogue in areas ranging from baptism and Eucharist to the place of the church of Rome in relation to the other churches. Most symbolically of all, perhaps, it looked for about fifteen minutes as if Catholics and Lutherans reached agreement on the doctrine of justification by faith that first divided them nearly five centuries ago.

A few sobering years into the twenty-first century it seems that our post-modern tribalism favors a more hard-nosed approach, both within and between the mainline denominations and also along the classic ecumenical fault lines of East and West, Protestant and Catholic. There are advocates of denomi-national retrenchment on the one hand, and on the other hand those who are keen to reconfigure received theology or ethics in the service of diverse cultural interest groups.

Now the church is once again racked by division. Cardinal Walter Kasper referred not long ago to the disillusionment and stagnation of the current "ecu-menical winter." Speaking to the Church of England's House of Bishops in 2006, he warned that certain decisions under consideration "would lead not only to a short-lived cold, but to a serious and long-lasting chill."[2] The Anglican com-munion has been staring into the abyss of schism as a result of events that have fractured internal fellowship and temporarily shut down high-level dialogue with Roman Catholic and Orthodox churches, and also with Muslim groups. Seem-ingly subsidiary themes about church order, discipline, and pastoral structure are widely experienced as church-dividing, even where other, apparently more central theological convictions may sometimes still be held in common.

But why is this? Is it perhaps the case that the substance of seemingly shared beliefs in fact evaporates on closer semantic scrutiny? If so, that in turn makes the disputes about the apparently peripheral suddenly stand out like tips of an iceberg of fundamental hermeneutical proportions. Vatican II and subsequent documents like the Catholic Catechism spoke movingly and perhaps optimistically about "separated churches and communities." But did that language assume the rudiments of a shared historic orthodox faith to be beyond all the mainstream denominations? Precisely that question is now in serious doubt. A few years ago the so-called Princeton Proposal for Christian Unity implied in part that conventional ecumenism no longer works because today the majority of the world's theologically engaged churches have in certain fundamentals more in common with each other than with the official structures of what was once called mainline Protestantism, structures to which some of them may continue officially to belong.[3]

2. See Kasper 2006 (with reference to women bishops).
3. Braaten and Jenson 2003; cf. Noll and Nystrom 2005.

We could go on for a long time in this vein, highlighting the problem of speaking meaningfully about "The Church." But does the New Testament have any guidance to offer? There are obviously many ways to answer that. As a way to reenergize reflection on this subject, I would like here to revisit a famous ecumenical debate about this question between two New Testament scholars at the time of the Second Vatican Council.

Revisiting the Käsemann-Brown Debate

In Montreal on Tuesday, 16 July 1963, the Fourth World Conference on Faith and Order convened for a session on the church in the New Testament. Two giants of New Testament scholarship had been invited to give presentations, Ernst Käsemann (1906–1998) and the relatively junior Raymond E. Brown (1928–1998). They represented a Protestant viewpoint and Catholic one, respectively; in fact, Brown noted at the start that he was the first Roman Catholic ever to have addressed such a conference. These two brief but powerful interpretations of the New Testament evidence turned out to be strikingly different. Almost half a century later there is inevitably something quaint and dated about the intellectual posture of these scholars: many of their certainties have ceased to be so certain; and other, especially reader-oriented considerations have become rather more central. There is a summary in the Proceedings of the Faith and Order conference, and both papers were later published separately.[4]

Käsemann

Käsemann spoke first, as arguably the doyen of German postwar New Testament scholarship, which was then still in full bloom. He spoke apparently unaware of what Brown would say; in fact, he made no reference to Brown at all. Käsemann focused on the intense historical particularity of any and all New Testament statements about the church, whose incessant change and contradiction allows us no more than a diversified range of ecclesiological archetypes. Jesus founded no global church, nor did he even express a desire that such a thing should exist. Any notion of ecclesiological coherence was lost as soon as the church reached out to gentiles because it was now "not possible to talk seriously of the renewed people of God, but only of the new in antithesis to the old."[5] Newly separated from its Jewish roots, gentile Christianity had to evolve a ritual and organizational structure to keep ecstatic excesses in check; it turned to the pagan mystery religions to help develop a notion of Christ as its cultic god, baptism as a ritual representation of the resurrection, and the

4. Rodger and Vischer 1964; Käsemann 1969; Brown 1963.
5. Käsemann 1969: 253.

Eucharist as the banquet of the elect. Establishing this was always a struggle, worked out over against the challenge from charismatic enthusiasts and from priestly sacramentalists. So, for example, Paul's driving concern is "to guard equally against Judaism and enthusiasm"[6]—continuity with Israel or the Old Testament, such as it is, functions at best as a continuity of "promise and miracle," relativized throughout by the history of unfaith.

Only in the post-Pauline period, Käsemann argued, did a form of church order emerge out of the need to combat what he calls "enthusiasm," and for this the church reverted to Jewish-Christian forms of government for its own development of a monarchical episcopate. Käsemann claimed that in the world of the post-Pauline epistles ecclesiology virtually displaces eschatology and becomes largely independent of Christology. Before long arises the claim of one holy and apostolic church that embodies the continuity of salvation history—the beginning of what German scholars in Käsemann's day still liked to call "early catholicism."

Johannine Christianity represents for Käsemann a "counter-offensive," both internally and vis-à-vis these Pauline and early catholic developments. For John, the dominant theme is the presence of Christ and the Word of Christ, which relativizes and indeed eclipses all other concerns, including church, ministry, and sacraments. (This is arguably the flip side of Käsemann's famous assertion that the Fourth Gospel's Christology is "naively docetic."[7])

Käsemann conceded that certain details of his survey might be debatable. But his overall conclusion was that the determining feature of the New Testament doctrine of the church is precisely its intense historical and social particularity and relativity, so that no uniform view of the church emerges. His relativism is not radical to the point of welcoming any and all diversity: at some level the question of Christian unity does remain for him "identical with the question of Christian truth."[8]

Käsemann's conclusion was famously stark and iconoclastic:

> No romantic postulate, however enveloped it may be in the cloak of salvation history, can be permitted to weaken the sober observation that the historian is unable to speak of an unbroken unity of New Testament ecclesiology. In that field he becomes aware of our own situation in microcosm—differences, difficulties, contradictions, at best an ancient ecumenical confederation without an Ecumenical Council.[9]

Then as now, "God's Spirit hovers over the waters of a chaos."[10]

Finally, however, Käsemann did note the paradox that despite the messy and contradictory phenomena, somehow early Christianity did proclaim "the one

6. Käsemann 1969: 254.
7. Käsemann 1968: 10.
8. Käsemann 1969: 256.
9. Käsemann 1969: 256–57.
10. Käsemann 1969: 257.

Church, not in the sense of a theory of organic development but in the name of the reality and the truth of the Holy Spirit."[11] His answer to that paradox was that the unity of the church has no visible reality but can be apprehended only by the eye of faith and as a reality that is yet to take hold in the world to come. The church as such has no substance at all; it is first and foremost an eschatological vision, above all a vision of Christology. Christology must increase, and ecclesiology must decrease: the Word of Christ must be given free access to facilitate for each individual Christian immediate access to Christ's presence—that, and that alone, must be the concern and the limit of any and all tradition and ministry within the church. Christ himself alone is the unity of his church.

Brown

Next up was Raymond E. Brown. He was then barely thirty-five years old; his subsequent major Johannine tomes were as yet a mere twinkle in his eye, not to mention his work on the birth and passion narratives or a host of other topics. Brown responded more overtly to Käsemann's tour de force, not always explicitly or point by point, but nonetheless unmistakably. (He may also have known an earlier published lecture that Käsemann had given in 1951.) Brown began by addressing three fundamental areas of disagreement:

1. Rather than reading the Gospels in isolation from the historical Jesus, appreciative interpretation of *all* the stages of tradition would lead one to "respect both the theological nature of the Gospels and the stages of their composition without needlessly undermining their value as witnesses to Jesus of Nazareth." This matters for ecclesiology as for other issues.
2. Brown stressed that Luke-Acts is an interpretation of received theological insights and cannot be reduced to a late harmonization of incompatible Palestinian and gentile views of the church into a coherent construct.
3. Brown emphasized, "A study of pseudepigrapha in the Bible seems to indicate that generally a pseudepigraphical work is attributed to an author because it is a continuation of his thought, style, or spirit, rather than because it is designed to *correct* his theology. Therefore, we must proceed with care in drawing a sharp line of demarcation between Pauline theology and that of the Pastorals."[12]

After thus putting a stretch of clear blue water between his own stance and that of Käsemann, Brown proceeded to affirm one of the main points of Käsemann's presentation: the New Testament documents offer no picture of

11. Käsemann 1969: 257.
12. Brown 1963: 298–99 (italics added).

linear progress toward a uniform position on the church. There most certainly is huge diversity and development, by no means always in an orderly manner. Yet that there are limits to this diversity is easily seen in the fact that the church was never broad enough to include either Ebionite or Marcionite excesses. The facts can be understood only dialectically: there are different theologies present in the New Testament, and yet their authors also show a clear consciousness of belonging to the one Christian church, and their different ecclesiologies affirm certain features strongly held in common.

This thesis directly contradicts a basic tenet of Käsemann, and Brown proceeded immediately to illustrate his claim in relation to three areas of common conviction: continuity with Israel, apostolicity, and baptism and Eucharist.

On Israel, Brown acknowledges the development of both continuity and newness with varying degrees of emphasis and of more or less spiritualizing development. The earliest Christian sources stress the restoration or the renewal of Israel, often through symbolism such as the church's base in Jerusalem, the Twelve, and the very title of *ekklēsia*, which is the same word used in the Septuagint of the people of God assembled at Mount Sinai. He accepts that there was a radical anti-Jewish group called the Hellenists, an idea that has since fallen out of fashion; but even so, he rejects the notion that they were the spokesmen for gentile Christianity. And Brown makes the obvious but often ignored point that the very fact of Paul's complicated explanation of descent from Abraham is proof of his conviction that continuity with Israel mattered to him.

On apostolicity, the Gospels' lists of the Twelve show their continuing symbolic import in the later first century, even as late as the book of Revelation (Rev. 21:14). This stress on the Twelve also demonstrates the fallacy of the cliché about an originally "spiritual" church being fossilized into a later authoritarian hierarchical church: Paul's letters show an apostolic structure from the very beginning, which in significant respects echoes Jewish organizational structures known from the Dead Sea Scrolls.[13]

Finally, Brown made a number of points on baptism in the New Testament as consistently rooted in notions of repentance and spiritual renewal (noting parallels in the Old Testament and at Qumran), and about the Eucharist, as a meal both of remembrance and of eschatological expectation.

In conclusion, and as if to underline the methodological chasm separating his approach from that of Käsemann, Brown stressed his conviction that "the subsequent history of the Church in the post-apostolic period is also a witness to the Church of the NT since the Spirit of Christ did not cease to work when the NT was completed and this Spirit in the Church guarantees continuity in essentials."[14] And in contrast to Käsemann's stress on individual faith, Brown

---

13. In the postwar period this interpretation was made popular by writers such as Bo Reicke (1946), Joachim Jeremias (1969: 260–63), and others (see, e.g., the list in Thiering 1981: 69–70n25), though its cogency was at times overstated.

14. Brown 1963: 307.

affirms, with other catholic interpreters, that Christian life is only ever found in a community bound to Christ.

Assessment

There is no doubt that biblical scholarship and ecumenical debate have moved on a long way since that evening in Montreal over forty-five years ago. Many of these judgments would be formulated rather differently now, while others have largely disappeared. And yet both of these sharply contrasting New Testament positions retain a powerful use as points of reference for contemporary ecclesial concerns, from postmodern ideological criticism to the emergent church, from catholic to Pentecostal megachurch ecclesiology, from liberal to communitarian readings of social order. It does seem to me that the fundamental hermeneutical postures of the two papers still have their respective sympathizers even today,[15] and this makes them useful discussion starters for the diverse spread of opinion represented in any contemporary audience. Here I will offer comments on the positive contributions of both lines of thought before going on to propose some possible avenues for discussion.

Strengths of Käsemann's Approach

Ernst Käsemann's position continues in some ways to be particularly suited to a postmodern account of meaning, in which claims of reference, truth, or unity are deferred, sometimes indefinitely, and instead are subordinated under political concerns associated with competing pursuits of power. Käsemann's position was in fact anticipated in two of his previous studies. The first was a 1949 lecture on ecclesial office in which he sharply contrasted the Pauline and the Lukan and deutero-Pauline notions of church order.[16] In another lecture, two years later at Göttingen, he had addressed the question "Does the canon of the New Testament constitute the foundation of the unity of the church?" Answer: "No."[17] Instead, in its irreconcilable diversity the New Testament canon "provides the basis for the multiplicity of the confessions."[18] In stressing the fundamental diversity of the New Testament's theological positions, Käsemann came to assert the irreducible relativity of the *kerygma*. On that reading, the intractable fragmentation of the churches today has its justification in the equally radical multiplicity of conflicting confessional positions within the New Testament itself.

15. A similar view was taken by Thomas Rausch (1988), who adopted Brown's criteria but added *koinōnia* and tolerance of diversity.
16. Käsemann 1960.
17. Käsemann 1964: 95 (German original, 1951).
18. Käsemann 1964: 103.

In Montreal the question was more specifically about the unity of the church rather than the canon, but the same hermeneutic prevailed. To our present question, "Does the New Testament have a doctrine of the church?" Käsemann's answer is also an emphatic no, and on much the same grounds: the divisions of the church reflect the New Testament's own inner contradictions about what the church is or should be. It is worth pondering that the claim here goes beyond the assertion of irreducible plurality, which was the subject of various other ecumenical studies around the time of Käsemann's presentation.[19] For Käsemann, a unity of the New Testament's conceptions of the church is not merely refracted through the "interrelation" of their plurality (as Paul Minear put it), but wholly impossible except in relation to the future kingdom of God. So we cannot really develop a New Testament ecclesiology at all.

A good deal of contemporary biblical scholarship tends to agree that there is nothing here to be discussed. One standard reference work, the *Anchor Bible Dictionary*, packs six thousand articles into 7,200 pages without finding any space for an entry entitled "Church." Elsewhere we find unsynthesized surveys of New Testament ecclesiologies.[20] Too often where scholars do speak of "the church," they typically mean either "my church" or else a devotional construct of catholic polity that does not, however, have real political existence. Käsemann's insistence on canonical or ecclesial unity as a purely eschatological conception has perhaps rather more integrity.

At the time, Käsemann's critically scintillating proposals both about the canon and about the church generated a great deal of interest, not least from a youthful Hans Küng, who drew on Käsemann's (and Küng's) Tübingen colleague Hans Diem to suggest a more constructive account of the role of *Frühkatholizismus* and the singularity of the New Testament canon.[21] Küng rightly notes that Käsemann's only way to safeguard his fiercely Lutheran position in the face of the New Testament's evident tendencies to catholicity is to resist them vigorously through a Protestant conspiracy of silent suppression or underinterpretation, a refusal to hear the New Testament as a whole.[22] As Küng puts it, Käsemann's hermeneutical normativity is deliberately to confuse a Protestant construal of *die Mitte der Schrift* (the center of Scripture) with the ecclesial transmission of *das Ganze der Schrift* (the whole of Scripture).[23]

---

19. See, for example, Patrick Dias's 1965 dissertation, published in the series Ökumenische Forschungen, jointly (!) edited by Hans Küng and Joseph Ratzinger (Dias 1968; cf. the later work Dias 1974). Compare previously, for example, Paul Minear (1960: 221–49), who speaks of *interrelated* "images," and Rudolf Schnackenburg (1965: 55–117 [German original, 1961]), who systematizes "theological guiding ideas" and their "basic unity."

20. I commissioned one such collection ten years ago. See Bockmuehl and Thompson 1997.

21. Küng 1962 (reprint, Küng 1964).

22. Küng 1964: 146–48

23. Küng 1964: 149, 153.

Käsemann himself appeared impenitent in his response: far from conceding that the wisdom of age might lead him to a more balanced position, he continued cheerfully to champion the virtue of theological polemicism.[24] In order to understand Käsemann's persistence in this hermeneutical stance late in life, we must consider that the torture and assassination of his daughter Elisabeth by Argentinian secret police in 1977 reinforced all his political instincts hatched forty years earlier, when the Gestapo had detained him for his pastoral support of communist miners.[25] His commitment to polemicism was motivated both personally and theologically: in a reflective essay in 1982 he described himself as an "angry old man" (*zorniger alter Mann*),[26] while in an interview on the occasion of his eightieth birthday in 1986 he asserted that "the Holy Spirit is a polemicist" (*der Heilige Geist ist ein Polemiker*).[27] Ten years later, his parting "last word and testament" at the University of Tübingen's celebration of his ninetieth birthday was "*Résistez!* Discipleship of the Crucified One necessarily leads to resistance against idolatry on every front; and that resistance is and must be the most important characteristic of Christian freedom."[28]

He was content to declare himself unable to hear the voice of the one Christ in the multiple New Testament sources and explicitly uninterested in the slightest whether the church's two thousand years of experience might suggest a different view.[29] Contrary to Küng's concern for *das Ganze*, Käsemann reverted to the doctrine of justification as the only principle that ensures the earnest but slippery Lutheran canon criticism of "what promotes Christ" (*was Christum treibet*).[30] In the end, Käsemann acknowledges that the Christian canon bears for him, as for Marcion, the superscript "To the Unknown God."[31]

Even after half a century it is not difficult to discern here hermeneutical options subsequently exercised by interpreters committed to privileging conflictual and power analyses as the preferred mode of interpreting early Christian texts, both within and beyond the canon. Daniel Harrington is right to

24. "The conciliatory and even-minded traits of old age never caught up with me, because I believe one really ought to get to the bottom of many things, and there is too much against which, precisely as a Christian and a theologian, one ought to polemicize" (Käsemann 1970: 357 [my translation]; see further pp. 361–62).

25. See, for example, Ulrichs 2001. The German government denied Käsemann support, and he was forced to pay a ransom of $22,000 to retrieve her badly abused body (which was then buried at Tübingen). In 2003 German prosecutors formally filed an extradition request for those responsible, but the Argentinian courts refused. See further Malcher 2003.

26. Cited in Ulrichs 2001; cf. Käsemann 1982: 244.

27. Cited in Küenzlen 2005.

28. Reprinted as Käsemann 1998 (my translation).

29. "Frankly, after a lifetime's preoccupation with the detail as well as the totality of New Testament theology, I am unable to hear the voice of the one Christ in all the witnesses. Even if the church's experience of two thousand years were to bear witness to it, that would not distract me in the slightest, nor even interest me" (Käsemann 1970: 365 [my translation]).

30. Käsemann 1970: 377.

31. Käsemann 1970: 410.

see in Käsemann a desire to exalt ecclesial and canonical diversity to a kind of metaphysical ideal;[32] yet what is for Harrington a criticism has in postmodern discourse been embraced, somewhat paradoxically, as the hegemonic metanarrative. Within English-speaking New Testament scholarship this mode of interpretation received a boost in the 1972 English translation of Walter Bauer's seminal 1934 work *Orthodoxy and Heresy in Earliest Christianity*, which came to be further reinforced by the dominant trends in much postmodern ideological criticism. But as John Webster shows in his contribution to this volume, even a leading orthodox theologian such as Rowan Williams, in his book *On Christian Theology*, advocates such an approach to Scripture as most faithful to the "literal sense," going on to interpret innercanonical conflict as providing the pattern for contemporary interpretations of the unity of the church.[33]

There is, in my view, no doubt that Käsemann's stance continues to speak powerfully to the hermeneutical inclinations of our present cultural moment. Whether one agrees with him or not, there is a genuine and dynamic contribution here. On the positive side, his approach facilitates the concern for a church fully committed to enfranchising minorities, a church that is spiritually energized from the bottom up rather than from the top down, fully particularized as to culture and social setting. And in his willingness to exploit tensions and contradictions to the fullest, Käsemann manages to bring to life the color and liveliness and instability that undoubtedly are present in the New Testament's diverse conceptions of the church. There are indeed a number of elements in tension that may seem irreconcilable even at the point where it might appear most fruitful to reconcile them. And it is clearly true, in fact it is a truism, that unity is meaningless where there is no diversity. For Christian faith, diversity and differentiation are built in some significant sense into the very being of God.[34] And as James Dunn has put it more recently, "*Diversity is as fundamental to the Christianity of the NT as is the unity of Easter and Pentecost . . . without it the Church cannot exist as Christ's body.*"[35]

Strengths of Brown's Approach

Raymond Brown, for his part, developed his own thought on these matters further after his initial paper in Montreal; he wrote considerably more on the same topic in his own subsequent scholarship. His book *The Churches the Apostles Left Behind* (1984), for example, filled out much of the evidence for his position and made it a good deal more nuanced. Although in that book

32. Harrington 1982: 41.
33. Williams 1991; 2000g: 44–59. Cf. Webster below, pp. 116–18, 121–22.
34. A point powerfully stated by Ioannis Zizioulas (2001: 57, and passim), who goes on in the same breath to demand theological criteria for distinguishing between legitimate and illegitimate diversity.
35. Dunn 2006: 455.

he cites neither his own earlier essay nor any of Käsemann's work, his conclusion remains compatible with what he said in Montreal: no one author gives us the New Testament doctrine of the church, and there is no consistent or uniform doctrine of the church that emerges even from the second-generation writings; indeed, aside from complementary strengths, it is remarkably easy to point out "glaring shortcomings" in each of the available ecclesiological perspectives taken in isolation. In a sense, he retraces his steps in greater detail to cover much of the New Testament evidence that Käsemann had used to bait the defenders of ecclesiological coherence in the canon. The key emphases that Brown here highlights are concerns for

- church structure in the Pastoral Epistles;
- the body of Christ in Colossians and Ephesians;
- the church in the Spirit in Luke-Acts;
- the one people of God in 1 Peter;
- a community of people individually in fellowship with Jesus in the Fourth Gospel, and individually guided by the Paraclete in the Johannine writings;
- a sense of authority that does not stifle Jesus in Matthew.

For today, Brown asserts, this New Testament diversity on ecclesiology makes it very problematic for any one church to claim absolute faithfulness to Scripture: New Testament ecclesiology makes us aware "that there are other ways of being faithful to which we do not do justice"; in that sense, "*every* Christian community . . . is neglecting part of the NT witness."[36] Nevertheless, Brown explicitly retains the conviction that "most of the NT was written before the major breaks in *koinōnia* detectable in the second century, and so NT diversity cannot be used to justify Christian division today."[37] This continues explicitly to contradict Käsemann's fundamental thesis.

New Testament Ecclesiology as Doctrinal Norm?
Three Observations

In a fuller treatment, various other areas of potential (and potentially contentious) ecclesiological convergence in the New Testament might fruitfully be explored, ranging from baptism and Eucharist, which Brown cited, to matters of eschatology or church discipline, which he did not.

Here, however, I want to suggest three ways of bringing this debate into sharper focus for this volume's reflection on the doctrinal normativity of what,

36. Brown 1984: 149.
37. Brown 1984: 147–48.

in chapter 12 below, Kevin Vanhoozer terms "the apostolic discourse and its developments." All three of my suggestions express concerns that have risen to much greater awareness in theological debate over the past half-century, even if all remain contested in biblical and theological scholarship and in the churches too. They appear here in no particular order of importance (though moving perhaps from least to most contested).

The Church as Israel

On the church's continuity with Israel and the God of Israel, subsequent developments in theology have identified here a far more pressing question than even Brown acknowledged. This is not just a matter of style or of interfaith diplomacy; it cuts to the heart of what it means to have faith in Jesus as the Messiah of the God of Israel.[38]

It is worth underlining the simple point that as soon as the New Testament writers used the word *ekklēsia* as a collective term in the singular, they were making a profound typological point about the community of Jews and gentiles, gathered around Israel's Christ, as identified with the Chosen People whom God has redeemed and commissioned for his salvation of the world. As William Horbury put it in a study of the Septuagintal connections, "To a great extent . . . , NT conceptions of the Church were ready-made before the apostles preached; and this is true not only of the imagery most readily applicable to the pre-existent or ideal Church, but also of descriptions of the empirical assembly."[39]

It is of course true that claims to be the people of God are in some texts asserted *polemically*, as against persecutors or other detractors of this faith in the God of Israel. There are difficult passages on this subject in the Fourth Gospel and other New Testament books; and similar polemics are also familiar between other first-century Jewish groups. But for all their undoubtedly problematic and volatile language of supersession, no New Testament texts apply Old Testament Israel language to the church in exclusion of Judaism per se, just as no authentically apostolic Christian group in the New Testament excommunicates any other such group from the Israel of God. We can put this point more strongly: for the New Testament authors, it is preposterous to think of the New Covenant people of the God of Israel in terms other than those of the one Chosen People, however fractured its relationship may be with the unfaithful within Israel.

The overwhelming consensus of the New Testament is best read as expressed in the Pauline conviction that what happened to "our fathers" in the

---

38. See studies such as Kinzer 2005; Lindbeck 2003; Marshall 2001; Soulen 2003 as well as the 2002 Vatican document on the Old Testament as Jewish and Christian Scripture (Pontifical Biblical Commission 2002).

39. Horbury 1997: 1.

wilderness of Sinai was "written for *our* instruction" in the New Covenant (1 Cor. 10:11)—a clear indication of an ecclesiology unapologetically conceived around the one elect people of God.[40] All this is compatible with recent Christian retrieval of the conviction that God has not revoked his covenant but rather has included gentile believers within it. Evidence of that retrieval is clear in post–World War II theology ranging from John Paul II to writers on Christian-Jewish dialogue.[41] But even within Christianity's normative founding text, from Matthew to Paul and Hebrews it is clear that the Old Testament fathers and mothers of the faith are *our* fathers and mothers of the faith. For the New Testament writers this is a conviction troubled but undeterred by its widespread if temporary rejection on the part of most Jews.

As George Lindbeck recently showed, that same conviction was imperiled on the Christian side by Marcionite anti-church-as-Israel reading in the second century but was confirmed by a renewed emphasis on the Old Testament in the third century.[42] There is no space here to run through the wealth of ecclesiological imagery that confirms this understanding, but I would add that to view the church as anti-Israel, or as anything other than Israel, is already to lose sight of its own identity as the body of Christ, a unity in diversity: Jesus is the unique Son of the God of Israel who in the parable of the vineyard inextricably linked his fate to the deliverance and renewal of Israel; and he is the one whom the New Testament affirms, precisely in his risen body, as saving Lord and Messiah of Israel (e.g., Rom. 1:3–4; Acts 2:36).[43]

Apostolicity and Witness

My second comment relates quite closely to the question about Israel and the church in relation to the Messiah of Israel. It seems to me that we should not lose sight of the significance of what appears for Brown under the heading of "apostolicity"; Käsemann considers it briefly under the rubric of "witness." The point here is fairly simple: despite claims to the contrary, from the earliest to the latest writings of the New Testament and into the second century there is a consistent sense that the Christian gospel is not reinvented ad hoc but rather consists of the message of Jesus as entrusted to individual and often named apostolic witnesses. Subsequent generations acknowledge themselves to be dependent on those witnesses, whether in Ephesians, in Hebrews, in 2 Peter, or in the Gospel of John. Although the ecclesial phenomena vary enormously, this apostolicity of the church, whether derived from a single founding figure or multiple figures, is not relativized by new revelations that some (like the later Montanists or gnostics) may claim.

---

40. For the construal of Pauline ecclesiology in terms of Israel, see Kraus 1995.
41. See further Bockmuehl 2006: 222–23 and n. 65; also Lohfink 1999.
42. Lindbeck 2003: 85, citing Harnack 1908: 2:279–89 and Pelikan 1971: 25–26.
43. See Bockmuehl 2006: 215–20, 227–28.

Interestingly, even some pseudepigraphal and later gnostic writings in their own way reinforce this trend, since many of their new revelations and assertions about the origin of the faith are clad in terms of encounters between Jesus and his closest disciples, albeit cast in a postresurrection mode that is generally uninterested in the earthly Jesus. For most second-century recipients of the first-century texts that we call the New Testament, it is impossible to be assured of authentic ecclesial life if one stands outside the tradition of the apostles; and for Irenaeus, that also means if one is not in communion with the church of the great apostolic foundations. This rule of faith is the consistent second-century voice that shapes the canon and is itself shaped by it. The living, enacted testimony of the apostles and their students embodied the empowered witness of Christ; for its adherents this is what made the church Christian, and this alone gave assurance that it stands in continuity with the church of the beginnings.

Käsemann, in my view, seriously underplays this point about the "tangibility" of apostolicity, which may today constitute a litmus test for the theological integrity of Protestant churches, whether their flavor is "old line" or "emergent." Even the witnesses of Hebrews 11 are sidelined in Käsemann's account when he asserts that "they are *only* his witnesses . . . *in so far as* they receive their witness from God and the Messiah."[44] To which the reply must be: true enough, but the point of such passages is precisely that the Old Testament saints are in fact the authentic witnesses of faith, and that they bear authentic witness to God and to Christ. The contingency of their witness takes nothing away from its authenticity. This is where good and serious discussion might engage Käsemann about what it means to affirm the apostolicity of authentic faith.

Did Jesus Have a Doctrine of the Church?

My third comment is in some ways just a teaser. It may sound innocuous and self-evident, but within New Testament scholarship it is perhaps the most controversial of all. Writers from the early twentieth-century French modernist Alfred Loisy (1857–1940) via Käsemann to the present day go out of their way to say that Jesus founded no church and intended no identifiable community. This is continually reaffirmed in various New Testament publications. As Loisy famously put it, "Jesus foretold the kingdom of God, and it was the church that came."[45] And even in a book published in 2006 James Dunn continues to insist, "There was no community as such functioning alongside or around Jesus."[46]

44. Käsemann 1964: 106 (italics added).
45. Loisy 1908: 166.
46. Dunn 2006: 115. The quotation continues: "but only larger or smaller groups of disciples either observing his mission or hindering his mission or participating in some small way in his mission."

Historically, of course, Christian communities of all denominational and creedal stripes have always tended to claim for their own particular ecclesial order the imprimatur of none other than Christ himself and his apostles. The reality is that there was never a time when diversity was not part of the very fabric of the Jesus movement; even Luke's harmonic account of the church in Jerusalem makes that clear. So did Jesus intend a messianic community or not? And does the New Testament have a notion of the church?

We can say with some confidence that Jesus' calling and commissioning of groups such as the Twelve and the Seventy was deliberately symbolic of an eschatological renewal of Sinaitic Israel gathered around twelve tribal princes and seventy elders—what Stephen in Acts 7 calls "the *ekklēsia* in the wilderness" (Acts 7:38).

All four Gospels affirm that Jesus singled out twelve men as an inner core of the larger group of disciples, although relatively less is made of this in John. New Testament scholarship generally regards their appointment as authentic, and their symbolism too is not in serious doubt.[47] In its biblical and Jewish setting this eschatological institution of the Twelve conveys a theocentric and specifically messianic reconstitution of the entire biblical Israel under the leadership of tribal judges and their king. This restoration of biblical Israel's twelve tribes was a message deeply rooted in the Old Testament and of some continuing interest in the early church, even after the demise of the Twelve. It would be salutary for contemporary ecclesiologies to be more attentive to the principle, evident in Acts and the Epistles as much as in the Gospels, that the church's apostolic *form* is a function of its apostolic *mission*.[48]

For Jesus, this was the hoped-for outcome of his mission on the Father's behalf, which would culminate in the Son of Man's messianic rule as Israel's king. In Jesus' case, his vision of the kingdom of God was characterized by an eschatological mission to gather in the leaderless "lost sheep" of the house of Israel (e.g., Mark 6:34; Matt. 9:36; 10:6; 15:24).[49] He summoned his disciples as well to his mission of good news to the poor, the blind, the deaf, the lame, and the lepers, who were to be initiated into the kingdom by washing away their sins in a baptism of repentance. This kingdom of the lost sheep of Israel is the one that Jesus would rule and whose tribes the Twelve would judge. His own innocent suffering and death were in some way instrumental to the realization of this vision; and although the New Testament writers do not offer a coherent statement about how or why this should be so, the Synoptics and Paul agree that Jesus expressed his own account of the mat-

47. See Meier 2001; Horbury 2003: 157–88; Davies and Sanders 1999: 635–36. For fuller documentation, including positions that dissent from the consensus, see Bockmuehl 2006: 211–15.

48. And not vice versa. The apostolic form without the apostolic mission invites death by orthodox sclerosis, while the latter without the former invites fermentation of a cult.

49. For a rather far-reaching attempt to expound political and geographic dimensions of Matthew's "lost sheep" logia, see Willitts 2007a (summarized in Willitts 2007b).

ter by instituting a eucharistic meal that became the focus of their corporate remembrance and worship.

Qumran too had a vision of the renewed Israel, a wilderness congregation (*qāhāl*) founded and built upon strict sectarian observance and separation from the unfaithful in Israel. Jesus, by contrast, told Peter that he would build his own messianic *ekklēsia* on the confession of faith in the Messiah of Israel (Matt. 16:18). Commentators are divided on the authenticity of that saying, but it captures the aims of Jesus' ministry brilliantly. Jesus, as the son of the vineyard owner, has as his mission the salvation of the vineyard, which task he served by his life, death, and resurrection.[50] And the apostles followed his footsteps in taking that mission to Israel and the nations. Can Jesus' story of the people of God be any less compelling for Christian dogmatics today?

---

50. Walter Kirchschläger (1995: 1336) rightly sees the gathering of a congregation of disciples (*Jüngergemeinde*), however loosely defined, as part of Jesus' *ipsissima intentio*. R. Alan Culpepper (2005) identifies further "church-building" metaphors in the passion narratives.

3

Johannine Christology
and Jewish-Christian Dialogue

R. W. L. Moberly

One of the contemporary growth areas of theology is interfaith dialogue. Although our particular focus here is Jewish-Christian dialogue, we should remember that this is situated within a wider context, not least dialogue also with Islam in encounters of the "three Abrahamic faiths."

This wider context is, of course, complex. For example, how far is dialogue a response to secularizing pressures, which perhaps lead to a desire to find common ground at the expense of traditional theological understandings? That is, is dialogue yet another nail in the coffin of theology, where theology must yield to ethical priorities, nonspecific spirituality, and an outlook of genial bonhomie in place of *odium theologicum*?[1] Alternatively, could the secular-

---

1. As I write this essay, I have just read Matthew Parris's latest periodic salvo against religion in *The Times* (Parris 2007). In response to those who ask why he continues to "bang on," he says, "An *ad hominem* response would be to remark that when the Church had the upper hand it was happy to persecute, imprison or behead non-believers and fight crusades against other religions. . . . On the back foot at last, it discovers (first) a brotherhood between all its sects. Then as the situation deteriorates Christianity discovers within itself a respect first for Judaism (suddenly we are all 'Judaeo-Christians'), then women with a Christian vocation, then for divorcees, and finally finds a common purpose with religions such as Islam, too (the 'faith' community). Needs must."

izing pressures lead to a refreshed understanding of traditional resources, especially Scripture, in which one is forced to relinquish the luxury of historic cultural prejudices and polemics in favor of a more searching engagement with the real subject matter of faith? To be sure, there could be no simple answers to such questions, and one can readily find examples of both trends. But we should at least note that our specific concern, the interface between doctrine and Scripture in relation to Jewish-Christian dialogue, is subject to many more influences than can be considered in this short essay.

Contemporary debate about theology, scriptural interpretation, and interfaith dialogue is extensive. One could valuably approach it by looking at the issues in relation to particular significant thinkers in the interfaith field, such as John Hick, Paul Knitter, Jacques Dupuis, Kenneth Cragg, and Gavin D'Costa. My focus, however, will be restricted to one famous New Testament text and aspects of its responsible appropriation.

Do Jews and Christians Worship "the Same God"?

I would like briefly to preface my study with one wider consideration. A fundamental presupposition of dialogue between the Abrahamic faiths[2] is that participants grant that within each respective faith tradition there is, in some way and to some degree, genuine engagement with God. The formulation of this presupposition can, however, be tricky.

The presupposition is sometimes formulated in terms of Jews, Christians, and Muslims all worshiping "the same God." For example, the important Jewish statement on Christianity, *Dabru Emet*, issued in the millennial year 2000,[3] has as the first of its eight theses that "Jews and Christians worship the same God."[4] Indeed, this can sound so obvious to dialogue-minded Jews and Christians that one risks some opprobrium by querying it—a case in point being the fate of Jon Levenson, a longtime participant in Jewish-Christian dialogue, when he suggested to his fellow Jews that there is good reason for Jews to resist any such formulation.[5] Levenson observed that, among other things, for traditional Christianity, Jesus is constitutive of the identity of God;

2. In an interfaith context, "Abrahamic" is an eirenically suggestive, rather than descriptively illuminating, epithet for the respective religious traditions.

3. The text is available online on the website of The Institute for Christian and Jewish Studies: www.icjs.org/what/njsp/dabruemet.html.

4. In the wider context there is also the distinguished precedent of Pope John Paul II, who said, in an address to Muslims on 9 May 1985 as part of a welcome to a colloquium on "Holiness in Christianity and Islam," "As I have often said in other meetings with Muslims, your God and ours is one and the same, and we are brothers and sisters in the faith of Abraham" (see www .vatican.va/holy_father/john_paul_ii/speeches/1985/may).

5. Frymer-Kensky et al. 2002. Levenson was accused of "bad faith as a Jewish thinker" (p. 8), and his argument was extensively (and astonishingly) misrepresented by scholars whose

in the words of the Nicene Creed, Jesus is "true God from true God." In summary, "participants in Jewish-Christian dialogue often speak as if Jews and Christians agreed about God but disagreed about Jesus. They have forgotten that in a very real sense, orthodox Christians believe Jesus *is* God."[6] Language about worshiping "the same God" is careless, as it elides the difference between God in himself and the understandings of distinct faith traditions. In its place it is surely preferable to speak of Jews, Christians, and Muslims as respectively worshiping "the one God." Such a formulation respects an affirmation that is central to each tradition and leaves one better placed to engage with differing construals of the nature and identity of that one God and their respective implications for belief and practice.

John 14:6 and Interpretative Strategies of Evasion

From a Christian perspective, interfaith dialogue necessarily raises questions of Christology. It is perhaps John's Gospel that poses the christological issues most sharply. Within John's Gospel, Jesus' words "I am the way, the truth, and the life; no one comes to the Father except through me" (John 14:6) most famously pose the issue of particularity and exclusivity and thus will constitute the focus here.[7]

This is a difficult text to handle well. Mainly this is because too many interpreters tend to take it as a freestanding axiom, in relative isolation from its Johannine frame of reference, and assume that it means (as I have heard not a few preachers say) "Nobody can know God apart from faith in Jesus Christ." My approach is to consider what the words do, and do not, mean within their Johannine context.

First, however, I want briefly to note two examples of how some interpreters can feel obliged to adopt an approach that is in essence a means of circumventing what the text appears to be saying.

The first is from Marcus Braybrooke, whose credentials in the area of interfaith dialogue are impressive. He has been executive director of the Council for Christians and Jews, is currently president of the World Congress of Faiths, and has been awarded a Lambeth Doctor of Divinity degree by the archbishop of Canterbury "in recognition of his contribution to the development of inter-religious co-operation and understanding throughout the world."[8] In his *Time to Meet* Braybrooke writes,

---

ability to read clearly seems to have been displaced by their indignation at his daring to wield the knife on some contemporary sacred cows.

6. Levenson 2001: 37. See also, more fully, Levenson 2004, especially pp. 6–10.

7. Scripture quotations throughout this chapter are the author's translation.

8. www.sternberg-foundation.co.uk/founders-bios.html#braybrooke.

At any meeting where the subject of the relationship of Christianity to other faiths is discussed, someone is sure to quote the words "No man cometh to the Father but through me" (John 14:6). Critical scholarship has made clear that the words of Jesus quoted in the Fourth Gospel should not be treated as his actual words. Equally important, although claims to unique authority were implicit in Jesus' teaching, historically at least, christological claims in the New Testament have to be treated with caution. . . . Many New Testament scholars now recognize that Jesus' own message centered on the kingdom of God rather than on himself. Further, traditional understandings of the doctrine of incarnation are being re-examined. Some writers suggest that overmuch emphasis on Jesus has obscured the fact that Jesus leads us to the Father, the one God of all humankind.[9]

Although the argument of this passage is implicit rather than explicit, its clear tenor is strongly resistant to finding continuing theological significance in John 14:6. On the one hand, Jesus did not say these words, and they misrepresent the message that he did bring. On the other hand, the traditional understanding of the incarnation being "re-examined" appears to mean that such a traditional understanding is now to be considered deficient rather than in need of faithful fresh rearticulation. In other words—to put somewhat crudely what Braybrooke implies more delicately—the Fourth Gospel represents a historic Christian mistake. It is an early misrepresentation of Jesus, and modern critical scholarship has enabled us to recognize this. Thereby a major obstacle from the path of interfaith dialogue is removed; critical history trumps classic theology.[10]

I will not discuss Braybrooke in detail but rather will simply observe that if Braybrooke were consistent, he would apply the same treatment to the Shema (Deut. 6:4–9). For the critical scholarship that shows that Jesus did not utter the words ascribed to him in the Fourth Gospel equally shows that Moses did not utter the words ascribed to him in Deuteronomy; nor can we suppose that the Shema accurately represents the message of "the historical Moses," because nothing confident can be said about "the historical Moses." Yet Braybrooke is warmly affirmative toward Judaism and nowhere even hints that perhaps Jews should abandon their historic core affirmation on the grounds of modern historical-critical scholarship. Yet if the fact that Moses most likely did not formulate the Shema is of little real significance for the Shema as constitutive of Jewish understanding and practice, why should not the same be the case if the wording of John 14:6 represents John's construal of Jesus? The really important question is not "Who formulated this wording?" but rather "Is it

9. Braybrooke 1990: 89–90.
10. Braybrooke takes a similar approach to Jesus' words of authorization of universal mission in Matthew 28:19 and Acts 1:8. His point that "both formulations . . . clearly do not go back to Jesus himself" comes in the context of providing reasons why Christians should "abandon a missionary approach" toward those of other faiths (Braybrooke 1990: 97).

true?" and historical-critical analysis can be only one factor among many in any serious attempt to answer the latter question.

Another strategy for Christians embarrassed by the apparent implications of Jesus' words in John 14:6 is to relativize their significance by a different kind of historical argument, one having to do with the original setting of John's Gospel. For there has been a remarkable shift in overall perception of the Gospel. Once it was seen as the most "universal" of the Gospels, for did not Jesus predicate of himself the catholic categories of bread, light, life, and so on? Now, however, it is widely seen as an inward-looking, sectarian composition. Instead of seeking to penetrate and win over the gentile world, it rather seeks to sustain Christian identity over against a hostile Jewish culture. To the best of my knowledge, Wayne Meeks made the decisive difference with his essay "The Man from Heaven in Johannine Sectarianism."[11] This putative frame of reference can be brought to bear in the kind of way that Moody Smith exemplifies in his commentary on John 14:6:

> This statement reflects a severe exclusivity, even intolerance. It should, however, be seen in light of John's presupposing a bitter polemic between Christ-confessing and Christ-denying Jews, in which confessors are being expelled from synagogues for their belief (9:22). Moreover, such polemic and mutual rejection were not unprecedented within ancient Judaism.[12]

If Jesus' wording is directed to in-house Jewish polemic in the late first century, then the implication appears to be that the words hardly qualify to have the enduring significance that should require them to be taken seriously in contemporary doctrinal formulation.

This historical hypothesis, which, however heuristically illuminating in certain aspects, remains a hypothesis, is directed toward the originating context of John's Gospel and does not address the question of its interpretation as a canonical text within the New Testament. Yet even if the formation of texts is sociologically and ideologically charged, the more texts are reused in a variety of contexts, the further their dynamics move from those of their originating context. The existence of a canon implies the importance of recontextualization, in which, although the originating context may still inform interpretation, other factors too become significant. The New Testament canon invites readers to consider John not as an independent composition for a particular context and/or community[13] but rather as the sequel to the three Synoptic

11. Meeks 1972 (reprinted in Ashton 1997: 169–205).

12. Smith 1999: 269. Admittedly, Smith subsequently offers a more positive construal of Jesus' words; though he does so by appeal to Hebrews 10:20 rather than to the intrinsic dynamic of Johannine Christology.

13. The essays in Bauckham 1998b suggestively highlight some of the difficulties that attach to certain common assumptions about the composition of the Gospels.

Gospels, within an authoritative collection of the church; the church's life settings are no longer those in which the canonical texts were composed, and yet these texts still function authoritatively. Within this context, a reading of John's Gospel as engaging a multinational audience for whom the universal symbols of bread, life, light, and so on can be realized in Jesus becomes a natural reading strategy.

John 14:6 in Its Johannine Context

We come now to a brief outline of what John 14:6 does, and does not, mean within the context of John's Gospel.[14]

1. The context of John 14:6 is Jesus' long "farewell" discourse, where he prepares his disciples for his going to the cross and the fact that they will have to face the future without his being among them as during his earthly ministry. Jesus' coming death is the horizon of his words here. In immediate context, after Judas's departure Jesus speaks of his coming "glorification," which involves his going where the disciples cannot, for the present, follow him (John 13:31–33). Nonetheless, they must live in love in the way that Jesus has loved them, and subsequently they will be able to follow Jesus in the way he is now going (John 13:34–36). Although the prospect of Jesus' going where the disciples cannot also go may be dismaying, the purpose of Jesus' words that follow is clearly to show why this need not be so.

2. Whatever the precise relationship between way, truth, and life,[15] it is clear that the leading idea is of Jesus as the way. For Jesus has just spoken of "going" (John 14:2, 3, 4, 5) and "way" (John 14:4, 5), and he next speaks of "going" to the Father. So the concern is that of knowing how to make a particular journey, a journey to God the Father. Since Jesus goes on to speak of knowing and seeing himself as tantamount to knowing and seeing the Father (John 14:7, 9), a major point of Jesus' words in John 14:6 is that the journey and the destination are, in some sense, identical—not identical in every way (as though there were no distinction between Father and Son), but identical in the sense that the nature of the journeying is entirely of a piece with the nature

---

14. At my time of writing, Rowan Williams also discusses John 14:6 in his Larkin Stuart Lecture, "The Bible Today: Reading and Hearing." He observes, among other things, "The point is that the actual question being asked is not about the fate of non-Christians; it is about how the disciples are to understand the death of Jesus as the necessary clearing of the way which they are to walk. . . . If we ask what the question is that the passage overall poses, or what the change is that needs to be taking place over the time of the passage's narration, it is about the move from desolation in the face of the cross (Jesus' cross and the implicit demand for the disciple to carry the cross also) to confidence that the process is the work of love coming from and leading to the Father" (Williams 2007).

15. On the possible significance of the repeated definite article, see Moule 1959: 112.

of the destination.[16] The response of faith to Jesus the Son,[17] which enables access to God the Father, also constitutes the substance of the relationship with God the Father that is thereby enabled.

3. The latter part of John 14:6, "No one comes to the Father except through me," is surely to be seen as restating negatively what the first part states positively, "I am the way, the truth, and the life," without making a further point about exclusivity. For if the way that Jesus constitutes is appropriately designated also by terms such as "truth" and "life," then that surely designates this particular way as incomparable and definitive. Or, in the language used elsewhere in the Gospel, John 14:6b reminds us that Jesus is not just "Son" (*huios*) but rather "only Son" (*monogenēs huios*);[18] in the famous words, "God so loved the world that he gave his only Son, so that all who believe in him should not perish but have eternal life" (John 3:16; cf. 1:14, 18; 3:18). In other words, it is because Jesus is the only Son that he is the only way to the Father.

4. The reason why faith in Jesus as Son enables, indeed constitutes, access to God as Father is given consistently elsewhere in the Gospel. In the language of John 5:19–24, it is because of the complete harmony of action between Father and Son, such that the Son only does what he sees the Father doing, and the Father therefore entrusts his authority and responsibility to the Son.[19] Or, in the words of the prologue, Jesus is the *logos*, who is so intimate with God that "all things were made through him" and he is the one who has made known the unseen God (John 1:3, 18). The logic, therefore, of "No one comes to the Father except through me" is that Jesus the Son is so intimate with God the Father that God is definitively represented by Jesus, and so one need not go elsewhere.

5. Despite the generalizing form of the wording "No one comes . . . ," the prime sense in context is that Jesus is telling his disciples about the nature of their journey in faith; that is, "None of you can come to the Father unless. . . ."[20] The generalizing form is indeed significant because it specifies that what applies to the disciples applies to others also. Nonetheless, it is important to see that the concern of the text is not an abstract axiom about people of other faiths but rather a drawing out of the wider significance of Jesus' words to his first disciples—what applies to the disciples applies to others also.

---

16. As Rudolf Bultmann (1971: 605–6) puts it, Jesus is the access to God not "in the sense that he mediated the access and then became superfluous," but rather "he is the way in such a manner as to be at the same time the goal."

17. Throughout John's Gospel "have faith, believe" (*pisteuō*) is the prime term of appropriate response to Jesus and introduces the paragraph on which we are focusing (John 14:1).

18. For a pithy presentation of the main issues in the debate about the meaning of *monogenēs* and its relation to *monogennētos* ("only-begotten"), see Bauer et al. 1999, s.v. *monogenēs*.

19. Compare the "Johannine thunderbolt" in the Synoptic Gospels (Matt. 11:25–27; Luke 10:21–22).

20. Thus there is an implicit *oudeis ex hymōn*, as in John 7:19.

In short, therefore, the concern of John 14:6 is to show that Jesus' going
to the Father via the cross is a way of self-giving love whose content becomes
definitive for others also to come to, and to know, God as Father.

Jesus as Light and Truth

At least two further passages are crucial to a right understanding of the Christology outlined thus far. The first is John's account of the "judgment" posed
by the coming of Jesus into the world (John 3:19–21). Here, as the prologue
puts it, Jesus is "the light that shines in the darkness" (John 1:5). The imagery
is of a torch being thrust into dark places. This poses a choice for those who
live in these dark places: do they come to the light, or do they shrink back
from it into a still-undisturbed area of darkness? Many do shrink back, and
this is because "people loved darkness rather than light because their deeds
were evil; for all who do evil hate the light and do not come to the light, so that
their deeds may not be exposed" (John 3:19–20). By contrast, "Those who do
the truth come to the light, so that it may be seen that their deeds have been
done in God" (John 3:21).

Three brief comments. First, the coming of Jesus poses an intrinsic challenge
for people that can no more be evaded or ignored than can those who inhabit
dark places ignore a torch thrust into their midst; some kind of response, of
turning toward or turning away, must be made. Second, the challenge posed
by Jesus is intrinsically moral, to embrace good rather than evil. Third, it is
possible in some sense to "do the truth" before coming to the light rather than
solely as a consequence of such coming. The issue at stake is not predestina-
tion, still less some notion that humans can perform good deeds independently
of grace (so that grace might appear to be, as it were, an optional extra).[21]
Rather, the point is that however great the darkness within the world, there
may be human dispositions and practices that are intrinsically open and at-
tuned to that light which is embodied in Jesus, even if they are not consciously
so conceived. A believing response to Jesus should affirm antecedent, as well
as enable subsequent, truthful living, even though, of course, explicit recognition of Jesus will give a more specific context and shape hereafter to that
which is affirmed.

The other passage to consider is the trial before Pilate, especially John
18:33–37, where there is a reconstrual of the meaning of Jesus as "king"
(*basileus*) that is comparable to the Synoptic account of Caesarea Philippi,
where the term "messiah/christ" (*christos*) as applied to Jesus also receives
fundamental reconstrual.

---

21. I discuss this elsewhere in terms of the principle that "the possibility of experiencing grace
and the possibility of experiencing grace *as* grace, are not the same thing" (Moberly 2006: 248);
the wording comes from Nicholas Lash in his construal of Karl Rahner's theology.

When Pilate presses on Jesus the question of whether or not he answers to being "king," the term apparently used in the Jewish leaders' charge against him, Jesus initially defines his kingship negatively: "My kingship/kingdom [*basileia*] is not from [*ek*] this world" (John 18:36). This language draws on the recurrent Johannine polarity between that which is "from above/from God/from the spirit" and that which is "from this world/from below/from the flesh" (cf. John 1:13; 3:6; 3:31; 8:23). The distinction is between that whose true nature is determined by God and that which is solely determined by the priorities of a created order that resists the will of its creator. So because Jesus' kingship is not "conventional," it does not involve his disciples fighting to protect him (Peter did strike out violently but was rebuked by Jesus [John 18:10–11]).

Pilate appears uninterested in Jesus' conceptual point and solely latches on to one implication of his words: if Jesus can speak of his "kingship," he must be conceding that he is a "king" and thus acknowledging the charge against him. Jesus' initial response, "You say that I am a king" (John 18:37), means "Yes, but 'king' is your term, not mine"; the implication is that the meaning of "king" is so different for Pilate and for Jesus that it prevents rather than assists real communication or understanding. So Jesus continues with words that must, in context, represent his own positive construal of his kingship: "For this I was born, and for this I have come into the world, that I might bear witness to the truth" (John 18:37). What it means for Jesus to be king (messiah) is given content in terms of representing a certain kind of reality, bearing witness to the truth—a reality that is not obvious to all, as the added rider makes clear: "Everyone who is from/of [*ek*, as in other formulations of the Johannine polarity] the truth listens to my voice."

There is an obvious similarity between John 3:19–21 and John 18:33–37. The clearest verbal resonance is the common use of "truth": those who do the truth come to the light, just as those who are of the truth listen to Jesus' voice. Thus, correspondingly, one should understand the light shining in the darkness as having the same dynamics as Jesus' bearing witness to the truth. In Jesus, people are confronted by a reality, a truth that compels a response toward or away from that reality—the reality of God.

What It Means to "Come to the Light"

The continuing trial narrative exemplifies important aspects of the dynamics of Jesus' account of his kingship, in relation both to Pilate and to those Jews who are present. First, Pilate. Although Pilate has a poor reputation (the "jesting Pilate" who asks Jesus about truth and does not wait for an answer [John 18:38]), he surely tries repeatedly to save Jesus, whom he recognizes to be innocent in terms of the charges brought against him. Pilate's declaration that he finds no case against Jesus is followed by reference to a custom of prisoner release at Passover that he clearly envisages as an opportunity to let Jesus go. When this is thwarted by the clamor for Barabbas, Pilate tries again. He has Jesus scourged and mockingly dressed up as a king, presumably in the hope that, among other things, this would satisfy the rancor against Jesus, for he then presents Jesus again and repeats that he finds no case against him. When further interchange with the chief priests proves fruitless, Pilate speaks again with Jesus, the upshot of which is a renewed effort to release him.

At this point the Jews who want Jesus crucified play their trump card. They in effect threaten Pilate by reminding him that to release a would-be king within the Roman Empire would diminish his credentials as "Caesar's friend"; it would be an act of disloyalty that they would be sure to let Caesar know about. So Pilate's own future is now involved. This leads to the dramatic climax, at the seat of judgment. Pilate initially presents the charge brought against Jesus, as "king," as ridiculous: how could this tortured object of mockery pose any threat? When they bay for him to be taken away and crucified, Pilate tries one last time, only to be confronted by the chief priests' definitive declaration of loyalty to Caesar, with its tacit reminder that Pilate would be disloyal should he release Jesus. And so Pilate capitulates and hands Jesus over for execution. All that is left then is a little spat with the chief priests over the wording on Jesus' cross.

We surely see here that Pilate initially tries, in his own way, to "do the truth" and "come to the light." But when it becomes potentially too costly for him to act upon his conviction that Jesus is innocent, self-interest prevails, and he capitulates; in Johannine terms, he withdraws into the darkness "because his deeds are evil." Pilate's drama is played out not in declarations of faith in Jesus or gross moral dereliction but rather in terms of mundane pressures where doing what is right is set over against self-interest; *this* is what Jesus as God's light and truth can represent.

There is less subtlety in the portrayal of those who call for Jesus' execution, who are depicted either generically as "the Jews" (John 18:31, 38; 19:7, 12, 14) or as "the chief priests" (John 19:6, 15); the picture is that of the religious leaders inciting a larger crowd. By this stage they consistently bay for Jesus' death, and their baying culminates in apostasy when the proclamation "We have no king but Caesar" not only puts pressure on Pilate but also in effect renounces God's covenant lordship over Israel. In John's portrayal, a baying mob is not only entirely blind to what is before their eyes—Jesus the king (messiah)—but also is willing to renounce its most basic allegiance in order to get its way. For in wanting the death of one who speaks the truth, their words and deeds are not "of God" but rather "of the devil" (John 8:40, 44). Their "deeds are evil" because their intentions and speech are murderous.

It is worth lingering briefly, however, on the question of what these Jews should have seen when Jesus was presented to them by Pilate. As in the Synoptic crucifixion scenes, the Johannine trial scene is full of the heaviest irony about Jesus' kingship and power. The irony depends, of course, on the Johannine perspective that "Jesus is the Messiah, the Son of God" (John 20:31). But without the benefit of Christian hindsight, what should these Jews have seen? In one sense, this is simply to pose the central problem of understanding the New Testament as a whole: How should the power and salvation of God be recognized in Jesus' lack of power as he is torturously executed by the Romans? Within John's portrayal we see at least two things. First, blindness is the culmination of a process of self-serving and hard-hearted decisions and actions, as succinctly portrayed in John 9, where the gaining of sight by the man born blind is paralleled by the religious authorities' progressive loss of sight; massive failure to see at the trial is the fruit of lesser failures previously. Second, recognition of Jesus during the trial would have, on any reckoning, required not only compassion for someone suffering but also a readiness to find truth and light in an unexpected place; without a willingness to open mind and heart in an uncomfortable way, one cannot recognize Jesus for who he really is.

On Understanding and Appropriating Johannine Christology

Let us look at some brief inferences from this exposition.

First, one will misunderstand Johannine Christology if one fails to see how John formulates paradoxical tensions as constitutive of that Christology. There is at least a double dynamic that must be held in place.

On the one hand, there is the tension of the particular and the universal. It is the particular figure of Jesus who embodies the universal truth of the one Creator God; the only Son reveals the God who is Father and enables coming to him. In a rather important sense, the "sectarian" reading of John (noted above) risks obscuring what is perhaps one of the most significant dimensions in John's whole portrayal: in coming to faith in Jesus, people are not, indeed cannot be, opting for something sectarian, for they are rather coming to realize the true nature of their being;[22] if they come to faith in the one who is the *logos*, "through whom all things were made," it cannot but follow that this faith enables the recognition and appropriation of reality as it is meant to be.

On the other hand, there is the tension of the ontological and the existential. The given, ontological reality of God the Father made known in and through the Son entails a constant, though unpredictable, existential challenge to creation to listen to the one who bears witness to the truth, to come toward the light that is thrust into dark places. Life is seen to be constituted by a struggle between light and darkness, in which the light is constantly challenging people

---

22. This is not, of course, to deny that Christian sectarianism is a recurrent phenomenon. The point is what a right understanding of Scripture entails.

to choose light rather than darkness—a challenge realized in the responsiveness of mind and heart, of conscience and action.

Second, it follows from this that although the truth of God in Jesus is entrusted to the church, enabling the church as it follows Jesus to bear witness
to truth and to be a light in darkness ("As the Father sent me, so I send you"
says the risen Jesus [John 20:21]), the truth is always greater than its particular
embodiments. There are various ways in which one can try to articulate this:
it is less that the church possesses the truth than that the truth constitutes the
church; it is not that God is on our side but rather that we may be on God's
side; even when one believes that Jesus is the Messiah, the Son of God, and
so one knows the truth, the reality is more than words alone can capture, the
words are easily misunderstood, the reality is easily misrepresented.[23]

John's prime depiction of these dynamics, and the gap that may open up
between profession and practice, is in terms of Jesus' Jewish contemporaries.
Yet to generalize and abstract this depiction, as though Jews intrinsically have a
problem because they do not believe in Jesus, while Christians are fine because
they do believe in Jesus, would be to misrepresent John's portrayal. For the
dynamics that are intrinsic to the recognition of God in Jesus entail listening
to the truth and coming to the light. If the Pharisees could know that God had
spoken to Moses and yet use this to close down rather than open up engagement with the implications of Jesus' actions,[24] Christians are no less liable to
know that God is revealed in Jesus and yet use that to close down rather than
open up engagement with the continuing shining of light in the darkness and
the bearing of witness to the truth. If Jews can be "of [ek] the devil" (John
8:44) because they want to resist, indeed put to death, one who bears witness
to the truth (and so the nature of their present reality is "evil"), if their eyes
can be closed to the reality of their king because they are too preoccupied
with baying for the one who speaks and embodies an uncomfortable truth to
be put to death, then, *mutatis mutandis*, the same can characterize Christians,
who can equally be "of the devil" and effectively apostatize through manipu-
lative and brutal actions performed in the name of Jesus. The Crusades and
the Inquisition are no more than notorious examples of a faithlessness that
operates constantly, albeit usually in less conspicuous ways.

Specifically with regard to the Johannine adversaries of Jesus, my contention is that the portrayal of the Jews as "of the devil" in John 8 is entirely

23. So too Rowan Williams, in his discussion of John 14:6, observes, "The text in question
indeed states that there is no way to the Father except in virtue of what Jesus does and suffers;
but precisely because that defines the way we must then follow, it is (to say the least) paradoxical if it is used as a simple self-affirmation for the exclusive claim of the Christian institution
or the Christian system. There is, in other words, a way of affirming the necessity of Christ's
crucified mediation that has the effect of undermining the very way it is supposed to operate"
(Williams 2007).

24. This is perhaps especially the case in the story of the man born blind (John 9).

correlative with their murderous intent toward Jesus, as eventually realized in John 19. To abstract and essentialize this portrayal and to suppose on that basis that John is "anti-Semitic" is to commit a major error. It is "of the devil" to be murderous, not to be Jewish.

On the Interface between Scripture and Doctrine

Finally, three brief comments about our overall concern, the interface between Scripture and doctrine.

First, John's Christology is surely a quintessential embodiment of the concept of mystery—where *mystery* refers not to a puzzle awaiting resolution (if only one knew a little more) but rather to a reality that expands the more one enters into it; as the well-known tag aptly puts it, "The more you know, the more you know you don't know."[25] Among other things, this reminds us that the purpose of doctrine/dogma is neither to produce certain kinds of premature "resolution" to life's challenges, as though believers should know the answer before the question is even asked, nor to encourage believers to become blinkered, as though they should either ignore those aspects of the world that do not obviously fit within a Christian frame of reference or misdescribe them so that they do. Rather, the purpose is to enable the heart and mind so to grasp definitive truth about God and humanity that it becomes possible to live more truthfully and self-givingly within God's world and be able to challenge darkness and untruth more searchingly and with less fear of the possible consequences.

Second, John's narrative illuminates how Christian doctrinal belief about Jesus should, and should not, be used. Johannine Christology surely is better captured by the historic doctrines of trinity and incarnation than by any other known formulations, for thus we maintain the emphasis that the reality and the mystery of God are definitively known and encountered in the particular person of Jesus. The not uncommon strategy of interfaith dialogue to set aside this belief is well intended, but surely it results from a failure of comprehension. Or, to put it differently, it turns the second-rate into the normative. For when Christianity becomes simply one religion alongside others, it has failed to recognize its true vocation, which is not to add to the world's religious diversity but rather to bear witness to the truth of what it means to have life in all its fullness in God's world.

Third, interfaith dialogue that is true to the doctrinal implications of Johannine Christology will necessarily embody both conviction about the nature of the truth of God in Jesus (a faith-derived understanding of ontological reality) and an openness to be surprised by others and to recognize that there

25. John does not use the Greek term *mysterion*. My point here concerns conceptuality rather than terminology.

may be things still to be learned about what this definitive truth really entails (an existential and epistemological sense of humility and incompleteness). As Michael Barnes puts it,

> While it is always tempting to think of the other as lacking something essential which I possess, the truth is that a certain darkness or otherness or lack of self-presence manifests itself in all human beings—especially in face-to-face dialogue. Paradoxically, perhaps, the truly universal experience in inter-faith dialogue is of that moment of disruption or surprise before the other which at certain moments in time reveals my own perplexity or incompleteness.[26]

Or, as Paul Griffiths puts it when commenting on the Johannine promise that the Spirit will lead Christ's followers into "the entire truth" (John 16:13),

> Note the future tense. This future reference is an essential point: the Holy Spirit has not yet taught the Church everything; and, it ought to be added, what the Holy Spirit has taught has not yet been fully comprehended by the church.[27]

This learning and comprehending involves a total way of being in the world, with openness and responsiveness to all those who speak the truth. Christ is the norm by which we seek here and now to discern right human responsiveness to the reality of God, wherever it is found; and this is a reality that involves learning and surprises for all.

26. Barnes 2002: 246.
27. Griffiths 2003: 24.

4

Reading Paul, Thinking Scripture

N. T. WRIGHT

Scripture, Doctrine, and Life: The Puzzle of Perception

For many in today's church, "doctrine," especially when labeled as "dogma," is the dry, lifeless thing that once seemed important but now fails to send people out to change the world. For some such people, it is Scripture that brings them to life—the book where they meet Jesus and find him speaking to them. They read, or listen to, Scripture in the way that they would listen to a favorite symphony or folk song. It recreates their world, the world where they and God get it together, the world where all things are possible to those who believe.

Not everybody sees things that way. For some, Scripture itself, except for highly select verses and passages, has become as dry and dusty as dogma itself. It is full of problems and puzzles, alternative readings and private theories of interpretation, and seems to them like a black hole that can suck down all the energy of otherwise good Christian people (exegetes and preachers) and give nothing much back in return. For them, what matters is invoking the Spirit, worshiping for longer and longer, extended prayer and praise meetings, telling others how wonderful it is to have a living relationship with Jesus. Such people assume (since the background of their tradition is broadly evangelical) that Scripture remains in some sense normative, but how it exercises that normativity, or how it "exercises" anything at all, or engages with their life and faith remains unclear.

The third category completes the circle. There are some for whom the books of devotion appear stale, but for whom, as C. S. Lewis once put it, the heart sings unbidden when working through a book of dogmatic theology with pipe in teeth and pencil in hand. For such people, as well, the endless and increasingly labyrinthine productions of the Great Exegetical Factory, especially the older Germans on the one hand and the newer Americans on the other, leave them cold. The lexicographical, historical, sociological, and rhetorical mountains of secular exegesis all move, and every so often there emerges a ridiculous mouse that squeaks some vaguely religious version of a currently popular self-help slogan. Meanwhile, the real mountains—the enormous, looming questions of God and the world, of church and society, of Jesus then and now, of death and resurrection—remain unaddressed. Salieri, in Peter Shaffer's *Amadeus*, looks at Mozart's operas and declares that Mozart has taken ordinary people—barbers, servant girls, footmen—and made them gods and heroes. He himself, however, has written operas about gods and heroes, and he has made them ordinary. A similar verdict awaits the contemporary "secular" exegete who dares to look into the mirror.

"Does it have to be this way?" asks not only the theologian but also the bishop. Where are the so-called ordinary people in all of this? Is there a better way not only of understanding the relationship between Scripture and doctrine but also of allowing either or both to bear fruit in the postmodern church and world?

Scripture and Narrative

To say that I want to begin to address this with some remarks about Scripture and narrative may provoke a sigh from at least some dogmaticians: "That is *so* last century, *so* postliberal. They are even giving it up at Yale now. Can any good thing come out of narrative?" Well, as a reader of Scripture, I perceive that the canon as it stands not only is irreducibly narrative in form, enclosing within that, of course, any number of other genres, but also displays an extraordinary, because unintentional to every single individual writer and redactor involved, overall storyline of astonishing power and consistency. You could say, of course, that this is all due to those who chose the books and shaped the canon, but if you look at the ones they left out, you would have to say either that even if you put them all in, you would still have the same narrative or that if you put some of them in (the gnostic Gospels, for instance), you would precisely deconstruct what would still be a huge, powerful narrative and offer instead a very different one from which, ultimately, you would have to exclude more or less everything else that is there. The gnostic Gospels, if made canonical, would eventually act like the baby cuckoo in the nest, kicking out all the native chicks, but if the chicks got together where they had landed on the ground, they would still have a massive family likeness. You cannot, in the end, take the anticanonical rhetoric of much contemporary writing to its logical conclusion without ending up having the canon again, only now as the alternative narrative. No: what we have, from Genesis to Revelation, is a massive narrative structure in which, though Paul, the evangelists, and John of Patmos are, of course, extremely well aware of the earlier parts, no single author saw the whole or knew about all its other parts. It is as though engineers from different workshops were invited to produce bits and pieces of cantilevers which ended up, when put together without the different workshops knowing of it, producing the Forth Bridge. And the case I have made elsewhere, to bring this into sharp focus, is that Paul was aware of enough of this large story at least to add his own bit and point to the completion, even though other writers, such as the seer of Revelation, finish the narrative sequence with a different metaphor: marriage, in Revelation 21, rather than birth, as in Romans 8. But with Paul, we are "thinking Scripture" all the way, and that means "thinking narrative."

I am thus taking the phrase "thinking Scripture" in, I think, two ways. First, that as we read Paul, we should be conscious that he is "thinking Scripture" in the sense that his mind is full of the great scriptural narrative and the great scriptural narratives, and that he is conscious of living in the climactic and newly explosive continuation and implementation of the first and also of living with the echoes and patterns of the second. But, second, part of the point is that as we read Paul, we should be conscious not only of "Paul said this, that, or the other" but also of "How can Paul's saying of this be Scripture for us; how can it, that is, function as the word that addresses, challenges, sustains us, putting us to death and bringing us to new life?"

Now of course, within the grand narrative from the first garden to the new city there are multiple smaller narratives, some of them pulling this way and that within the larger one, sometimes even seemingly in opposite directions. That is to be expected, and actually it is only if we shrink the grand narrative from its full proportions that this becomes a problem. And of course, since the narrative itself is precisely about God's extraordinary, vibrant, and multifaceted creation, we find poetry, prophecy, and wisdom firmly embedded, embodying what the story is saying about creativity and procreativity, about humans bearing God's image, about God's generous overspilling love, and so on. And within this narrative, and sometimes within its subgenres, there are statements of overarching truth or inalienable moral duty: the Ten Commandments come within the Exodus narrative (and are themselves prefaced by, and sometimes refer back to, bits of the larger narrative), and huge yet simple statements such as "Christ died for our sins according to the scriptures" are framed within the implicit narrative of Paul's ongoing relationship with the feisty and factious Corinthians. And because I hold, as I always have done, a very high view of Scripture, not only as dogma but also as method, I find myself bound to ask whether doctrine, including, be it said, doctrine about Scripture itself, has really taken on board this element. It is not simply a question of "How can a narrative be authoritative?" I have written a book about that already.[1] The question, rather, is "How can a narrative, or more specifically this narrative, relate to the abstract questions, cast frequently in nonnarratival mode, that have formed the staple diet of doctrine and dogma?"

Is this even the right question to be asking? Might it not seem to imply (1) that it is doctrine that really matters, that will give life and energy and focus to the church; (2) that Scripture is the authority for our doctrine, since that is itself a foundational doctrine, but (3) that Scripture as we find it seems singularly unsuited for the purpose (as Winston Churchill said about a golf club in relation to the task of conveying a ball into a small and distant hole)? And, granted that modern and often postmodern exegesis has left Scripture in bits all over the floor, each labeled "early Q" or "deutero-Paul" or "Hellenistic moral *topos*" or whatever—as though that settled anything—will it help (and if so, how?) to draw attention to Scripture's most prominent characteristic, or will this too collapse into another pile of mere narrative theories, with actantial analyses like the spars of the skeleton ship in *The Rime of the Ancient Mariner*, giving the initial appearance of being seaworthy but actually carrying only Death and Life-in-Death?

Doctrine as "Portable Story"

I think not. I want to propose what may be a way forward—not a particularly original one, but one that I have found helpful in reflecting recently on that strange doctrine called "the atonement." I want to propose that we see doctrines as being, in principle, *portable narratives*. What do I mean?

When I am at home, my clothes live in wardrobes, and my books on bookshelves. But when I need to be away from home, I put them in bags and suitcases. It is not easy to carry suits, robes, and shoes, let alone books and notebooks, a laptop computer, an MP3 player, and so on, all loose, on and off the London Underground. The bags and suitcases perform a vital function. But when I get to my destination, even if I am only there for a single night, I get almost everything out, hang up the clothes and robes, and arrange the books on a desk or table, not because the suitcases were not important, but rather because they were. The bits and pieces have got where they were going and must be allowed to be themselves again.

1. Wright 2005.

This model suggests a to-and-fro between Scripture and doctrine that goes something like the following. It may be very important for the internal life of the church, or for the church's witness to the world, that we address a question about the meaning of Jesus' death that has come up at some point in debate. How are we going to do it? It is hard, each time you want even to refer to Jesus' death itself, to quote even a few verses from Mark 15, Matthew 27, Luke 23, or John 19. If, each time I wanted to refer in a discussion to the archbishop of Canterbury, I had to spell out the complete biography of that great and good man as set out in *Who's Who*, the discussion would get impossibly clogged up. The title—the phrase "archbishop of Canterbury"—is a portable version of this, implying it all without telling the full story; but at any point it might be important that people were aware that this title refers to someone who was born in Wales, to someone who once held a chair at Oxford, to someone who has written a book on the resurrection, and so on. The narrative is implicitly carried within the title; at any point, you can reach in and get the bit of the story you need. Thus, in the same way, and thinking about Paul and the cross, it is quite cumbersome, each time you want to refer to the atonement, to have to say something like "Paul's teaching that 'Christ died for our sins according to the scriptures.'" So we bundle all of this, and the much fuller statements as well, up into a suitcase labeled "atonement," which we can carry on and off the trains and buses of our various arguments and discussions, and which really does perform a vital function in enabling discourse to proceed. However, when we get to the other end, we need to unpack it all again, so that what we are left with is not a single word—"atonement" or "reconciliation" or *Versöhnung* or whatever it might be—but rather the whole story: John 18–19 as it stands, Romans 3, Galatians 3, 2 Corinthians 5, and so on. Such passages, I suggest, are the ground-level reality. The word "atonement" itself and its near equivalents, and the various theories about atonement, are of service only insofar as they enable us to bundle up the passion narratives and the key New Testament witnesses to the meaning of the cross, not in order to muzzle them or only to "live out of a suitcase," snatching an item here and there but keeping everything else crumpled up and invisible inside the zipped-up leather dogma, but rather to bring them out again and live off them, live with them, put them on and wear them, line them up and use them.

At this point, already, I must introduce a further element. The conviction has been growing in me that when Jesus wanted to explain to his followers what he thought would be the meaning of his death, he did not give them a theory; he gave them a meal. And the meal itself, by being a Passover-meal-with-a-difference, already indicates a massive and complex implied narrative: a story about a long history reaching a new, shocking, and decisive fulfillment; a story about slavery and freedom, about Israel and the pagans, about God fulfilling his promises, about covenant renewal and forgiveness of sins. And this encoded story, this meal-as-narrative, works by doing it. Breaking the bread and drinking from the cup are not *about* something else, unless that something else is simply called "Jesus." Rather, we might better say that theories about atonement are, at their very best, abstractions from the Eucharist, which is itself the grid of interpretation that we have been given—by Jesus himself!—for Jesus' death. This makes life much more complicated, of course, since we have suddenly introduced a third and disturbing element into the "Scripture and doctrine" debate, but at least in the case of the atonement, we have, I think, no choice.

Creeds as Portable Story—and Therefore as Symbol

I will come back to this presently, because it might be that the atonement is, in this respect and perhaps in others, something of a special case. But first I want to state the obvious and then develop it a little. The idea that doctrines are portable stories is, of course, already present in the classic statements of Christian doctrines, the great early creeds. They are not simply checklists that could in principle be presented in any order at all. They consciously tell the story—precisely the scriptural story!—from creation to new creation, focusing particularly, of course, on Jesus and summing up what Scripture says about him in a powerful, brief narrative (a process that we can already see happening within the New Testament itself). When the larger story needs to be put within a particular discourse, for argumentative, didactic, rhetorical, or whatever other purpose, it makes sense, and is not inimical to its own character, to telescope it together and allow it, suitably bagged up, to take its place in that new context—just as long as we realize that it will collect mildew if we leave it in its bag forever.

One of the things that creeds enable Scripture to do, by being thus compressed into a much, much briefer narrative framework, is to allow the entire story to function as symbol. It is no accident that *symbol* was one of the words that the early Christians used to denote their creeds. The creeds were not simply a list of things that Christians happened to believe. They were a badge to be worn, a symbol that, like the scholar's gown that tells you what this person is about, declares, "This is who we are." That is, of course, why the creeds are recited in liturgy: not so much to check that everyone present is signed up to them but rather to draw together, and express corporately, the church's response to the reading and praying of Scripture in terms of "Yes! As we listen to these texts, we are renewed as *this* people, the people who live within *this* great story, the people who are identified precisely as people-of-this-story, rather than as the people of one of the many other stories that clamor for attention all around." And this, I think, is the role of doctrine, or one of its crucial and central roles: to ensure that when people say the creeds, they know what they are talking about and why it matters, and also to ensure that when some part of the larger story is under attack or is being distorted, we cannot just come to the rescue and, as it were, put a finger in the dyke, but rather we can discern why the attack has come at this moment and at this point and can work to eliminate the weakness that has allowed it to gain access.

Part of my general point about Paul is precisely that he is constantly doing this packing and unpacking, compressing and expanding, hinting in one place and offering a somewhat fuller statement of the same point elsewhere. A good example of this is in 1 Corinthians 15:56–57, where Paul says (bewilderingly, since he has not been talking about these things), "The sting of death is sin, and the power of sin is the law; but thanks be to God, who gives us the victory through our Lord Jesus Christ." By itself, this is more or less incomprehensible, since nowhere else in his writings to date has Paul said anything about the law being "the power of sin." We might just about have inferred it from Galatians 3, but it would be stronger than anything there. But in Romans 7 Paul explains precisely this point at much greater length, ending with the same shout of triumph. In other words, it is not simply the case that Scripture gives miscellaneous teaching about various topics that the church can codify into portable statements and then decodify back into Scripture again. We can see the same process going on within Scripture itself, not least in Paul himself, and not least at this point, when we are thinking about sin, the law, and the victory of Christ—in other words, about atonement.

All this leads us to another important general point about the nature of doctrine, Scripture, and narrative.

Checklists and Connect-the-Dots

It dawns on me, uncomfortably, that it is possible to treat doctrines, not (as the creeds do) as basically a narrative but simply as a kind of abstract checklist, dogmas to which one must subscribe but which do not really belong at all within a story, or, more insidious perhaps still, do belong within a story but within a story that, because it is not usually seen as such, is quietly doing its powerful work of reshaping what these admittedly true doctrines will now mean and why. In other words, simply putting a checkmark beside all twenty-nine (or however many) true doctrines is not good enough. It could be that you are like a child faced with a connect-the-dots puzzle, realizing that you have to link the dots but not understanding what the numbers are there for. You can indeed draw a picture in which all the dots are connected, but it may bear little relation to the picture that was intended. You can, in fact, link all the dots, both in the classic early creeds and most of the later ones (e.g., the post-Reformation confessions and articles), and still be many a mile away from affirming what the biblical writers, all through, were wanting people to affirm. You can connect all the dots and still produce, shall we say, a thistle instead of a rose. To take a different but related example: if I come upon the letters "BC" written down somewhere, it is only the larger context, the larger implicit narrative, that can tell me whether they mean "Bishop's Council" (in an entry in my calendar), "British Columbia" (in my cousin's mailing address), "Before Christ" (in a book about ancient history), or the two musical notes that bear those names (about the conclusion of Sibelius's seventh symphony). Implicit narrative is all. If you affirm a doctrine but place it in the wrong implicit narrative, you potentially falsify it as fully and thoroughly as if you denied it altogether.

This point is not dissimilar to one made by Robert Jenson,[2] though I think he has not done enough to ward off the suspicion that his own proffered solution is subject to the same critique that he has offered of other theories. Writing about the doctrine of the atonement, he suggests that what is wrong with the three main models—Anselm, Abelard, and Christus Victor, to put it bluntly—is that all of them are placing the death of Jesus within a narrative other than the one that Scripture itself proposes. Scripture is not talking about the honor or shame of a medieval nobleman, or about a program to educate people in how to love God, or about monstrous mythical powers and how they might be defeated. I think, actually, that Scripture is more obviously talking about the last of those, but that is another question to which we may return. My difficulty with Jenson (and I suspect that he is building up to addressing this in a fuller work for which the 2006 article is a brief flyer) is that his alternative narrative, which is about the relationships between the three persons of the Trinity, while very interesting and not at all unrelated to the story that Scripture tells, is still not that story itself and still avoids the really important part of the whole thing, the thing to which the church has persistently given far too little attention (including, I believe, the classic creeds themselves): the story of Israel.

It is this story that drives the whole of the New Testament, which is not surprising, because it is what drove Jesus himself. When Paul says that "the Messiah died for our sins according to the scriptures," he does not mean that if we look hard enough, we can find a few helpful proof texts. What he means—and what we see in the great sermons in Acts, particularly chapters 7 and 13 and the subsequent summaries of similar material—is that the story of Israel from Abraham to the Messiah is seen as the plan of the one Creator God to save the whole world. It is remarkable how difficult it is to get this across to people who are deeply embedded in a rather different story, one that reads simply "creation, sin, Jesus, salvation." Interestingly, of course, if you miss the "Israel" stage of the story, not only do you become a de facto Marcionite, as many, alas, in both Protestant and Catholic traditions seem to be, but you also leave yourself, most likely, without an ecclesiology or with

2. Jenson 2006.

having to construct one from scratch far too late in the narrative. There are, of course, all kinds of clues in the New Testament to indicate that something is badly wrong here, and the story of exegesis, not least in the Protestant and evangelical worlds, has sadly included several quite clever moves for rendering these clues (e.g., Rom. 9–11) irrelevant. The story of Israel is assumed to be at best exemplary and at worst irrelevant, except for odd flashes of prophetic inspiration, rather than having anything to do with the meaning of the story of Jesus himself. And with this all pretense of actually paying attention to Scripture itself has vanished.

The question presses, of course, as to how paying attention to the story of Israel enables us to understand what the New Testament writers are saying about the cross, not to mention how we might, having understood, work toward a more biblical formulation; or how all this integrates, as it must if it is to be true to Jesus and the New Testament authors, with the Eucharist and the life of the community that is formed around it. But the same point could, and perhaps should, be made in relation to other doctrines, not only the atonement. Christology, for instance, has, in my view, suffered in the Western tradition because of people simply putting a checkmark in the "Jesus is divine" box without really stopping to think which god they are talking about, what it means within the biblical narrative to say such a thing, and how this integrates properly, not merely accidentally, as it were, with the other box that people will usually check, the "Jesus is human" box. The signs that all is not well include, on the one hand, a kind of "superman" theology wherein Jesus is "the man from outside" coming with miraculous, "supernatural" power to "zap" everything that is wrong, all conceived within a strictly dualistic view that ends, not surprisingly, in his followers being miraculously "raptured" up to join him in "heaven," and, on the other hand, an official acknowledgment that Jesus was human, which nevertheless leads to no engagement whatsoever with the question of what it meant to be *Jesus of Nazareth*, to live and think as a first-century Jew longing for God's kingdom, to be possessed of a deep and radical vocation and to construe that in terms and stories available to a first-century Jew, and so on. The enormous resistance to this latter project tells its own story, which cannot be reduced, in my view, simply to reaction against, say, the Jesus Seminar and some of its sillier forebears.

The mention of the "rapture" points to a further example of how not to connect the dots. For many Christians, the question "Do you believe in the second coming?" means, quite simply, "Do you believe in the dispensationalist rapture doctrine?" and indeed there are some who would love to believe in the genuine New Testament doctrine of the second coming who feel obliged not to put a checkmark in the box because they cannot and will not swallow the rapture. Rapture theology is what you get, in other words, when you take the doctrine ("He will come again with glory to judge the living and the dead, and of his kingdom there will be no end") and put it, first, within a heaven-and-earth dualism in which the only point of human existence on earth is to work out how to leave it with a ticket to the right destination, and, second, within a very localized nineteenth-century reading of one particular set of texts, especially 1 Thessalonians 4:17, which flesh out, within that larger (wrong) story, what the "second coming" might look like. Again, there is enormous resistance to any attempt within these supposedly biblical circles to tell the genuinely biblical story about heaven and earth, and new heavens and new earth, and about the good Creator God, who has promised to unite them into one in Christ Jesus (Eph. 1:10, which itself stands at the heart of a prayer story that is a Christ-and-Spirit-shaped version of a Jewish creation-and-exodus celebration).

Many other examples could be given, but I trust the point is taken. This leads me to a final observation.

What Does "Listening to Scripture" Actually Mean?

Part of the long-term debilitating result of a moribund and overly footnoted exegetical tradition—somewhat, we may suppose, like the endless annotations upon annotations of the late medieval period—is the apparent failure in many parts of today's church actually to engage with Scripture or to listen to it with any seriousness. Here, of course, the normal locus might be thought to be the sermon; however, in many Western churches, the exegesis offered from the pulpit is bare and uninspiring and often is either rather obvious or just plain eccentric. No doubt there are noble exceptions in every direction, but I have an uncomfortable suspicion that most Western Christians, at least in mainline denominations, know what I am talking about. And if that pushes the emphasis elsewhere, where is that "elsewhere"? In small Bible study groups? Fine, but do they produce fresh, vibrant readings of Scripture that then can be passed up the food chain to the larger community? In other groups of clergy and other ministers? Fine, but is this an exercise in mutually assisted devotion rather than a real grappling with key passages and issues with a view to taking some action? In synods? We draw a discreet veil over the mere suggestion. In doctrine commissions and other similar groups? Well, perhaps; but I must say, as one who has been a member of several such bodies, that the best that one can normally hope for is flashes of insight mixed with heavily negotiated compromise statements that end up reflecting not just last century's exegesis, but the wrong bits of last century's exegesis.

Yet most churches include in their formularies and/or statements of intent something about "listening to Scripture" or even "listening to Scripture together," and church members regularly refer back to this in their synod debates and the like. Yes, sometimes noble efforts are made, such as at successive Lambeth Conferences, where serious Bible study has, thank God, been a major, important, and cross-cultural feature. But my concern, granted that that is an exception, is twofold. First, ought we not to be thinking hard about what could and perhaps should be done in this area, aside from what we are currently doing (and not doing very well)? Second, is it not at this point that there is a real danger of those who want to get the church refocused and reenergized trying to do so by, as it were, going behind the back of Scripture (lest we get bogged down in that moribund exegetical tradition again!) and leaping straight for something called "doctrine" instead?

That may be a false fear, but it should perhaps be named just in case. I will not attempt to answer it, but, in answer to the former question, it is worth drawing attention, within the more catholic end of the church, to two phenomena. First, there is the "Ignatian method" of reading Scripture, normally done individually and normally for personal devotional engagement and enrichment but sometimes perhaps in groups and with more wide-ranging results. I am not aware that people tend to emerge from an Ignatian meditation eager to go and put some fine-tuning into one or another of the church's doctrines, but perhaps they should. Second, there is the liturgical reading of Scripture, and particularly of the Gospel reading, as the climax and focus of Scripture, seen as one mode of the personal presence of Jesus with the worshiping congregation, symbolized by making the sign of the cross at the Gospel reading during the Eucharist and at the "Gospel canticle" in morning and evening prayer. I suspect that this phenomenon remains inarticulate for most worshipers even in the traditions where it is the norm, but it is likewise worth drawing out and reflecting upon.

Moreover, I am suggesting that the Eucharist is in fact the primary and indeed dominical grid for understanding Jesus' death. I recognize that the word *understanding* is actually changing in meaning as I say that, so that it is forced to encompass physical and social actions and realities as well as mental states and abstract ideas. It is therefore perhaps germane to my more focused question that we might contemplate the eucharistic reading of Scripture in terms of that reading being one part of the necessary and formative action within which the Eucharist means what it means. It thus enables God's people to "understand," in this deeper sense of being grasped by the reality at every level, who Jesus the Messiah was and is and what his death really did accomplish.

Scripture, Exegesis, Dogma, and Church:
Some Concluding Pauline Proposals

I know only too well, from both sides of the table, as it were, the frustration felt by the preacher or dogmatician who is told by the exegete, "The text does not actually say that." I hope that the dogmatician also recognizes the frustration that the exegete feels when told, precisely in his or her effort to be obedient to one of the primary Reformation dogmas, about Scripture itself, "Do not give us that exegetical mish-mash; we want results, good solid doctrines that we can use and preach from." (Ernst Käsemann commented on this point in a typical statement about those who are concerned only with "results" needing to keep their hands off exegesis, because it has no use for them, nor they for it.[3] I understand his point, but I insist that we must keep on trying.)

I return, instead, to the category of narrative. Rather than trying to filter out the actual arguments that Paul is mounting in order to "get at" the doctrines that, it is assumed, he is "expounding," I have stressed that we must pay attention to those larger arguments and to the great story of God, the world, Israel, and Jesus, giving special attention to the "Israel" dimension, which is regularly screened out in dogma but is regularly vital for Paul, and within which the cross means for him what it means for him.

Closer exegetical attention would show that what the tradition has usually called "the atonement"—that "portable story" within which so much implicit exegesis and dogma has been baggaged up, sometimes uncomfortably—is not a suitcase that Paul employs. It is, perhaps, a sub-suitcase, a compartment within his larger luggage—perhaps something akin to the way Schweitzer saw justification as a *Nebenkrater* within the "main crater" of "being in Christ," though of course I disagree importantly if obliquely with his particular point. But it is not the main thing that Paul is talking about.

Where does that leave us in terms of the questions posed earlier on? To begin with, it means that we must constantly struggle to hear Paul within the world of his implicit, and often explicit, narratives, especially the great story that starts with Abraham (itself understood as the new moment within the story that starts with Adam and, indeed, with creation itself) and continues through Moses to David and ultimately to the Messiah. Protecting Paul from that story—that is not too strong a way to put the matter—has been a major preoccupation both of some academic exegetes who have wanted to locate him solely within a Hellenistic world and of some dogmaticians and preachers who have wanted to make sure that he is relevant to, and addresses clearly, the pastoral and evangelistic issues of which they are aware. But it is precisely at this point, as I have stressed, that the doctrine of Scripture's own authority presses upon us. By what right do we take Scripture and find ways to make it talk about the things that we want it to talk about?

I suggest, in fact, that the key point is to develop more particularly our reflections on the way in which Scripture is used, heard, and lived with within the actual life of the actual church. The belittling of Scripture into a short and puzzling noise that intrudes upon our liturgy here and there is dangerous and destructive, especially, of course, in churches where there is not even much strong dogma to take its place. And the use of Scripture as the peg to preach

3. Käsemann 1980: viii.

sermons that the tradition, even the evangelical or Protestant tradition, has decreed we ought to preach is always in danger of self-delusion. In short, we have to discern and attempt ways of letting Scripture be heard not only when it says something that we understand but want to disagree with (that is where "the authority of Scripture" normally bites), but also when it says something that we do not understand because we have carefully screened out, or never even imagined, the narrative world within which it makes sense.

One of the main ways this needs to be done is, of course, through sustained teaching by preachers and teachers who are themselves soaked in Scripture. Fair enough. But I do think that our churches and parachurch organizations could and should do more to help people understand the great narrative of Scripture, by sustained readings, public and private, by drawing attention to the great narrative themes and encouraging people to explore them, by discouraging the nonnarratival or deconstructive songs that have swept in through today's cheerful and unthinking postmodernity, and by encouraging and creating new words and music to get the great themes into people's heads and hearts. All these suggestions remain a great challenge at the level of pastoral and ecclesial practice. But I think, as well, that at the academic level we need to see far more open exchange between serious historical exegesis—not done in a corner or by bracketing out questions of meaning, doctrine, and life but instead engaging with the realities of which the text speaks—and a dogmatic theology that itself remains open to being told that it has misread some of its own key texts. This, in other words, will be a dogmatic theology that itself does not hide in a corner or bracket out questions of history, text, and original sense.

We are once again at the fault line bequeathed to us by our Western culture, not just in modernity but going back at least as far as the medieval period; and if we are ever to have any hope of straddling that crack without falling down into it, the doctrine called "authority of Scripture" (which declares that Scripture is the way through which God the Holy Trinity activates, through the Spirit, the authority that the Father has delegated to the Son) insists that it is by paying attention to Scripture itself that we will find not only the bridges over the chasm but also the means to make the earth move once more and bring back together what should never have been separated in the first place. If reflecting briefly on Paul's doctrine of reconciliation helps us to glimpse a pathway toward the reconciliation of two camps within the church that have been circling one another suspiciously for far too long, and perhaps two personality types that have projected themselves a little too enthusiastically into that polarization, I think that Paul himself would heave a sigh of relief and suggest that now, reunited, it might be time to get on with the task of coherent living and preaching the gospel.

PART 2

Theology's Bible

5

The Religious Authority
of Albert Schweitzer's Jesus

JAMES CARLETON PAGET

On 15 November 1928 Karl Barth, then professor in systematic theology at the University of Münster, wrote to Eduard Thurneysen to say that he had met Albert Schweitzer some eight days before. "I told him [Schweitzer]," Barth writes, "that his [lecture] was crude works-righteousness and that he was a man of the eighteenth century, but other than that we got on very well. There's no point picking a squabble with him . . . I have to go to a seminar. I'm speaking today about the damaging nature of eternal truths."[1]

In a somewhat barbed way the letter raises the question of the appropriateness of discussing Albert Schweitzer in a volume concerned with the question of the normative role of the New Testament in the discussion and formulation of Christian doctrine. For there is definitely a sense in which Barth's implied judgment of Schweitzer as a liberal is right, in particular as this relates to Schweitzer's view of the role of Christian doctrine in the formulation of the Christian message.

In a public lecture in early 1902, delivered in Strasbourg and entitled *Protestantismus und die theologische Wissenschaft* ("Protestantism and Theological

1. Barth 1974: 628.

Science"), Schweitzer outlined his critical attitude toward Christian dogma. Schweitzer notes that theological scholarship

> has gifted to us . . . true freedom from dogmas. We do not stand as slaves under their rule [*Herrschaft*] . . . but as free men we understand and attend to them. We understand them as something that was necessary; we respect them as holy vessels in which past generations have housed the water of life and in which we taste such. But because of their historical nature, they are not binding norms. We find ourselves in relation to them in the situation of a nation which has fought itself free of an absolute monarchy and come under the rule of an ideal monarch. The dogmas stand in place of the monarch. We bring to them noble respect. But the parliament, which represents us, these are the ideas and needs of our age. In the political and also in the religious-spiritual area this is the only solution of the conflict between the old and the new.[2]

And in another lecture, written four years later, entitled *Jesus und Wir*, Schweitzer, more trenchantly, notes that the church has placed a dogma over Jesus.

> As an historian I would certainly say that they [the leaders of the church] had to do so, that viewed from a historical perspective they could do nothing else. But as we are here concerned to speak about what is the case, I state that the churches have encased a vibrant man in a building of dogmas, have destroyed his simple living humanity, and made him inaccessible to those who do not stand in the building. It cannot and dare not be said enough: Jesus belongs as a man to men.[3]

In none of this does Schweitzer reject the need for Christian doctrines; indeed, on one occasion he can talk about the need for the church to have what he terms *Ehrfurcht vor der Überlieferung* ("reverence for tradition"), here reflecting what he says about the noble respect accorded a monarch, and this means the need for a thoughtful engagement with such traditions, for a need to reexpress them in terms that take account of the new context to which they are being addressed (nowhere does he speak of *undogmatisches Christentum*).[4] But there is an easily located impatience, a sense that, as with a monarch in a parliamentary democracy, traditional Christian doctrines are almost irrelevant. In this respect, it is striking that in spite of the implied need for an interaction between religious tradition and thought, Schweitzer almost never mentions or discusses such significant Christian doctrinal concepts as the incarnation or the Trinity. It is the biblical tradition, understood essentially as the New

---

2. Schweitzer 2003: 246.
3. Schweitzer 2003: 272.
4. For a more measured, but brief, discussion of the subject, see Schweitzer 1973: 5.375–77. See also Rössler 1990.

Testament tradition, that engages Schweitzer in his belief that tradition is best understood without reference to Christian dogmatic categories. And although he is interested, at least in broad terms, in how that tradition came to be transformed into ideas associated with the second century and beyond, he subscribes, at least in a moderate form, to the view that such transformation led Christians away from what was central (and by implication, biblical) in their faith.[5]

So, given all this, why discuss Albert Schweitzer in a volume dedicated to the place of the New Testament in the formulation of Christian doctrine? First, Schweitzer could, on one reading, be said to represent one pole of the discussion, and any serious engagement with this subject needs to be conducted from a variety of quarters. The liberal tradition's perspective on the development of Christian doctrine, whether viewed through the eyes of Harnack, Troeltsch, Schweitzer, or Werner, is a significant part of our theological heritage, even if it is not in vogue at present. Second, Schweitzer's interaction with that tradition is singular and striking, and few people in the period out of which he emerged reflected as fervently, and as problematically, as he did upon the ongoing significance of Jesus and Paul for the Christian faith and its articulation. Third, Schweitzer remained fundamentally concerned with the Bible, and in particular the New Testament, throughout his life, and this in spite of the fact that many of his later writings are philosophical in orientation.

In this respect we should note that even as late as 1930, well after his career as a New Testament scholar had ended, he felt the need to finish his work on the mysticism of the apostle Paul. He felt this need because he was strongly convinced of the fact that this book, with its focus on a central figure of biblical history, had something to say that went beyond the confines of its supposed academic contribution—a point that becomes very clear if one reads the dense, lapidary, almost sermonic conclusion of that work.[6] Related to this is the fact that toward the end of his life, at a very busy time, he began to pen a lengthy book on the kingdom of God (*Reich Gottes und Christentum*).[7] Schweitzer's philosophical position is often associated with "reverence for life," but it is striking that he also saw the need to express similar sentiments in terms of a straightforwardly biblical metaphor.[8]

In this context we need to note one final point. There are good grounds for thinking that Schweitzer's own philosophical enterprise is notably theological; that is, it cannot be understood if its theological substructure is not

5. Note here Schweitzer's close relationship with Martin Werner (they corresponded on a regular basis from the 1920s onward), and Werner's dedication of *Die Entstehung des christlichen Dogmas* (Werner 1941; ET, *The Formation of Christian Dogma* [Werner 1957]) to his friendship with Schweitzer.

6. See Matlock 1996, especially pp. 58–59.

7. Schweitzer 1995.

8. See Schulik 1990: 275.

acknowledged.[9] As Schweitzer was to write to his friend D. E. Rölffs in 1931,[10] his philosophy of reverence for life was no more than the outworking of things he had written in the conclusion of the second edition of his *Quest for the Historical Jesus*—a point confirmed in his at first pseudonymously published *Selbstdarstellung* of 1926. There he writes, "In the moment when Schweitzer concluded *The Quest* his philosophy was already complete."[11]

Schweitzer and Jesus: The Sounds of a Christian Pietist

Few doubt the central place in Schweitzer's consciousness of the figure of Jesus. Schweitzer decided to go to West Africa, specifically Lambaréné in the Gabon, under the auspices of the Paris Missionary Society, an organization with strongly evangelical tendencies. This was a strange decision, one might think, given his liberal leanings. And yet it was precisely the advertisement in the Society's own bulletin, with its strong call to serve Jesus, that attracted Schweitzer to it—a point that he implicitly makes in a letter, dated 9 July 1905, to Alfred Boegner, the director of the Society: "I have become ever simpler, more and more a child and I have begun to realize increasingly clearly that the only truth and the only happiness lie in serving Jesus Christ there where he needs us." Something of this sense of the calling of Jesus is vividly captured in correspondence with his wife, Helene Bresslau, from the period 1902–1913.[12] In a letter dated 24 December 1904 he tells her that he wants to buy her a *Christus-Medaille* (a medal on which was a depiction of Christ's head) like the one that he possesses. "I look at this so often, this medal," he writes. "It is remarkable to look at a man and to know that one is his slave."[13] In another letter, dated 23 December 1903, he gives us a sense of the way in which Christ has taken possession of him against his will:

> Is it not remarkable that this great figure [Jesus] has suborned us and put us in chains? Sometimes I think of revolting. Yes, he has given us powers but he has also taken them from us! He has taken our personality from us; out of free men he has made us slaves. How many talents has he suffocated—and look how he has created wretched people, for without him we would have been glorious characters. That is blasphemy if you want to call it so, but he is sufficiently great to tolerate it.[14]

9. See Barsam 2001 (see now the published version, Barsam 2007, which appeared too late for consultation here).
10. Schweitzer 1987: 118–19.
11. Schweitzer 2003: 370.
12. Schweitzer and Bresslau 1992.
13. Schweitzer and Bresslau 1992: 79.
14. Schweitzer and Bresslau 1992: 53.

Elsewhere he speaks of being taken prisoner (*gefangen*) by Christ, and then he continues, "Because of this obedience, Jesus will forgive me my heresy: I am a bit like one of those satraps who has been sent to the borders of the kingdom and allowed somewhat of a free hand, because they defend and protect it."[15] In the aforementioned letter to Rölffs he writes, "Jesus has simply taken me prisoner [*gefangengenommen*] since my childhood."[16] Here, in a variety of settings, the pious and the radical mix in odd ways, but common to all of them is a relentless, sometimes uneasy, commitment to Jesus.

The Hermeneutics of Schweitzer on Jesus

But in what does this commitment rest? Here we must turn to Schweitzer's scholarly work on Jesus.

Schweitzer's thesis about the motivating forces behind, and the course of, Jesus' ministry can be found in a variety of works dating back to 1901.[17] The rudiments of his view can be succinctly summarized. Jesus preaches the arrival of a coming kingdom in which he will be manifested as the Messiah. He demands from those who will enter the kingdom an absolute ethic of love as proof that they belong to God and the Messiah, what Schweitzer controversially termed an "interim ethic." At a certain point in his ministry, when he believes that the kingdom is about to come, Jesus sends out his disciples to spread this news, but when they return, the kingdom has not come. In this moment of crisis he concludes that the kingdom can come only when he, by suffering and death, has made atonement for those who have been elected to the kingdom and thus saved them from having to go through the premessianic tribulation. He goes up to Jerusalem in the full knowledge that death awaits him. At the final supper he declares to his disciples that he will not drink again of the fruit of the vine until he drinks of it again in his father's kingdom. His death on the cross does not bring about the series of events that he expected, and he dies on the cross with a cry of despair.[18]

It is not my intention to critique Schweitzer's thesis from a scholarly perspective. What is more important is to examine Schweitzer's attempt to derive something lasting for Christian life from what he admits is a set of disturbing conclusions. It is precisely in Schweitzer's willingness to reflect hermeneutically that he differs so strongly from Johannes Weiss, with whose *Die Predigt Jesu vom Reiche Gottes* (1892) he agreed so strongly, but which lacked, even

15. Schweitzer and Bresslau 1992: 70.
16. Schweitzer 1987: 118–19.
17. See especially Schweitzer 1901; 1906 (also the enlarged second edition, Schweitzer 1913 [ET, Schweitzer 2000]).
18. For a summary, see Grässer 1979.

in its second edition, a real engagement with the theological consequences of its historical conclusions.[19]

In what follows I will explore Schweitzer's hermeneutical response to his apparently shocking set of conclusions. Rather than showing how those views evolved,[20] I will outline their central claims as these are found in the second edition of *Von Reimarus zu Wrede*, which was published in 1913 as *Geschichte der Leben-Jesu-Forschung*. In the process I will refer to other writings that seem relevant.[21]

Schweitzer was clear that historical work on Jesus—that is, the work of Schweitzer and other advocates of "thoroughgoing eschatology"—had delivered a shattering blow to theology. Jesus, as historically reconstructed, will no longer be a figure to whom the religion of the present can ascribe its own thoughts and who can appear sympathetic and universally intelligible to the multitude. The historical Jesus can only be to our time a stranger and an enigma. The mistake of previous generations of scholars lay in assuming that Jesus could mean more to us by entering the world in the form of a man like ourselves, by believing that history could in some sense contribute to the making of the present. In the first edition the expression of such views had led Schweitzer to seek to transcend the claims of the historical Jesus by appealing to the mighty spiritual force streaming forth from him: it was this fact that could be neither shaken nor confirmed by any historical discovery. This somewhat problematic statement, which remains unchanged from the original conclusion in *Von Reimarus zu Wrede*, is not developed here. As we will see, Schweitzer prefers to concentrate on the complex of Jesus' will.

In the same conclusion Schweitzer states, "We thought that we had to lead our time by a roundabout way through the historical Jesus, as we understood him, in order to bring it to the Jesus who is a spiritual power in the present. This detour has now been closed by true history."[22] Schweitzer asserts that the liberal presentations of Jesus' life, with their enfeebling tendency to self-projection, have succeeded in robbing Jesus of much of his power, precisely because they have watered down "his imperative world-denying demands on individuals so that he did not come into conflict with our ethical ideals."[23] This leads to a sharply hermeneutical question: "What does the historical Jesus mean for us when we dissociate him from all false justification of the past from the present?"[24] Schweitzer's response is positive: we are immediately aware that in spite of its strangeness, Jesus' personality has great significance

19. See Lannert 1989: 196–97.
20. For this, see Pleitner 1992.
21. Quotations are taken from the English translation, Schweitzer 2000.
22. Schweitzer 2000: 479.
23. Schweitzer 2000: 480.
24. Schweitzer 2000: 480.

for us, and it may profoundly enrich our religion. But in what way? It is here that Schweitzer introduces the idea of the will.

> Each world-view comprises elements determined by its own time and elements undetermined by time. These are intermingled and exist alongside each other, so that a world-view consists of a will penetrating and shaping the body of available contemporary thought-forms. This body of ideas is subject to change. . . . But the will is timeless. . . . However much change there may be in the thought forms of a period, and however extensive the differences between old and new world-views may be as a result, in fact these differences go only so far as there is a difference in the direction taken by the will determining the view.[25]

The aim of interpretation, then, is to enable an accord to be reached between will and will, specifically between Jesus' will and the will of the reader.[26] But how do we go about translating or understanding the will of Jesus, expressed as it is in "primitive late-Jewish metaphysics"? Schweitzer rejects the idea that we separate out transitory from permanent elements; the results of this procedure so detract from the greatness and unity of Jesus' thinking that it only appears to enrich our religion without really doing so. Jesus is "greater if he is allowed to remain in his own eschatological setting and, despite all that is strange to us in that way of thinking, can influence us then at a more elementary and powerful level."[27] Schweitzer continues, "If we only allow the compelling force of his personality and his preaching of the kingdom their full expression, the alien and offensive elements can be quite calmly recognized. This happens automatically as soon as the inevitable limitations of the thought forms available to him are acknowledged."[28] In other words, "Actually it cannot be a matter of separating between the transitory and the permanent, but only of translating the basic thought of that ideology into our concepts"; but such a "translation" can come about only if we begin to move "towards a disposition not dissimilar to Jesus."[29]

Individuals within a specific time period can have a real and living relationship with Jesus only to the extent to which they think ethically and eschatologically within their own categories and can produce in their own worldviews the equivalents of those desires and expectations that hold such a prominent position in his—that is, when they are dominated by ideas that correspond to those that govern Jesus' conception of the kingdom of God.[30]

25. Schweitzer 2000: 481.
26. Schweitzer 2000: 484.
27. Schweitzer 2000: 481. See also words from 1926 in Schweitzer 2003: 368.
28. Schweitzer 2000: 482.
29. Schweitzer 2000: 483.
30. Schweitzer 2000: 483. Note his words from 1903: "The eternal nature of Jesus cannot be described but can only be conceivable to those who are bound to him in community" (Schweitzer 2003: 275).

Such a disposition contrasts sharply with the present state of society, which "lacks all sense of immediacy and all enthusiasm for the ultimate goals of mankind and of being," and it is precisely this lack of inner similarity between Jesus' "ethical enthusiasm and the directness and powerful quality of his way of thinking" that rendered exegetes of the present age incapable of understanding him, forcing them to make him a man and theologian modern in every way.[31] Schweitzer goes on, perhaps paradoxically, to assert that once we have connected our will with that of Jesus, his message no longer appears offensive; in fact, its call for a consummation of the world makes perfect sense. Schweitzer continues, "We give history its due and liberate ourselves from the thought-forms which were available to him. But we bow to the powerful will which lies behind them."[32] But after these expostulations that save Jesus for the world through a kind of metaphysics of the will, Schweitzer maintains, "But, let it be clear, the idea of the moral consummation of all things and of what we must do in our time has not come down to us from him through historical revelation. It is inherent in us and is part of the moral will"; "but," he continues, "because Jesus, following the great among the prophets, grasped the entire truth and immediacy of it and imbued it with his will and personality, he can help us to master it and to become moral forces for our time."[33]

We can achieve a relationship to such a personality only when we become united with him in the knowledge of a shared aspiration, when we feel that our will is clarified, enriched and enlivened by his will, and when we rediscover ourselves through him. Our religion, insofar as it proves to be specifically Christian, is therefore not so much a Jesus-cult as a Jesus-mysticism (*Jesusmystik*).[34]

Several observations arise from this summary.

1. Schweitzer's turn from the liberal view that history was the locus in which to locate the meaning of Jesus for us now, the place that would allow us in some particular way direct access to the figure himself, was a gradual one.[35] Of course, Schweitzer is clear that the historical enterprise cannot be avoided (in this context much of Schweitzer's rhetoric concerning the business of historical investigation in terms of a *Wahrhaftigkeitstat* ["act of truthfulness"] reminds us of the language of the theological liberalism from which he emerged); it is simply that it cannot energize the present. In all of this Schweitzer is reflective of a growing conviction within strands of Protestantism that was to reach its zenith, admittedly from different presuppositions, in the work of Barth and Bultmann.

31. Schweitzer 2000: 483, 482.
32. Schweitzer 2000: 486.
33. Schweitzer 2000: 486.
34. Schweitzer 2000: 486.
35. See Pleitner 1992.

2. Schweitzer is keen to avoid, at least explicitly, a sieving process whereby the supposedly permanent and the transitory aspects of Jesus' message are separated one from another—an interpretative move that liberal scholars were often quick to make. For a full appreciation of the character of Jesus' will, there is for Schweitzer a sense in which he should be seen in a unified light, and this means in his full eschatological setting. After all, according to Schweitzer, we achieve our hermeneutical goal by a translation of the basic thought of that ideology into our concepts. Such an approach better preserves the absoluteness of Jesus' convictions, the enthusiasm of his ethical disposition (described as an absolute ethic), which is entirely set upon the establishment of the kingdom. It is precisely in this form that Jesus becomes a force in the present world.

In this context we should note how Schweitzer, here brandishing an antiliberal cudgel, plays up the role of Jesus' difference from the world and its prevailing values. Schweitzer, unlike his liberal predecessor Ritschl, saw the world as in decline and saw its transformation as lying not in the values of human society but rather in a type of eschatological ethics that had as its core the conviction of "not being conformed to the world." Jesus as a man whose mind is set upon the kingdom of God rises above the values of the world. "The kingdom of God," as Schweitzer asserted in a series of pieces for laymen written in an Alsatian Liberal theological magazine, "is untimely work for the future" (*unzeitgemässe Arbeit in der Zukunft*),[36] although none of this should be seen to imply an indifference to the world, for, *pace* Schweitzer, it is precisely because of Jesus' difference from the world that he is able to work effectively within it.[37] Here Schweitzer's work as New Testament scholar converges with his work as cultural critic. But there is a sense also in which Schweitzer's solution to the problem of the situatedness of the historical Jesus has the whiff of a liberal solution about it, for by his appeal to a sort of metaphysics of the will, Schweitzer is seeking out something eternal to bridge the gap between the past and the present. This is why Henning Pleitner can describe Schweitzer's work as *Das Ende der liberalen Hermeneutik*.[38]

3. Inspired in part by the involved debate that had taken place at the beginning of the twentieth century about the existence of Jesus,[39] in *Geschichte der Leben-Jesu-Forschung* Schweitzer had reflected more extensively on the question of the importance of the historical Jesus, what he termed a "philosophico-religious question," and in a way that revealed tensions in his thinking on the subject.

36. Schweitzer 1988: 124. For a more vehement expression of Jesus' relationship to the world, see Schweitzer 2003: 280.

37. "To the question, How can a man be in the world and in God at one and the same time, we find this answer in the Gospel of Jesus: 'By being and working in this world as one who is not of the world'" (Schweitzer 1951: 73–74). See further Frey 1993: 158.

38. Pleitner 1992.

39. For a short account of this, see Weaver 1999: 45–71.

From what Schweitzer termed "a purely logical point of view," whether Jesus existed or not remained purely hypothetical. And, according to Schweitzer, any theology that did not take account of that observation would make itself unduly dependent on the most incalculable contingencies. "Modern Christianity," he writes, "must always reckon with the possibility of having to abandon the historical figure of Jesus. Hence it must not artificially increase his importance by referring all theological knowledge to him and developing a christocentric religion: the Lord may always be a mere element in religion, but should never be considered its foundation."[40] It was Christian scholars' fixation with history, over against metaphysics, that had led many of them to fashion a Jesus who, in Schweitzer's opinion, had more to do with their own modernizing presuppositions than with the real historical figure. Or put differently, it was, ironically, the obsession with history that had led scholars, perhaps unconsciously, to seek to overcome the specificity of Jesus' own historical circumstances and to paint a picture of him that smoothed the rough edges of his unacceptable and, in Schweitzer's opinion, eschatological viewpoint. As he states,

> The remarkable thing about the problem which confronts the philosophy of religion is that all compromises which lie between the two extremes are basically worthless. We must come to terms with either one or the other. Religion has to reckon either with an unhistorical Jesus or with a too historical Jesus. All intermediate solutions can have only an appearance of plausibility.[41]

It is for this reason that Christianity must take more seriously than it has the possibility of living without this all-too-historical and contingent Jesus, and that it must develop a metaphysics—"that is, a basic view of the nature and significance of being which is entirely independent of history and of knowledge transmitted from the past, and which can be recreated afresh at every moment and in every religious subject."[42] It is to this section of *Geschichte der Leben-Jesu-Forschung* that Schweitzer alludes when he writes in his conclusion the words already cited: "But, let it be clear, the idea of the moral consummation of all things and of what we must do in our time has not come down to us from him through historical revelation. It is inherent in us and is part of the moral will." But what is remarkable is that in spite of such utterances, Schweitzer still maintains that our will can be clarified and enriched by that of Jesus, "for a living personality means a remarkable enrichment of religion," and so he can, almost in spite of himself, insist on an ongoing role for Jesus. In this respect, it is interesting to note that in *Geschichte der Leben-Jesu-Forschung* he dismisses the neoorthodox views of Wobbermin,[43] which partly reflected

40. Schweitzer 2000: 405.
41. Schweitzer 2000: 405–6.
42. Schweitzer 2000: 402.
43. Schweitzer 2000: 407–8.

those of Kähler, that a distinction should be made between the historical Jesus and the historic Christ, and he is similarly harsh on Bousset and Troeltsch's differently expressed opinion that there is a need for Jesus to have a symbolic role within Christianity.[44] This emerges, in my opinion, precisely from the commitment that Schweitzer has to the person of Jesus and to the sense, however conceived, of relating to him.[45] In this context we should attend not only to the more striking remarks that Schweitzer made about his own relationship with Jesus, already referred to, but also to the comment found in his earliest account of the life of Jesus, *Das Messianitäts- und Leidensgeheimnis: Eine Skizze des Lebens Jesu.* "With the aim of the book may they not find fault: to depict the figure of Jesus in its overwhelming heroic greatness and to impress it upon the modern age and upon modern theology. . . . Before this mysterious person, who, in the form of his time, knew that he was creating upon the foundation of his life and death a moral world which bears his name, we must be forced to lay our faces in the dust, without daring even to wish to understand his nature."[46]

4. In all of this it is important to note what should be clear from observation 3 above: Jesus is something not because of who he is in some metaphysical sense, or because of the eternal validity of what he teaches, but because of the will that he shows, which has the capacity to transform. As Schweitzer notes in a letter dated 24 December 1910, "He is my Lord in spite of the fact that inwardly I stand free in relation to his ideas and opinions. . . . He is my Lord through the great and pure will in which my will finds its way and becomes brilliantly simple."[47]

Schweitzer and Paul

As is well known, Schweitzer argued strongly against the prevailing tendency in Pauline scholarship to divide Jesus from Paul.[48] What binds them together is their eschatological vision; what distinguishes them is the different points at which they find themselves in eschatological history. Jesus waits for God's consummation of things in the coming of the kingdom; Paul waits for the same thing but argues for the view that Christians, through the death and resurrection of Jesus, have begun to experience the reality of the kingdom, precisely because being in Christ, they have begun to share in the benefits of his saving activity

44. On Troeltsch, and the general theological background of the period, see Claussen 1997.

45. Schweitzer's concern with the personality of Jesus, understood in terms of his will, is precisely what differentiates him from Bultmann with his insistence on the central role of the kerygmatic Christ and his negligible interest in ethics. See Grässer 1984: 67–68.

46. Schweitzer 1914: 274–75 (German original, 1901).

47. Schweitzer and Bresslau 1992: 130.

48. For accounts of Schweitzer's work on Paul, see Matlock 1996; Grässer 2003.

expressed through the Spirit. This is what Schweitzer calls "Christ-mysticism," and one of the chief ways in which it manifests itself is in ethical activity.

> While for other believers ecstatic discourses and convulsive raptures mean the surest proof of the possession of the spirit, St. Paul turns the doctrine of the spirit into ethical channels. According to him the spirit which believers possess is the spirit of Jesus. . . . This spirit of Jesus is the heavenly life force which is preparing them for existence in the post-resurrection condition, just as it effected the resurrection in itself in him. At the same time it is the power which compels them, through their being different from the world, to approve themselves as men who have ceased to belong to this world. The highest proof of the spirit is love.[49]

In all of this Schweitzer, like Bultmann later, makes much of the fact that Paul is not dependent upon the earthly Jesus for his teaching but rather is dependent upon and living in the authority of the spiritually arisen Jesus. "For Christianity," writes Schweitzer in the sonorous conclusion of *Die Mystik des Apostels Paulus*,

> is a Christ-Mysticism, that is to say, a belonging together with Christ as our Lord, grasped in thought and realized in experience. By simply designating Jesus "our Lord" Paul raises him above all the temporally conditioned conceptions in which the mystery of his personality might be grasped, and sets him forth as the spiritual being who transcends all human definitions, to whom we have to surrender ourselves in order to experience in him the true law of our existence and our being.[50]

Schweitzer continues,

> All attempts to rob Christianity of Christ-mysticism are nothing more or less than a useless resistance to that spirit of knowledge and truth, which finds expression in the teaching of the first and greatest of Christian thinkers. Just as philosophy, after all its aberrations has always to return to the primary truth that every genuinely profound and living world-view is of mystical character, in the sense that it consists of some kind of conscious and willing surrender to the mysterious and infinite will-to-live, from which we are; so thought of an essentially Christian character cannot do other than conceive this surrender to God, as Paul conceived it long ago, as coming to pass in union with the being of Jesus Christ.[51]

The modern Christian cannot conceive of that union in exactly the same way as Paul did, but just as Paul sought to conceive of it in terms that were different

49. Schweitzer 1951: 214–15.
50. Schweitzer 1955: 378 (German original, 1930).
51. Schweitzer 1955: 378.

from those of Jesus and responded to the conditions in which he found himself, so do we have the right to do the same. Paul's *thoughtful* engagement justifies our own thoughtful engagement, which will lead to the conclusion that

> our faith, like that of primitive Christianity, must grasp the appearance and the dying of Jesus as the beginning of the realization of the kingdom of God. . . . To believe in the Gospel of Jesus means for us to let the belief in the Kingdom of God which he preached become a living reality within the belief in him and the redemption experienced in him. Paul, in his Christ-mysticism, was the first to accomplish this: is it reasonable for us to neglect the gains which he has secured, and attempt to reach the same result in our own strength and by independent thought?[52]

Paul, for Schweitzer, becomes the first protagonist of a Christ-mysticism whose interpretative shape, if not its presuppositions (Schweitzer's Paul is an eschatological realist), is close to what Schweitzer had understood as central to any appropriation of Jesus' eschatological worldview. Paul, for Schweitzer, is principally a figure of greatness because he is a thinker—the patron saint of thinkers, as he strikingly puts it. Paul becomes, in some senses, the first Christian rationalist, and Schweitzer, by implication, his worthy successor.[53]

Philosophical Postscript

Schweitzer's philosophical work had been a significant presence in his life from the beginning of his academic career and came to preoccupy him from 1913 onward, but it rarely attracts attention. And yet, I would contend, it remains relevant to the subject of this volume.[54] In this work Schweitzer argues that human beings should understand themselves as wills-to-live who live in the midst of life that wills-to-live. Such an affirmation involves identification, a sense of commonality, with all other wills-to-live conceived as all living phenomena in the world. Schweitzer moves from this to argue that all is a part of a cosmic will-to-live, which completes what he terms the mystical element of his thought. Union with such a will is reached not through contemplation but through ethical action, expressed as service to life. All of these conclusions are reached not through contemplation of the world (the world, according to Schweitzer, manifests itself as a sad and hideous competition between life, as cruelty and suffering) but rather through apprehension of what Schweitzer holds to be the will within us, which is ethical in character. But this cannot

52. Schweitzer 1951: 394.
53. On this and the general "Enlightenment" tone of Schweitzer's work, see Matlock 1996: 58–59.
54. For a recent account, see Günzler 1996.

be seen to be a self-evident conclusion. Both Schopenhauer and Nietzsche, who in different ways influenced Schweitzer, had arrived at quite different conclusions based on their own beliefs about humans as wills—in the case of Schopenhauer it seemed, in a sense, that life denial was the best option open to a human being, and in the case of Nietzsche in a grand assertion of the will to power. Schweitzer can arrive at his conclusion only because he has a sense of God as the will-to-love manifest in his Son Jesus Christ.[55] As Schweitzer was to write in *The Mysticism of Paul the Apostle*, "In Jesus Christ God is manifested [*offenbart*] as Will-to-Love."[56] Christ, in Schweitzer's thought, is a transformative moral force, and in some respects his philosophical contentions can work only if that is the case. In such instances, writes Barsam, we are reminded of Schopenhauer's image of a conjurer who pulls out of his hat something that had always been there.[57]

The germs, then, of Schweitzer's philosophical solution for the regeneration of culture are to be found in his work on the New Testament. His eschatological solution to the problems of the New Testament can easily be translated into his central philosophical claim that it is only by reflection upon one's inner core as will that one can act upon the world in an effective way; or put eschatologically, it is only by setting one's eyes upon the future kingdom, by leaving the world, that one has the capacity to work upon it. The view that that self-reflecting will can act ethically only as it conceives of itself as one will-to-live acting in the midst of other wills-to-live seems in a variety of ways to depend on Schweitzer's own view of Jesus as will-to-love, inchoately expressed in *Geschichte der Leben-Jesu-Forschung* and more completely in *The Mysticism of Paul the Apostle*.[58]

Conclusions

"Whether from a position of faith or of unbelief, how can biblical scholars do justice to historically and culturally contingent human figures like Jesus of Nazareth or his apostle Saul of Tarsus—and yet make sense of the texts' insistence on these same figures as, respectively, 'Son of God' or divinely appointed apostolic witness?"[59] In one sense, Albert Schweitzer took this question very seriously: he sought to show how historically and culturally contingent Jesus was, and therefore how problematic history is as the locus in which to discover who he really was. He also took this question seriously

55. Barsam 2001: 42–43.
56. Schweitzer 1955: 379.
57. Barsam 2001: 32–33.
58. Note this comment by Schweitzer: "All living knowledge of God rests upon this foundation: that we experience Him in our lives as will-to-love" (1933: 277).
59. Bockmuehl 2006: 20.

insofar as he sought to overcome historicism and show how Jesus, in spite of his strangeness, indeed because of it, continued to have a hold on those in the present. Analogous conclusions could apply to his discussion of Paul, who becomes the model upon which all those who are serious about *thoughtfully* engaging with Jesus need to reflect, and which they need to imitate. But the term that emerges out of his hermeneutical foray, *Jesusmystik*, appears to deny the importance of straightforwardly conceived christological questions (we should note, for instance, that one of the severest criticisms leveled at Schweitzer's book on Paul is its failure to discuss Paul's Christology). After all, Schweitzer contrasts *Jesusmystik* with *Jesuskult* in such a way as apparently to reduce Jesus' role to that of moral exemplar of the will, to one of clarifying and activating the will within us. And as we noted earlier, we look in vain in his work for engagement with terms such as "Son of God" and with incarnation or related christological themes even at the level of pallid demythologization.

But Schweitzer's engagement with the question above, however tangential, is illuminating. First, it witnesses to one of the important beginning points in the gradual movement away from a broadly liberal Protestant hermeneutical enterprise conducted, strangely enough, by a theologian with liberal assumptions. This is *fin de siècle* liberal hermeneutics with the volume turned up and a sharply critical voice-over, which partially explains why aspects of what Schweitzer argues seem to anticipate things that Barth and Bultmann say but that also look so different from their theology. Second, Schweitzer is a biblical critic who remains strongly attached to the Bible, in particular the New Testament, all his life; and in many ways he continues to express his concerns and hopes with biblical metaphors such as the "kingdom of God." Third, his work betrays striking tensions as it witnesses to a Christian's attempt to think out a final and lasting principle that will guide the world to cultural revival. The tension exists between, on the one hand, Schweitzer's extraordinary statements that speak of his ongoing commitment to Jesus and, on the other hand, his unfinished effort to discover a lasting cross-cultural principle with which to aid human cultural renewal. For Schweitzer, there was no tension between religion on the one hand and philosophy on the other. As he was to write to his friend D. E. Rölffs, in the previously noted 1931 letter,

> My conviction is that thought arrives at all the deep truths of religion and that human beings become religious when they become thoughtful. The ethic of reverence for life is nothing other than Jesus' great commandment of love reached by means of thought. Religion and thought meet each other in the mystery of belonging to God through love.[60]

60. Schweitzer 1987: 118–19.

But as I have stated, it is unclear that Schweitzer's philosophical position can be arrived at without Christ; and if that is the case, it is equally unclear that Schweitzer could have seen Jesus' role only as exemplary. His Christology may, in the end, be higher than he ever explicitly states.[61]

61. In a sermon dated 22 March 1903 Schweitzer explicitly rejects the idea that Jesus is simply a moral exemplar: "He wants to be more than an example, he will be the force [*Kraft*] which a new world hopes for" (2001: 457).

6

Karl Barth and Friedrich Mildenberger on Scripture in Doctrine

JAN MUIS

Does the New Testament prescribe Christian theology? It seems to me that this question should be distinguished from the question of whether the New Testament is normative, because norms and prescriptions are different things. A norm is a standard to test a doctrine; a prescription is a rule for how to construct doctrine. The New Testament is normative if doctrine cannot contradict it; it is prescriptive if doctrine must be derived from it. Doctrine can be derived from the New Testament in two ways: either its content is taken from the New Testament as a whole, or both its content and its conceptual form are directly deduced from specific New Testament statements and key terms.

Could "*the* New Testament" be prescriptive? Not only does the New Testament contain statements of different kinds, but also there are many statements with differing content. Where do we have to look for their unity: in the text of the New Testament itself, in the history behind the text, or in some other reality beyond the text? And how do the different statements relate to this unifying factor? Are some statements more closely linked to this factor than others are? Are they more central and therefore more normative and prescriptive? Can we classify the texts by the degree to which they are central, normative, and prescriptive?[1]

That we need Scripture in order to believe and live as Christians can hardly be denied, but do we need doctrine at all when we listen to the gospel, when we pray to God, when we confess the Lord, when we live a Christian life? In a sense, this is a hypothetical question because the terms of the Nicene Creed, "God of God, Light of Light," and of the Chalcedonian formula, "truly God, truly man," are part of the vocabulary of the church. Confessions and doctrines exist and are used by believers on occasion. So actually there are two questions here: do we need traditional doctrine(s); do we need new doctrine(s)?

I will discuss the answers to these questions in the work of Karl Barth and Friedrich Mildenberger. I will analyze their frame of reference before I describe their view on the relation between Scripture[2] and doctrine and the role of exegesis.

Barth

The Framework

According to Barth, the task of church dogmatics is to test the actual proc-lamation of the church (*CD* I/1, 3–5, 249–50).[3] This test can be carried out by confronting the proclamation of the church with Scripture and with Jesus Christ, the two other forms of the Word of God (*CD* I/1, 265; I/2, 802). The first and fundamental form of the Word of God is God's self-revelation in Jesus Christ; the second form is Holy Scripture. It is important to note the difference between Scripture and revelation and the difference between the Word of God and revelation. Scripture is not identical with revelation; it is a witness to revelation. Revelation is the Word of God, but the Word of God is not identical with revelation. Revelation is a "form" of the Word of God, just as Scripture and ecclesial proclamation are. "Form" denotes a unity that is not identity, a dual unity or an indirect identity.[4] Christ, Scripture, and the proclamation of the church remain different but can become one and the same Word of God for us if and only if God speaks through them. This divine speech-act, the Word of God, is eternal and cannot become part of human

---

1. For instance, Hendrikus Berkhof (1990: 97–98) distinguishes four categories: texts about God's saving and revealing acts; texts about necessary implications of these events; texts that present an image of these events or their implications; texts that represent the outdated world-view of their time.

2. In this essay I will speak of Scripture instead of the New Testament because both Barth and Mildenberger treat the New Testament not as a separate entity but rather as part of Scripture.

3. Numbers in the text refer to Barth's *Church Dogmatics* (*CD*).

4. For an analysis of the different uses of the term *Gestalt* ("form") in Barth's reflections, see Muis 1999: 138–44.

time and consciousness; the hearing of God's Word in time is an elusive human experience. Time cannot contain eternity. As human beings in time, we can only remember and expect the Word of God (CD I/1, 249; I/2, 502, 513–14, 527, 530, 532).[5]

At the same time, Word and revelation are more intrinsically connected than are Word and Scripture and Word and proclamation. This is because Jesus Christ is the Word of God in a sense that Scripture and proclamation are not (CD I/1, 304–5).[6] He is the eternal Word of John 1:1, the eternal Son of the Father together with the Holy Spirit. As I have argued elsewhere, Barth interlocks a *Logos* model (revelation as incarnation) and a speech model (speech as address) of the Word of God. "Word of God" has different meanings in both models: the eternal Son of God and the divine act of speech. Only the *Logos* model is worked out in a trinitarian account: God reveals himself in his eternal Son Jesus Christ to us through the Holy Spirit.[7]

Barth's answer to the question of how the proclamation of the church can be tested is surprising: the norm for the proclamation of the church is not Scripture, not even Jesus Christ as God's self-revelation, but rather the Word of God (CD I/2, 801), the eternal act of God's speaking, which can never fully be grasped and contained by the human mind in a timely consciousness (CD I/1, 12–14). Because the divine speech-act is not directly available as an object of human experience, the Word of God can only indirectly function as norm. Theologians can confront the actual proclamation of the church with the Word of God when they themselves hear the Word of God in Scripture and teach what they hear to others as a witness (CD I/2, 814–15). It is the hearing and teaching of the teacher that points to the Word of God as the norm of proclamation. This act of teaching that emerges from hearing is what Barth calls "doctrine" (CD I/2, 853–54).

The Word of God is new each and every time we hear it; therefore, traditional doctrine cannot be normative for proclamation (CD I/2, 802–5). Hearing requires the biblical attitude of the witness who hears and speaks. So the Word of God becomes indirectly available as a norm for doctrine in the form of the biblical attitude, not in the form of the biblical text as such (CD I/2, 816–21)! Barth calls this *formal* heteronomy. By teaching what they have heard, theologians make this norm indirectly available as a doctrine. Barth calls this *material* autonomy. Both the formal heteronomy and the material autonomy reflect the theonomy of the Word of God (CD I/2, 815–16, 857–58). In this way, the transcendent norm of the divine act of speech becomes indirectly available in human acts of hearing and speaking.

5. See Muis 1999: 150–53.
6. This means that Christ is categorically different from Scripture and proclamation; it is misleading to subsume the three under the concept "Word." See Barr 1999: 692n18; Muis 2000: 63.
7. Muis 1999: 138–50.

It is striking that Barth does not speak about material heteronomy. He connects heteronomy and autonomy analogously to the way he connects authority and freedom in the church in his concept of obedience (CD I/2, 781–82); thus, he associates heteronomy with objectivity, and autonomy with subjectivity. As a result, the norm for doctrine becomes formal and objective; the content of doctrine becomes subjective. The reason for this conceptuality is Barth's distinction between what we think about God (*Inhalt*) and God himself (*Gegenstand*), between our concepts of God and the reality to which they refer. Barth links material content to subjectivity not to safeguard human autonomy but rather to safeguard God's transcendence.

God's transcendence does not prevent God from becoming immanent. The Word of God has become flesh. The eternal Son of God has become a human being. The divine subject has become a human object of human experience in space and time. In this way, God has made himself known to us. Because the God who has revealed himself in Jesus Christ is the creator of heavens and earth, he exists in a freely chosen relation to his creation. However, he is no part of creation; his existence does not depend on the existence of creation. Therefore, if we know God as he is by revelation, we know him as an independent reality. This knowledge can be expressed in concepts and statements. A doctrine of the transcendent, eternal creator is possible on the basis of his self-revelation in creation, in history and time.

Scripture in Doctrine

Dogmatics is concerned with the content of actual proclamation, biblical theology with the biblical foundation of it, and practical theology with its application (CD I/1, 4–5, 16; I/2, 766). Dogmatics not only discusses questions posed by Scripture but also tries to solve problems that emerge in the life of the church (CD I/2, 821–22). It is not primarily concerned with the biblical texts: Scripture is a presupposition, not a theme of dogmatics.[8] Even so, dogmatic reflection without exegesis is impossible (CD I/2, 821). On the one hand, dogmatics is more speculative and abstract than both exegesis and application; on the other hand, it remains more closely connected with exegesis than with proclamation in an actual context (CD I/2, 884).

Dogmatic reflection focuses on God's revelation to which Scripture bears witness. Scripture becomes a unity only when it actually witnesses to the revelation of the Father in the Son through the Holy Spirit—that is, when it refers to Jesus Christ, the risen Lord. Its unity is an event, not a *datum* (a fixed given) but rather a *dandum* (something still to be actively given). Therefore, doctrine cannot be deduced from biblical salvation history or from the biblical texts. We have no bird's-eye view of such a history and cannot have an overview of the

8. Barth 1975a: 40–44.

living Jesus Christ as part of that history (*CD* I/2, 481–85). Nor can we take one single biblical concept as the core of this history or the center of doctrine. No single theme can be the center of a system (*CD* I/2, 869–75).

Reflection is impossible without certain epistemological and ontological presuppositions. Barth rejects any attempt to think theologically without such presuppositions as biblicism. He does not look for so-called biblical presuppositions instead of philosophical ones. We are committed not to the philosophy of Scripture but rather to its witness. To think biblically is to think as a witness of Jesus Christ. Philosophical elements in the witness of Scripture are not necessarily linked with its central content, God's revelation in Christ (*CD* I/2, 727–36, 818–19). The impossibility of deducing doctrine directly from Scripture and of thinking purely biblically means that Scripture cannot be directly prescriptive for doctrine, but only indirectly as witness of the self-revelation of the Triune God in Christ.

Although he does not try to infer new doctrine directly from Scripture, Barth often uses biblical texts to evaluate and reconstruct traditional Reformed doctrine.[9] This reconstructing method can be seen in his treatment of pre-destination, based on a detailed exegesis of Romans 9–11, among other texts (*CD* II/2, 195–305); in his view on the relation between creation and covenant history, based on the separate reading of Genesis 1 and Genesis 2 (*CD* III/1, 94–329); and in his reinterpretation of the doctrine of the divine and human nature in terms of event and *Geschichte* on the basis of the narrative of Jesus' life, death, and resurrection (*CD* IV/2, 20–154). In the context of the doctrinal topic that he is working on, Barth selects and orders texts[10] and carefully reads them in order to solve systematic problems. This means that Scripture is much more than a general presupposition of doctrine; biblical texts offer guidelines and conceptual tools for the (re)construction of doctrine.

Mildenberger

The Framework

Mildenberger's *Biblische Dogmatik*[11] is focused on the use of Scripture in the language of faith, which he calls "simple God-talk." Simple God-talk is not restricted to proclamation; it includes prayers, confessions, praise, and stories, and these different forms of God-talk function in different situations (*BD* I, 14–20).[12] Scripture proves to be the effective Word of God in its use in simple God-talk (*BD* I, 93). A text becomes Word of God when it can describe what is going to happen in our life in such a way that we can see God at work

9. See McCormack 1995: 331–37.
10. See Bächli 1987: 99–100.
11. Mildenberger 1991–1993.
12. Numbers in the text refer to Mildenberger's *Biblische Dogmatik* (*BD*).

in what is going on (*BD* I, 18, 63). The working of Scripture as Word of God in our actual lifetime is determined both by Jesus Christ, in whom God has reconciled the world to himself, and by the coming of the Spirit, who makes Jesus Christ present and makes us believe in him (*BD* I, 116, 127). Besides this christological and pneumatological determination of our history, our history is determined by God the Creator, who determines all time (*BD* I, 130). Ultimately, our lives belong to God's history with us (*BD* I, 172–73, 201).

The description of an actual situation by a biblical text is analogous to metaphorical description. In this description the biblical text acquires a double reference: it refers to both the biblical history and to what is going to happen in our own life and history (*BD* I, 195–201, 260). We understand a biblical text if we discover a situation that it can describe. The reverse is also true: we understand our situation *coram Deo* ("before the face of God"), if we discover a biblical text that can describe it as a situation in which God is present. Thus, understanding is application. It is not always possible to find the right situation for the text, or the right text for the situation; in this case we had better be silent about God: God can also be absent (*BD* I, 12, 20, 220, 225, 248, 260). Mildenberger thinks that we cannot talk adequately about God without biblical texts and apart from the events in life and history in which God is present or absent. This means that Christian God-talk is indirect in two ways: it is about our situation in which God is working, not about God apart from his working and our situation, and it needs biblical language for an adequate description, not abstract concepts (*BD* I, 168, 178, 199).

This view implies that the actual speech (*parole* [de Saussure]) of the Bible can be used as a language (*langue*) to describe our life and history in relation to God (*BD* I, 212–24). But biblical language cannot be used without understanding its original historical context. We never apply "the Bible"; we always apply specific biblical texts from a specific, original context to a specific, actual context. We might call this recontextualization. Consequently, historical-critical analysis of the biblical texts is indispensable for their use as Word of God. Mildenberger's use of the historical-critical method does not presuppose that we can conceive of God's presence and assistance as part of history understood as a chronological order of equal, interrelated events. The Christ event is an act of God, which disrupts any homogeneous conception of time and space (*BD* I, 222). Therefore, critical reflection about ontological presuppositions is part of theology.

Simple God-talk is true if it happens that our use of biblical texts really is about the presence of God in our life and history. This truth is an event, not a state. This event is performed not by the believer but ultimately by the inspiration of the Holy Spirit (*BD* I, 15, 21, 113, 229, 272). The actual inspiration of the Holy Spirit is as constitutive for simple God-talk as is the Word of God in Christ. According to Mildenberger, this is not clear enough in Barth's theory of the three forms of the Word of God (*BD* I, 117).

There is no objective test to decide whether the application of a text to our life and history is true.[13] The Bible itself cannot be an independent, objective norm, because what we have is in fact an interpreted Bible (*BD* I, 266). Although there is no single independent and accessible criterion, there is the general criterion that our understanding of a text should be in line with the Bible and the experiences with single God-talk that have resulted in some basic decisions that underlie the confessions of the church. For Mildenberger, these basic decisions are the unity of the Creator and the Redeemer (early church), justification as the work of God alone (Reformation), and access to God by Christ alone (Barmen Declaration). These normative factors are interdependent and regulate the process of understanding in a general way (*BD* I, 265–71).

Mildenberger does not interlock the notion of Christ as the Word of God with the notion of Christ as the eternal *Logos*, which is the eternal Son. In other words, in his account of the Word of God Mildenberger only uses the speech model, whereas Barth combines the *Logos* model and the speech model. There are two reasons for this. First, the notion of divine self-revelation is not essential for Mildenberger's view on the Word of God as inspired use of biblical texts.[14] Second, Mildenberger does not consider the classical *Logos* Christology of Nicea an irreversible doctrine.[15] He is aware that the *Logos* Christology is rooted in the Bible and not in Hellenistic philosophy (*BD* I, 133), but he underscores the doxological character of John 1. A hymn does not merely describe what is the case; it anticipates what must and will be eschatologically, and it cannot be transformed into a metaphysical statement (*BD* I, 134, 152, 190). Mildenberger thinks that in the later development of doctrine a change of subject has taken place: one started claiming that the man Jesus Christ is divine, but one ended in saying that the divine *Logos* has assumed human being. The concrete subject of the first statement has become the abstract predicate of the second, and its abstract predicate has become the subject of the second. Thus, the focus of Christology has changed: the Son of God became God the Son (*BD* II, 386–88; III, 427). Christology has to focus on the divinity of the man Jesus, not on the humanity of a transcendent, divine being. That is why Mildenberger develops a *Pneuma* Christology instead of a *Logos* Christology (*BD* III, 111–91).[16]

---

13. As a consequence, Mildenberger offers "no discussion of ways in which the use of the Bible within the [theological] scheme may be *assessed, verified* or *falsified* on the basis of the biblical texts themselves" (Barr 1999: 528).

14. See Barr 1999: 519, 526.

15. For the term "reversible," see Lindbeck 1984: 85, 87. Mildenberger (*BD* I, 216) can incidentally call Jesus the Word of God that has become flesh, but this does not determine his thought.

16. Mildenberger (*BD* II, 389–91) acknowledges that the *Logos* Christology of the early church is a break with Hellenistic metaphysics. Even so, it uses metaphysical concepts to say who Jesus Christ is for us, and in this way it remains indebted to the metaphysical tradition and its insoluble problems. In his view, this is also the case in Barth's Christology.

Mildenberger does not try to develop a doctrine about God. He is focused on the right application of biblical texts, not on doctrine. Actual God-talk in terms of biblical texts can be abstracted neither from the concrete situation in which the text originated nor from the concrete events to which it is applied. God-talk is talk about events in our life in which God works. There is no metaphysical escape from our timely being in the world by means of timeless and abstract concepts. Therefore, Mildenberger refuses both a metaphysical theory about God as necessary and independent being apart from our contingent world and a modern conception of man as a self apart from the outer world (BD I, 97, 188, 204, 244, 273; II, 12–31; III, 54–60).

Scripture in Doctrine

Like Barth, Mildenberger thinks that dogmatics plays an intermediary role between biblical and practical theology. Unlike Barth, he considers this role not only normative but also prescriptive—prescriptive, that is, not for doctrine but rather for simple God-talk. Mildenberger's dogmatics is an inquiry into the right way to apply the biblical texts to new situations. It offers theological readings of texts, which are examples of the possible use of these texts in simple God-talk (BD I, 269). Thus, the goal of dogmatic reflection is not the proposal of new doctrine.

But the way we talk about God is always influenced and determined by traditional doctrine. Traditional doctrine, which gave answers to questions about faith that emerged in the life of the church, is a sediment of the experiences with Scripture over time. These past experiences cannot be neglected when we talk about God in our day. We have to reflect on these experiences and their doctrinal expressions. Although, as we have seen, Mildenberger considers the basic decisions of the early church, the Reformation, and the synod of Barmen as normative, he uses the traditional doctrines of the church primarily as a means to articulate our questions about the presence of God in our lives. He develops a complex method to use traditional doctrines as questions for the theological reading of biblical texts. The questions of traditional doctrinal *theologia* concerning God as creator and preserver of world and humankind are answered by the biblical *oikonomia*, texts about reconciliation with God by Christ and communication with God by the Spirit; the questions of traditional doctrinal *oikonomia* concerning salvation of humankind and world are answered by the biblical *theologia*, texts about humankind and world as true creation of God (BD I, 243–46).

Mildenberger's dogmatics is a reflection on the texts themselves. Although they all belong to one Bible, biblical texts are very diverse. Mildenberger tries to do justice to the diversity of their origins and applications.[17] The original

---

17. James Dunn (2006: xxxix) says that the diversity in the New Testament "should be something liberating and exciting, since it undergirds the affirmation that God continues to speak to the diverse and specific situations of today."

cotext and context may be more relevant to our situation than the cotext and context of the canon.[18] The unity of the texts lies not in the inspired character of the Bible as a whole, or in a developing biblical history of salvation behind the texts, but rather in their use in simple God-talk that is inspired by the Holy Spirit.

Biblical texts are read as possible answers to questions articulated by traditional doctrine. In Mildenberger's dogmatics biblical texts perform the role that doctrine plays in Barth's: the texts are not used as foundations or guidelines for doctrinal answers; they are the answers themselves (BD I, 244). In contrast with Barth, Mildenberger does not collect diverse texts; instead, he reads larger text units as a whole (BD I, 245). Mildenberger calls this theological reading: dogmatic reflection as, that is, in the way of, exegesis (BD I, 244). For example, reflection on justification is developed in an ongoing reading of Romans (BD II, 160–84, 327–62).

Discussion

Barth thinks it impossible to use Scripture directly as a norm and a prescription for doctrine. The ultimate norm is the eternal Word of God, which is not directly available in time and history. Only revelation, the living Christ himself in unity with the Father and the Spirit, could prescribe doctrine, but he is beyond Scripture. Mildenberger considers Scripture as normative for traditional doctrine and prescriptive for simple God-talk, but he sees no need for new doctrine. Thus, both authors deny that Scripture prescribes new Christian doctrine.

I think that the answers of Barth and Mildenberger are unconvincing and do not follow from their own premises. Mildenberger accepts traditional doctrine as answers to questions about faith and as documentation of past experiences with Scripture, but he does not argue why the tradition of giving doctrinal answers to questions about faith should stop. If simple God-talk goes on, new questions will arise and new answers will be needed. Moreover, simple God-talk itself needs doctrine in order to make our diverse uses of different texts in different contexts coherent. It seems to me that Mildenberger's own account of the use of texts in simple God-talk asks for doctrine. If repeated use of similar biblical texts in similar situations is successful—that is, if it actually describes the presence of God in our lives—a pattern emerges. When we try to describe such general patterns, we develop concepts and relations between them. This is a conceptual account—a conceptual imagination, if you like—of God in relation with his creatures; that is, it is doctrine. Mildenberger rightly stresses that God is present and active in many different ways and situations,

18. See Mildenberger's (BD I, 256–57) interaction with Brevard Childs about Amos's proclamation of divine judgment.

but God's agency is characterized by some general basic relations, implied by his being Father, King, Creator. A conceptual account of these relations can help regulate and test the application of particular texts.

In Barth's reconstruction of traditional doctrine Scripture is much more than a general presupposition. His exegesis often offers guidelines for reflection and conceptual tools for theological reconstruction. Sometimes this reconstruction is so radical that we must speak of creative construction of new doctrine—for example, when he relates the divine decrees of election and rejection to resurrection and cross, or when he interprets the humility of God as the obedience of the eternal Son to the eternal Father in the doctrine of the immanent Trinity. These doctrinal innovations as such are speculative in character, but they are also the result of a theological reading of biblical texts in search for answers to doctrinal questions. This means that, despite Barth's own theory, Scripture has not only formal heteronomy but also material heteronomy.

I conclude that Scripture is indirectly prescriptive for doctrine, because biblical texts provide guidelines and conceptual tools for the construction of doctrine. Could Barth's and Mildenberger's theories help us understand this prescriptive character of Scripture? I will focus the discussion of this question on two related issues: the diversity of the texts and the concept of revelation. Mildenberger is particularly helpful in that he undertakes to do exegetical and hermeneutical justice to the rich diversity of the biblical texts and to make this diversity fruitful for simple God-talk. This diversity should not be wiped away by doctrine, because it points to the diverse ways in which God is present and active in his history with his people. This reminds us that doctrine can never replace Scripture itself.

On this point, Barth's exegesis is sometimes vulnerable or even weak. It is legitimate to focus a general theological reading of the biblical texts on their transcendent center, the risen Lord.[19] A reading of the Bible as a whole at "middle distance,"[20] in which diverse texts are read "simultaneously," as it were, is fruitful for doctrine. However, such a reading must not be conflated with the exegesis of single texts. Sometimes Barth seems to be in danger of blurring the distinction between general theological reading and exegesis of specific texts. An example of this is found in his explanation of "Your kingdom come" in the ethics of reconciliation. Barth concludes from the diverse New Testament texts that God's kingdom is a unique eschatological reality and event.[21] However, this eschatological reality has come near in Jesus Christ. "'The kingdom of God has come near,' means: 'The Word has become flesh.'"[22] In a doctrinal discourse it may be allowable to juxtapose the coming kingdom and

19. The exalted man Jesus is the center of the New Testament (Dunn 2006: 247, 405–6).
20. I take this term from David Ford (1979: 78), who uses it in a different context.
21. Barth 1976a: 407–8.
22. Barth 1976a: 429. To be fair, in small print Barth (1976a: 432–35) discusses carefully the relevant New Testament texts about the kingdom of Christ and explores the implicit evidence in the New Testament as a whole for his bold claim.

the incarnation, but one cannot identify the two in an exegesis of Mark 1:15 and of John 1:14, because this simply neglects the diversity of these texts. The unifying tendency of Barth's reading is the result of his focus on Christ. To be sure, Jesus Christ is the core of the New Testament, but what the various texts say about him can be quite diverse.[23] Is it possible to do justice to this diversity in Barth's framework?

This may seem impossible because Barth's unifying and harmonizing reading of biblical texts as one witness of God's self-revelation in Christ is based on his concept of revelation in terms of incarnation: Jesus Christ is the eternal Word who has become flesh, and the eternal Word is the eternal Son. Are Barth's trinitarian account of God's self-revelation and his identification of Word and Son biblical? There are reasons for doubt, both with respect to Barth's doctrine of revelation and with respect to the New Testament. Regarding Barth, Bruce McCormack has shown that the doctrine of incarnation provided Barth with a solution to the problem, posed by Kantian philosophy, that we cannot know God.[24] This was not the problem of the authors of the New Testament. Is Barth's doctrine of incarnation in the framework of his trinitarian doctrine of self-revelation a speculative new construction foreign to the New Testament? When Barth developed this doctrine for the first time in his lectures in Göttingen in 1924, he was fully aware that it was a construct.[25] But a doctrinal construct that is not directly inferred from the New Testament does not necessarily contradict the New Testament. In Münster, a year later, Barth gave an exegetical foundation for his doctrine of revelation in his lectures on John.[26]

In the New Testament the identification of Word with Son is found only in John 1.[27] The development that resulted in this identification is quite complex.[28] In the various parts of the New Testament the belief that the crucified one is risen from the dead is central. Modern Christologies reflect on the relation between resurrection of the crucified and incarnation. The question is whether incarnation is a necessary implication of the eschatological exaltation of Jesus as the Son of God. Some say no,[29] but others affirm this,[30] arguing that the historical development of the notion "Son of God" shows an inner

23. See Dunn 2006: 31, 406–8.

24. McCormack 1995: 207, 223–24, 249–50, 312–13, 359–60, 367.

25. Barth 1991: 131–41.

26. Barth 1976b. Cf. *CD* II/2, 95–99.

27. Marinus de Jonge (1988: 79–88) even doubts whether we can really speak about incarnation here.

28. Dunn 1989; Dalferth 1994: 106–18.

29. Berkhof (1990: 97–98, 289–98) considers preexistence and incarnation as nonnecessary images, apparently belonging to his third category of texts (see n. 1 above). Dalferth (1994: 31) considers incarnation as a secondary interpretation of the primary confession and interpretation of God's eschatological, saving agency in Christ as resurrection.

30. Pannenberg 1977: 150–53; Kasper 1976: 174–76.

logic: the man who became the Son of God by resurrection must have been the Son of God from the beginning, and the Son of God from the beginning can be no other than God the Son.[31] Barth does not discuss these issues. It seems that he takes a particular New Testament doctrine of revelation as a canon in the canon.[32]

Indeed, Barth's account of revelation in terms of incarnation is a dogmatic construct that cannot be deduced directly from Scripture. However, this is an argument against it only if one requires that every doctrine be derived directly from biblical texts, or even from common and central claims in various parts of the New Testament, which is a rather biblicist position. Barth's doctrine of revelation in terms of incarnation and Trinity and his combination of the *Logos* model and the speech model of the Word of God provide an explanation of why Jesus Christ is God's ultimate and definitive self-revelation. We should distinguish here between *explanans* (what explains) and *explanandum* (what is to be explained). Barth's doctrine is the *explanans*; the self-revelation of the Father in Christ through the Holy Spirit that is experienced in faith is the *explanandum*. It seems to me that the claim that Jesus Christ is the ultimate and definitive self-revelation of God is basic to Christian belief, irrespective of the relation between resurrection and incarnation and of the way the *Logos* Christology has been worked out in classical christological and trinitarian doctrines.[33] This belief cannot be omitted in an account of the use of Scripture in doctrine.

But this is exactly what happens in Mildenberger's account. Mildenberger separates the *Logos* model of the Word of God from the speech model and rejects the *Logos* Christology, but he offers no alternative explanation of why and how Jesus Christ is the definitive revelation of God. More than that, not only does he reject Barth's *explanans*, but also, in the end, he seems to reject the *explanandum* as well: it is not God's revelation in Christ that is constitutive for the use of Scripture as Word of God in simple God-talk but rather the inspiration of the Spirit. When, with Barth, he identifies Christ as the only Word of God (*BD* I, 182, 270–71), this means only that this Word of God determines our time and history. Why would Christ be the only Word and determine our history if he did not reveal ultimately and definitively who and how God is?

Could Barth's concept of revelation do exegetical justice to the diversity of the biblical texts and of the actual contexts in which they are used? In other words, could Mildenberger's method of recontextualization be considered

31. Dunn (2006: 246) seems to support this argument, but elsewhere (Dunn 1989: 63, 259) he rejects it.

32. See Dunn 2006: 420; Sykes 1979: 41–42, 47–51.

33. Interestingly, there has been a shift in Dunn's view on the relation between John and Nicea: the importance of incarnation as God's self-revelation has become more and more clear to him on the basis of the whole of John's Gospel. Cf. Dunn 2006: 249, 412; 1989: xxvii–xxviii, 261–65.

as a concretization and extension of Barth's doctrine of Scripture as witness of revelation and as a form of the Word of God? I see no reason why it could not. If we strictly maintain Barth's distinction between the living Christ and the texts of the New Testament and actual ecclesial proclamation, we can do justice to the diversity of the texts in their original context and of their application in new, actual contexts. Christ differs from all situations and can be present in all different situations. Thus, the focus on Christ gives room for contextual exegesis and contextual application of diverse texts. The only constraint on this is that the exegesis of different texts should not render the witness of the living Christ impossible. Indeed, exegesis of the texts of the New Testament that precludes one from seeing Jesus Christ in the mirror of these texts is unbiblical.[34]

34. I am grateful to Dr. Gerrit van Ek for his helpful comments on the first draft of this essay.

7

Rowan Williams on Scripture

JOHN WEBSTER

Background

Rowan Williams has a considerable and justly deserved reputation as a constructive Christian theologian. For over twenty years he has unobtrusively pushed
theological practice away from the twin intellectual and spiritual dangers of
irony and sclerosis. He has done this by commending a certain theological
temper: sophisticated but not mannered; self-critical without being hopelessly
self-subverting; often associative but not merely random; curious about a wide
range of intellectual fields (especially the arts, social and cultural theory, and
philosophy of a nonanalytical sort); ranging widely through the history of
Christian thought and spiritual practice, with only the Calvinist tradition
remaining largely out of sight; patiently displaying the spiritual cogency of
classical orthodoxy and its capacity to illuminate. He is not a *ressourcement*
after the manner of de Lubac or Congar, being more troubled by the dangers
of closure and more interested to chase up echoes of the gospel outside the
church, more open to being extended from beyond the tradition. But he shares
the sense that—patiently stated and detached from some of the compulsions
by which it has been rendered unserviceable—conciliar teaching about the
Trinity and incarnation can help unravel a good many knots.

His primary theological commitments were formed early, set out in books such as *The Wound of Knowledge* and *Resurrection*, or in the first published essays on Lossky and Barth; later work, though it amplifies and extends the scope of his thinking and brings in new conversation partners, continues the same vision with consistency. There also is a consistent style: fluent, disarmingly informal at some points, at others technical and compressed, shuttling between the devotional and the analytic, composed in long sentences with frequent apposition and benign catachresis, fugal,[1] with a rather dense surface, persuading by elaborating upon a striking insight or by cumulative suggestion rather than by sequence of demonstration; only sometimes does the writing give way to a tendency to overload. As with any theological writer of power, the style unfolds from the matter—in this case, a catholic vision of all things caught up in the creative and redemptive love of God enacted in Christ and represented in the church.

Williams is not a commentarial theologian but rather a conversational one; that is, he does not think on the basis of, and in deference to, a given text but rather moves, as it were, toward it, or, perhaps, generates a set of variations upon it. In this he is, of course, no exception: commentarial theology is pretty rare these days (T. F. Torrance's *The Trinitarian Faith* is probably the last really distinguished British example). Commentarial theology tends to flourish in theological cultures that are characterized by wide agreement about the *positum* of the Christian faith, and that accord priority to the catechetical dimensions of theological work. As we will see, Williams is uneasy with conceiving of the theologian's task as one of immersion in a determinate textual world, even if the text is a biblical one. Texts open the world and are open to the world; they are not an enclave, a bordered territory, but rather a wide field of possibilities whose meaning is disclosed as we attend to and extend their resonances beyond themselves. This explains in part why there is rather little sequential exegesis in Williams's work and, instead, a leaning toward thematic interpretation in which the "patterns" of a biblical text stimulate reflective expansion—exegesis is not the end of theology. It is also part of why Williams sits fairly loose to questions concerning the nature of Scripture—that is, bibliology proper—and speaks more readily of the hermeneutical afterlife of texts. And, as we will see, this is connected in turn to some deep doctrinal commitments.

Williams's work is a good illustration of a more general feature of theological thought about the nature of the Bible: a "doctrine" of Scripture cannot be extracted from the web of theological convictions of which it is part. Doctrines of Scripture are never freestanding—even in those modern neorationalist theological schemes in which bibliology undertakes the role of epistemological foundation for everything that follows. Rather, doctrines of Scripture are bound up with (sometimes driven by pressure from) theological teaching

---

1. See Williams 2005a: 135–36.

about the nature of God and God's communicative or revelatory acts, about Christ, Spirit, church, salvation, faith, and much else. Moreover, it is not only doctrinal convictions that exercise this kind of pressure on how the nature of Scripture is construed, but also other basic (and often subterranean) attitudes that form the particular dogmatic "dialect" with which a theologian speaks—views about distinction between God and the world, about the human historical condition, about knowledge and its media, about the operations of language. One of the most instructive aspects of Williams's work is his alertness to these matters, his sense of the wider intellectual environment of theological accounts of Scripture. Our first task, then, is to indicate something of the setting of what Williams has to say about the Bible before we move to issues of the nature and interpretation of the Bible proper.

Setting

"Human beings," Williams writes, "have their identity in history and appropriate their salvation in history."[2] It is a remark made in passing, but it indicates a deeply held conviction, one that opens up into a theological account of the nature of creatures and their relations to God, as well as one that sheds a good deal of light on some of the intellectual, cultural, and spiritual pathologies that he seeks to uncover. Contingent temporal processes are fundamental to human creatures; their identity or substance is not something beneath the surface of historical transactions but rather *is* that surface—bodily, linguistic, social, cultural. Human selfhood is not "a spring of action determined by a pure will or . . . a timeless substance operating by pure reason";[3] it is, rather, that which is built up over time. "The self lives and moves in, only in, acts of telling—in the time taken to set out and articulate a memory, the time that is a kind of representation . . . of the time my material and mental life has taken, the time that has brought me here."[4] Creatureliness is thus inseparable from the historical-material processes of learning and, in a sense, producing one's self; it is a matter of "*making* one's life, making one's soul, in a certain fashion, deciding, developing, intending and desiring, in cooperation, *synergeia*, with God."[5] This emphasis on creaturely contingency as irreducible to some ahistorical essence is ubiquitous in Williams's work. It is an early conviction: his first book, *The Wound of Knowledge*, writes the history of Christian spirituality from the New Testament to the Spanish mystics largely around this theme, with, for example, Irenaeus and the Cappadocians grasping that

2. Williams 2005b: 95.
3. Williams 1982: 30.
4. Williams 2000e: 144.
5. Williams 1979b: 63.

the locus of God's saving presence is "the world of historical decision,"[6] and Clement or Origen drawing the spiritual life away from confrontation with "the contingencies of the human situation."[7] The same conviction surfaces elsewhere in his writing, not only in theological work but also in spiritual and political tracts such as *The Truce of God* or *Resurrection*, which frequently return to the theme of human refusal of contingency and flight into defensiveness.

There are important consequences here for how knowledge, and especially knowledge of God, is to be conceived. Knowledge is inseparable from the process of its production or acquisition, because to know is to be engaged in a set of unfinished practices of coming to see and extend connections rather than to possess the world through conceptual representations. "We understand by chains of association, not by the deliverance of a self-standing concept."[8] Seeking to know is not the same as seeking resolution, because

> that part of the natural world that is the human system of knowing cannot be spoken of except as a spiral of self-extending symbolic activity; its relation to its environment is inescapably mobile, time-related. There is no abstracting from the passage of time some necessary, non-revisable and exhaustive correlation between an inside and an outside, a set of determinate, entirely "objective" stimuli and a "correct" reception of and reaction to them.[9]

More simply: "Truthfulness unfolds—it doesn't happen all at once—and makes possible different levels of appropriating or sharing in the activity that is in the world."[10] To this pragmatic-idealist or historical view of the generation of knowledge in time, knowledge of God is no exception. From the first, Williams has laid some emphasis on this point, often in the course of drawing attention to a negative effect of theological systematization: a territorial cast of mind that closes possibilities, arresting the temporal connections in which truth occurs. Here he deploys the notion of *apophasis*, indicating not so much a skepticism about the possibility of encounter with the divine essence but rather a mode of knowing encounter with God "beyond the bondage of a closed, conceptual system" that involves "the renunciation of a world of determined essences."[11] Apophasis indicates not so much unknowing as acceptance of both the mobility of the creaturely condition and the impossibility of representing God in a single contingent form: God's "everlasting act is as little capable of being a determinate object to our minds as the wind in our faces and lungs can be held still and distant in front of our eyes."[12]

6. Williams 1979b: 30.
7. Williams 1979b: 46.
8. Williams 2001b: 6.
9. Williams 2005a: 137.
10. Williams 2005a: 137.
11. Williams 1980: 107.
12. Williams 1987: 242.

This redefinition of apophasis in terms of the indeterminable and unsystematic character of knowledge of God in time has its roots in the doctrine of God, upon which Williams has written suggestively, though we await a full treatment of both theology proper and Christology. The force of the catholic doctrines of the Trinity and incarnation is to press for a reconstruction of deity as fullness of relation, both *in se* and *ad extra*. Drastically compressed, the central insight is this: "Because [God's] activity and life are self-differentiating, a pattern of initiating gift, perfect response, and the distinct and 'new' energy that is the harmony of these two movements, created difference, otherness, multiplicity, may find place in God."[13] Further, God's being in itself is utterly full and inexhaustibly generative, never depleted, always the source of life. This coincidence of plenitude and generativity in God means that "the divine nature cannot be abstracted from God's active relationship with the world."[14] God's identity is full, not inchoate; but because that fullness embraces filiation, spiration, and creation, we are required to say that "God is, of his nature, 'generative'";[15] "the God encountered in the history of Israel and the life of Christ must of necessity be involved in the generating of otherness because of the radical, self-dispossessing of the love that God displays."[16]

This, in turn, leads to christological matters. Jesus is that human historical existence which is "so related to the eternal relation of the Son to the Father that his human life is the embodiment in time of that eternal relation."[17] Thus, in reflecting on icons of Christ, Williams notes that Christ is commonly represented as "*coming out* from an immeasurable depth; behind or within him, infinity opens up."[18] This expresses the fact that "Jesus' human life is shot through with God's, he is carried on the tide of God's eternal life, and borne toward us on that tide, bringing with him all the fullness of the creator";[19] and so, "the fact of Jesus' history, part of our history, is a doorway into the endlessness of God's life and resource."[20] The word *resource* is important, indicating that Jesus, because of his relation to God, is a "transfiguring reality."[21] The incarnation catches up within itself creation, matter, time, charging them with possibilities: "the world of matter and time is not finally and authoritatively closed on itself; the boundaries are unsettled."[22] In christological terms, this means that Williams lays a good deal of emphasis on the unrestricted character of Jesus' pertinence, availability, and agency—in effect, a way of speaking of

13. Williams 1987: 243.
14. Williams 1987: 242.
15. Williams 2005a: 149.
16. Williams 2005a: 158.
17. Williams 2001b: 10.
18. Williams 2003a: 4–5.
19. Williams 2003a: 6–7.
20. Williams 2003a: 14.
21. Williams 2003a: xx.
22. Williams 2003a: 14.

the eternal deity of Jesus, which is such that his historical reality cannot in any straightforward sense be the terminus of Christian devotion.

> Jesus is manifestly the focus of the renewed sense of God that constitutes the distinctive news that Christianity brings; it is through his life and death and resurrection as an historical individual that change occurs in our standing in relation to God. But that change is precisely a movement into the relation Jesus always and already has to God: he is and is not the "terminus" of devotion, and there is . . . an *absence* at the centre of the Christian imagination, a space opening up to the final otherness and final intimacy of encounter with the Father.[23]

But there is a further consequence here, of some significance for how church, tradition, and Scripture are understood: we may not separate the person of Jesus from what Williams calls a "further space of encounter, from the gift of adoption and participation in divine life that is central to the New Testament and the patristic tradition."[24] If Christology reaches back into the divine infinity, it equally reaches forward into creaturely time, culture, and society. And Jesus, in his outreach to us, does not remain a wholly external figure stretching across an abyss but rather one whose life gives itself to us and enters into us, evoking an endless set of correspondences in which the pattern of his own relation to the Father is extended through human time.

This is, perhaps, not very far from those "extension of the incarnation" or *totus Christus* ecclesiologies with which Anglicans often flirt and by which they are sometimes seduced. If Williams resists the blandishments, it is partly because he stresses, if not the "finished" nature of Christ and his work, then their strangeness, their over-againstness, which is such that Christ and the church are not simply two points on a continuum on which he is ecclesially reproduced. "The union between the Church and Jesus is what gives form and integrity to the history of an empirically human community, so that this human community makes present and effective the action of Jesus";[25] yet all this is possible only on the basis of the church's "persistent return to the prior agency of Jesus."[26] Only on this basis is it possible to speak of the church in epiphanic terms as "the place where he is shown."[27] But, with these cautions, the ecclesiology can flow, most of all in relation to catholicity, a mark of the church that for Williams condenses much of what he wants to say about time and community opened to the infinity of God by the risen one. A catholic church is

23. Williams 2001a: 230.
24. Williams 2001a: 230.
25. Williams 2001b: 12.
26. Williams 2001b: 13.
27. Williams 1982: 63; see also Williams 1995b (essay on Michael Ramsey).

endlessly sensitive, contemplatively alert to human and personal diversity, tirelessly seeking new horizons in its own experience and understanding by engaging with this diversity, searching to see how the gospel is to be lived and confessed in new and unfamiliar situations, and doing so because of its conviction that each fresh situation is already within the ambiance of Jesus' cross and resurrection, open to his agency under his kingship.[28]

This process—the process of human life transfigured by appropriating Christ's resourcefulness—is what Williams understands as revelation. In a couple of early essays, one on Barth's doctrine of the Trinity and one on "Word and Spirit,"[29] he is troubled by "communication" models of revelation in which the Spirit's revealing activity is construed as the Spirit crossing an epistemological gulf to secure absolute knowledge on the part of creatures. The locus of revelation is, rather, that set of events in which human history is drawn to share in Jesus' relation to the Father. The question to which revelation offers an answer is not "How [can] the transcendent God (who is *elsewhere*) . . . be communicated here?" but rather "By what agency is human life transfigured?"[30] Revelation is thus neither episodic nor oracular but rather ecclesial; revelation indicates the "translatability" of Jesus' relation to the Father "into the contingent diversity of history."[31] Revelation is transformation, not simply a means to deliver apodictic certainty. These things are picked up in a later essay, "Trinity and Revelation," which distances revelation from the idea that "the given represented the finished, the fixed,"[32] so bypassing "the question of how [theology] *learns* its own language."[33] Rather, "revelation . . . is essentially to do with what is generative in our experience—events or transactions in language that break existing frames of reference and initiate new possibilities of life."[34] Because of this, revelation cannot be isolated from tradition, from the historical processes in which Jesus' significance "is apprehended by way of what it means to belong to the community whose character and limits he defines."[35]

With this we return to the emphasis on temporality with which we began: revelation is the community's transfiguration through Christ over time. Williams has a number of searching essays that, taken together, explore what the church might look like if temporality goes all the way down rather than being a surface beneath which the church has integrity and unity untroubled by tem-

28. Williams 1982: 63–64.
29. Williams 1979a; 2000l (German original, 1980).
30. Williams 2000l: 123.
31. Williams 2000l: 126.
32. Williams 2000j: 132.
33. Williams 2000j: 131.
34. Williams 2000j: 134.
35. Williams 2000j: 136.

poral defection.[36] His quarrel with George Lindbeck concerns his conception of the church's identity or orthodoxy, not as a sort of inner truthfulness behind material history and conflict, or some "locative" cultural pattern, but rather as a history in which, as he puts it elsewhere, "learning and exchange must continue"[37]—precisely because at the church's heart is the story of Jesus and his relation to God, which is "not exhaustible in word or system."[38] Orthodoxy preserves the interrogative element or revelatory interruption of the church's life, and so Williams recommends "a church whose unity lies primarily . . . in shared attention to the questioning story of a crucified and resurrected Lord, *and* an attention to how that story is being assimilated in diverse and distant communities, culturally and historically strange."[39]

There are Anglican dimensions to this, as can be seen from the elegant set of lectures and papers recently collected as *Anglican Identities*, which are a cumulative apology for "a theologically informed and spiritually sustained *patience*."[40] Williams's chosen Anglicans "know that as Christians they live among immensities of meaning, live in the wake of a divine action which defies summary explanation. They take it for granted that the believer is always learning, moving in and out of speech and silence in a continuous wonder and a continuous turning inside-out of mind and feeling."[41] Two chapters on Hooker are representative, setting him forth as a "contemplative pragmatist," reticent about "comprehensive formulations,"[42] yet sufficiently confident that the church's shaping of its own life is not independent of a given divine wisdom focused in the incarnate Word. More than anything, "to know God . . . involves elements of flexibility and corrigibility," not because of some trivial relativism but rather because "God remains God . . . and can only be discerned in the 'following' of the divine action within the mutable world, in a process of learning, not a moment of transparent vision or of simple submission to a decree."[43] This makes our response to revelation at once unfinished and political, bound up with a set of lives gathered around a given, though unfathomable, memory and presence—that of Jesus himself.

A quotation draws together the threads of this survey of some elements of Williams's theology:

> We have already the actual and substantive answer to the question of what God and humanity mean for each other, how God communicates with us and we with

36. Williams 1983; 1989a; 1993; 2000a; 2000d; 2000h.
37. Williams 1989a: 15.
38. Williams 1989a: 17.
39. Williams 1989a: 18.
40. Williams 2004: 7.
41. Williams 2004: 7.
42. Williams 2004: 26.
43. Williams 2004: 45.

God: Jesus Christ, the incarnation of God's eternal self-sharing and self-emptying wisdom. But because Jesus is word and image and mystery, because his truth is inseparable from involvement in the life of faith, the way we articulate this meaning is always shifting somewhat and never appears as a total system.[44]

Christian faith is a *set of associations* (social, linguistic, cognitive) generated by and from a particular event of limitless creative power and reach. If Christianity is thus, what is to be said about the nature and interpretation of Holy Scripture?

Scripture

Williams offers no extended treatment of the doctrine of Scripture; what he has to say can be gleaned from occasional remarks on the topic and from reflections on a range of neighboring themes: hermeneutics, history, the unity of the church. Further, he is reluctant to invoke language about God in a direct way in talking of Scripture: appeals to inspiration, canon, and illumination are rare, and when they do appear, usually they are reworked to emphasize the mediation of God's activity through creaturely cultural processes (and the attendant human obscuring of divine presence and act). As we may expect from what he has to say of the historical character of human encounter with revelation, Williams is quite deeply unsympathetic to any conception of the biblical text as "undialectically transparent to God's self-imparted meaning."[45] The economy of revelation is not such that Scripture is an oracle, and its interpretation a matter of immediate, passive absorption by a text that exercises governance apart from the history of its production and use. "The 'world of Scripture,'" he writes against Lindbeck, "so far from being a clear and readily definable territory, is an *historical* world in which meanings are discovered and recovered in action and encounter. To challenge the Church to immerse itself in its 'text' is to encourage it to engage with a history of such actions and encounters."[46]

It is important to realize, however, that this is a kind of historical realism rather than historical naturalism of the sort operative in those styles of biblical scholarship focused upon textual origins. This latter approach troubles Williams, not so much because it demystifies the processes of textual production but rather because it lacks alertness to the abundance of the text and the processes by which it is received. "We need a sensitivity to what in the text is 'excessive,' and therefore unsettled, to its representation of a question, of a tension for which the words are not yet clear."[47] This is a familiar enough

44. Williams 2001b: 5.
45. Williams 2003b: 226.
46. Williams 2000d: 30.
47. Williams 2003b: 223.

point from Ricœur, but it is shaped by a construal of the divine economy that we have sketched—and ultimately by a doctrine of God—in such a way that text and interpretation, Scripture and the cumulative life-acts of the church, cannot be teased apart. It is these relations that lie at the center of Williams's thinking about Scripture. He offers two rather different, though in the end convergent, approaches to depicting Scripture in the life of the church. One is more pacific, directed primarily by a phenomenology of signs, artistic labor, and the active reception of meaning; another, more critical in idiom, is concerned to suggest that the revelatory potency of the gospel presents itself, sometimes *malgré tout*, through the church's production and use of a set of texts that are caught up in the Spirit's representation of the utter resourcefulness of Jesus.

Scripture can, first, be explicated in terms of some more general features of sign-making. Williams's thinking here is developed in relation to sacraments, and, more recently, to artistic labor in one of his best pieces, *Grace and Necessity*, but it coheres well with suggestions elsewhere about the nature and interpretation of the Bible. Pondering the work of Jacques Maritain, he suggests that art operates in a quasi-revelatory way.

By engaging us in an unforeseen pattern of coherence or integrity, art uncovers relations and resonances in the field of perception that "ordinary" seeing and expressing obscure or even deny. Thus, art in one sense "dispossesses" us of our habitual perception and restores to reality a dimension that necessarily escapes our control. It makes the world strange. So, finally, it opens up the dimension in which "things are more than they are," "give more than they have."[48]

He illustrates this from the work of the poet and engraver David Jones, preoccupied with "the showing of the excess that pervades appearances":[49] "Art shows that form is utterly bound to matter, yet also that this matter does not exhaust the possibility of form."[50] This "abundant" character of form in its necessary relation to matter is, we will see shortly, an important element in grasping how Scripture operates. For the present, we note that artistic labor, sign-making, is explicated out of a theology of incarnation and God's "excessive" presence.

> God makes himself other; the world is a world in which things make themselves or are made other (they are more than they are and give more than they have); human beings are those creatures who uniquely have the capacity and responsibility to uncover for one another the nature of the world in which sameness and otherness constantly flow into each other, and in which there is no final reading of a "surface."[51]

48. Williams 2005a: 37–38.
49. Williams 2005a: 60.
50. Williams 2005a: 61.
51. Williams 2005a: 82–83.

Human life, acts, "makings," may become "significant form,"[52] ultimately because of "the Word become sign."[53]

The attractiveness of this for a certain kind of sacramental theology is evident, especially because of the emphasis laid upon acts of sign-making rather than on consecrated objects. A paper from the mid-1980s on "The Nature of a Sacrament" argues that

> the hope of the world becoming other is anchored, in the Christian sacraments, by the conviction that all human significant action arises from the primordial action, the art and sign, of a God committed to drawing our lives into the order of healing and communion. . . . He makes the world to be his "sign," a form of living and acting that embodies his nature and purpose. Christian sign-making . . . is a working with that creative energy.[54]

But what of Scripture? How is the Bible an instance of the way in which sign-making is "caught up in God's own will, God's own 'longing,' to share divine truth"?[55] We are to "read" the world and the cultural activities and products by which we make sense of the world as signs in which God extends toward us: "Everything in creation is a divine outreaching to us. To know something is to become alert to God's outreach in it."[56] Scripture, read in the light of Jesus' risen presence, which is the supreme divinely given sign that orders all others, has its significance as a sign within the history of the revisioning of the world that Jesus' incarnation, death, and, above all, resurrection bring about. The Bible is to be approached "as if it were . . . held open before us by the living Christ."[57] More closely: "The resurrection . . . is to do with the creation of the new humanity, where resentment and hostility are 'unfrozen,' and with the establishment of scriptural revelation as a living relationship within the new humanity."[58] Scripture is a sign functioning within the new society generated by the resurrection.

How does this operate in the use of Scripture? Reading Scripture as a sign in the sphere of reality opened by the resurrection means being alert to significant patterns, not necessarily on the surface of the text, and not capable of being isolated apart from acts of interpretation and living in the community that gathers around Jesus. In the terms indicated earlier, the "form" of Scripture exceeds its matters; Scripture has a privileged place in a chain of sign-making that does not terminate with inscripturation or canonization; the boundaries between the text as sign and the symbolic acts of readers are porous, precisely

---

52. Williams 2005a: 89.
53. Williams 2005a: 90.
54. Williams 2000f: 207–8.
55. Williams 2003a: 74.
56. Williams 2003a: 74.
57. Williams 2003a: 77.
58. Williams 2003a: 35.

because both exist in the sphere of Christ's transformation of all things. Williams's early work *Resurrection* offers the fullest working out of these ideas. The book seeks to show "how, as narratives, these Easter texts present us with a variety of 'significant patterns,' imaginative approaches to the question what it meant and means to say that Jesus who was deserted and executed is alive to God and also present with his followers."[59] And so, for example, the Gospel stories of the resurrection are seen as explorations of themes such as "absolution by God"[60] or "recognizing one's victim as one's hope,"[61] to be read through categories and experiences of oppression, victimization, and exclusion. Scripture is to be read in light of the way in which, in the economy of God's "outreach," "the particularity of Jesus crucified and proclaimed as savior in Jerusalem becomes a universal symbol, the focus and pivot of a fresh and transforming interpretation of all human reality."[62] This is a loose statement that invites unfavorable comment; however, what Williams is doing with the biblical narratives is something rather different from, say, what Schleiermacher does in the Christmas Eve dialogue: the matter of the text is not so reduced to its form that it could be translated without residue into a psychology or sociology of convertedness. The text does indeed signify personal and communal renewal; it is not an enclave apart from its effective history. But the functioning of the text as sign is contingent upon the action of God. It is

> a narrative structure in which we can locate our recovery of identity and human possibility, a "paradigm" of the saving process; yet not only a paradigm. It is a story which is itself an indispensable *agent* in the completion of this process, because it witnesses to the one personal agent, that is, the risen Christ.[63]

The concern to prevent closure is never far from Williams's mind, and one real advantage of an understanding of Scripture as sign is its coherence with a deep conviction that the life of Jesus risen "is not a life exhausted in any text or assemblage of texts": "The empty throne, the space between the cherubim, is filled by identifying Jesus with a dead teacher or a living memory—with a human construct or the object of human mental activity, rather than with the aniconic and paradoxical 'presence' of the God of the covenant."[64]

This leads to the second, more critical, account of the nature of Scripture. The making of signs, especially textual signs, is not innocent; it includes a

---

59. Williams 1982: 1.
60. Williams 1982: 2.
61. Williams 1982: 11.
62. Williams 1982: 26.
63. Williams 1982: 49. It is worth noting that in setting out this understanding of Scripture as sign, Williams most commonly speaks of narrative texts, especially the resurrection narratives, whose indeterminacy and obliqueness cohere well with his presentation; it is not easy to see how Romans or Hebrews would fare on this account.
64. Williams 2000b: 193, 194–95.

history of conflict, suppression, or exclusion. Put differently: there is a history of textual production, from which Scripture is by no means exempt, a history that is ideologically freighted and of which the text itself offers only an obscure representation. A rather troubled paper on "Historical Criticism and Sacred Text" is the sharpest statement of this.[65] In it Williams tries to disabuse us of a common assumption of "the transparency of text to what it represents."[66] The biblical text, far from being a "finished textual synthesis,"[67] is a collection of discrete units that indicate an unresolved intertextual struggle about what the various texts seek to indicate.

> The nature of the biblical text allows us to give due weight to what we might call a pathos of reading: the new textual movement emerges from the unmanageable contradictions of available speech in a changing situation; but it is also an attempt to resolve or remove a contradiction, potentially a moment of *loss*, diminution of meaning. We read this composite biblical text to understand not only the proposed resolutions, but to be aware of what losses occur as text responds to text.[68]

The hermeneutical consequence here is that we are to read a particular biblical text "with an eye to tensions within the text, to the voices on its edge, to what it opposes or suppresses, so far as we can discern. It takes its place within the entire composite text of Scripture as an element already communicating the meanings of God through its inner conversations and stresses and self-reflection or self-subversion."[69] If the first account of Scripture makes its appeal to a phenomenology of sign-making, this second account applies a rule that Williams announces elsewhere: "There is nothing untouched by culture and the contestation of power."[70] But it is important to note that, according to Williams, even an ideologically freighted text can be considered to be, and used as, sacred. A sacred text is "one for which the context is always more than the social-ideological matrix," one of which it can be said that "reader and text are responding to a gift, an address or summons not derived from the totality of the empirical environment."[71] Accordingly, in engaging a sacred text we not only encounter false consciousness; we also converse "with a presence that is not a rival speaker,"[72] beyond the competition that the text indicates. Listening for that speaker entails seeking "those contradictions between intention and performance, those marks of excess and of intra-textual

65. Williams 2003b; see also Williams 2000c: 53–55.
66. Williams 2003b: 220.
67. Williams 2003b: 221.
68. Williams 2003b: 222.
69. Williams 2003b: 223.
70. Williams 2003b: 248.
71. Williams 2003b: 224.
72. Williams 2003b: 224.

strain that might have to do not only with immediate ideological context but with God."[73] In short:

> the sacred text enacts its sacred character not by its transparency but by its nature as unresolved, unfinished, self-reflexive or self-questioning. It is through these things that its "excess" appears—its character as not determined by the matrix from which it historically comes or by the conceptual framework it constructs.[74]

What is pressing upon Williams here is not, I suspect, sensibilities about textual indeterminacy but rather an aggressively political construal of textual activity, whether of authors or readers, that requires of him the same kind of subversive interrogation of settled representations of God's presence into which Donald MacKinnon schooled his listeners. There is no "knowledge without representation,"[75] and so, no text without ideology. If the text is sacred—if there is, indeed, *Holy* Scripture—it is only so in spite of itself.

Thus far we have been exploring the nature of Scripture. What of its interpretation? By now it ought to be clear that, for Williams, interpretation—reading and making sense of a text—is indispensable to the process of coming to know God through the Bible. Partly this is because texts have their meaning in "the world of temporal engagement and growth,"[76] such that the reading of them cannot be finished in a comprehensive "totalising interpretation";[77] partly, also, it is because a biblical text is not "simply an oracle"[78] but rather requires appropriation. In Williams's hands, however, this is not simply a general hermeneutical commitment; it is an extension of christological and soteriological teaching: Scripture has its place in the divine economy in which human lives are being drawn into correspondence to Christ, and so "Scripture is not simply a long record of finished business."[79]

Two key terms emerge from various writings on these topics: *diachronic* (or *dramatic*) reading and *analogy*. In line with what is said elsewhere about the inescapably time-laden character of knowing, diachronic reading takes seriously the fact that Scripture cannot be taken in all at once; its reading must therefore involve "a movement in time"[80] or "a process of learning to perceive."[81] The appropriation of the text's meaning cannot be restricted to an isolated present moment but rather must be seen as part of

73. Williams 2003b: 225.
74. Williams 2003b: 227.
75. Williams 2003b: 225.
76. Williams 1988: 44.
77. Williams 1988: 40.
78. Williams 1995a: 134.
79. Williams 1995a: 136.
80. Williams 2000c: 46.
81. Williams 2000c: 47.

the process of learning and producing meanings. . . . The meanings in our reading are like the meanings in the rest of our experience, they are to be discovered,
unfolded. . . . So long as our humanity remains unintelligible except as a life of
material change, irreversible movement, it is unlikely . . . that we could establish
non-diachronic modes of reading as primary.[82]

This is, of course, close to understandings of the relation between text and
interpretation found in some kinds of reader-response theory or in appeal
to "performance" as a metaphor for reading the Bible;[83] there is the same
resistance to making the text a determinate communicative act, and the same
anxiety about viewing the text as a closed textual "world" (as Lindbeck or
Childs are believed to do). But, though the warrants for diachronic reading
certainly include a general theory of the provisionality of history and meaning, there is more: the governing principle is christological and, by derivation,
ecclesiological. "Reading Scripture in faith is reading it as moving towards
or around a unifying narrative moment, the story of the work of Jesus; *how*
it does so, how we are to carry through such a reading in points of detail, is
constantly elusive."[84]

Here the term *analogy* begins to do its work. The term is partly a way of
pointing out the correspondences between that which is brought to speech in
the text and our own histories. This is what Williams calls *analogia duratio-
nis*, "a continuity between the time(s) of the text and what we recognize as
movement and production in our own lives."[85] But the term also articulates
the correspondences between different readings of the Bible within the conversation that is the history of the Christian tradition. To speak of analogy
is thus to indicate both the mutually constituting character of Scripture and
tradition, and also the proper unity displayed by the tradition of interpretation in the church, poised between, on the one hand, a shapeless pluralism
and, on the other hand, closure. To read with the rule of analogy in mind
means, therefore, that "we are not the first or the only readers."[86] But it also
indicates, more profoundly, a hermeneutic rooted in what might be called
Jesus' *catholicity*.

To explore the continuities of Christian patterns of holiness is to explore the
effect of Jesus, living, dying and rising; and it is inevitable that the tradition
about Jesus is re-read and re-worked so that it will make sense of these lived
patterns as they evolve. We constantly return to imagine the life of Jesus in

82. Williams 2000c: 49.
83. See Lash 1986; Young 1990.
84. Williams 2000c: 56–57.
85. Williams 2000c: 52.
86. Williams 2000k: 24.

a way that will help us to understand how it sets up a continuous pattern of human living before God.[87]

It is just that—rereading Jesus, imagining his resourcefulness—which is, for Williams, the core of scriptural interpretation.

Reflections

Williams is free of the dualism that commonly afflicts accounts of Scripture and interpretative practice, for the simple reason that he does not think that theology is forced to choose between divine revelatory causality and material-cultural processes. Revelation and its scriptural witness do not need to be "supernatural" in order effectively to communicate the gospel. Williams's theology of Scripture and his embrace of the contingencies of interpretation in history form part of a larger theological venture in which the choice between "natural" and "transcendent" is considered an expression of theological disorder—the fruit of a half-Christian metaphysic in which God and creatures are centers of will standing on either side of a gulf. For Williams, taking the Trinity and incarnation seriously means denying the bifurcation of the spiritual and the historical-cultural. Further, he suggests that the proper location of Scripture is in the economy of God's gracious transformation of creatures; Scripture is not artifact or report or oracle but rather is a text occupying a place in the new relations of God to creatures and between creatures themselves that are brought about by the gospel.

Williams is reluctant to say much about God's relation to the processes of text production or reception. As a rule, God is spoken of as obliquely or indirectly related to the text that mediates him but in whose production he is not involved at other than a background level. Classical Protestant theologies talked of God's relation to textual production through the doctrine of inspiration; Williams shares the general modern unease with that tract of Christian teaching, though not because he is an historical naturalist but rather because for him divine causality is immanent within creaturely production of texts and meaning. Yet sometimes divine agency is so retired as to be scarcely visible, and the relation of text and divine communication appears, at the very least, to lack intentionality and at times to be an arbitrary annexation of one bit of the church's sign-making. If, however, God's relation to textual production is to be more than one in which God picks up Christian making of meaning, a treatment of inspiration can scarcely be avoided. Inspiration, moreover, can be supplemented in a number of ways. We can articulate scriptural authorship as prophetic and apostolic activity—that is, as cultural production that originates in divine commissioning and whose agency is centered in the communicative

87. Williams 2000k: 25.

activity of God, who bends authorial intentions to serve his own. Or again, we might invoke the notion of the sanctification of Scripture, not as a natural property of biblical texts but rather as a relation to God that extends across the entire range of its production, authorization, and reception.[88]

Williams makes a good deal of the complicity of Scripture and its interpretation in ideology, and his correction to this is to stress the indeterminacy of Scripture in the life of the church, in that Scripture keeps certain questions alive rather than offering definitive solutions (a point seized upon by critics eager to prove that Augustine's chair is occupied by a skeptic). At this point, however, appeal might be made to the divine promise that accompanies Scripture and its reading: Holy Scripture will be part of God's gift of truth to the church. That gift is certainly a gift in time, not a moment of sheer transparency. However, it cannot be deferred to the eschaton: the church may *expect* God to use its uses of Scripture and so to complete the prophetic work begun in the authors themselves. The church is authorized to confess that Scripture is *Holy* Scripture. "Holy Scripture" does not, of course, mean that Scripture is a closed bit of textual territory that affords us a "total perspective" on everything,[89] but it does mean that Scripture is sanctified and therefore guarded by God, that truthful speech is not just an eschatological possibility but rather a calling and task that the church can fulfill as it trusts the divine promise. Is there a threat of false consciousness in all this? Of course. But the safeguard is not historical or hermeneutical indeterminacy; rather, it is an operative doctrine of the superintendence of the Holy Spirit, who guides the church into the truth.

Similar questions about divine intentionality might be raised in response to Williams's curious insistence on polyphony, conflict, and incoherence within the canon. Some of his sensitivities here might be met by a more theologically oriented description of canon as an act of churchly deference to a divine calling and authorization of witnesses. Further, as Markus Bockmuehl points out,[90] Williams's reluctance to allow canon any role in shaping exegesis makes it hard for him to produce the sort of exegetically driven theology that was common across the Christian tradition until at least the early modern period, because canonical indeterminacy erodes the sense that theology has a concrete object. "Fugal" theology—theology as "chains of association" of the sort that Williams commends—is certainly not without its proper matter, namely, the transforming potency of the story of Jesus, which reaches back into the depths

---

88. Williams's recent Larkin Stuart Lecture "The Bible Today: Reading and Hearing" gives some space to these matters in speaking of Scripture as the address of the risen Christ, partly in response to critics who heard earlier statements as a claim that "we are given only a method of interpretation by the form of Scripture—a method that, by pointing us to the conflict and tension between texts simply leaves us with theologically unresolvable debate as a universal norm for Christian discourse" (Williams 2007).

89. Williams 2000h: 13.

90. Bockmuehl 2006: 82–86.

of God's uncreated creativity. But part of the force of both canon and the doctrine of the sufficiency of Scripture is to restrict indeterminacy or, perhaps better, to indicate the channel along which the meaning of the gospel flows, the place where it might be expected, the shapes that it will assume.

This connects to a christological question: Does the emphasis on the sheer inexhaustibility of Jesus miss something about his perfection? In Williams's view, Scripture is not a determinate speech-act by the risen one whose identity is fully achieved; it is, instead, the sign and occasion of his resourcefulness, his endlessly suggestive character, his capacity to generate variations. Scripture is a function of the catholicity of Christ as God. None of this means that Williams sits loose on the particularity of Jesus: no less than Barth or Frei, he is insistent on Jesus' unsubstitutability. But Jesus is a concrete universal.

> The creative act of God . . . can only be articulated in terms of two quite irreducible moments: the establishing in the life of Jesus of a unifying point of reference, and the necessarily unfinished ensemble of human stories drawn together and given shape in relation to Jesus. This means that the actual concrete meaning of Logos in the world, the pattern decisively and transformingly embodied in Jesus, could only be seen and realised through the entire process of the history to which the event of Jesus gives rise, with all its fluidity and unpredictability.[91]

What is curious here is the slenderness of Jesus' agency in the history of his reception in the church's sign-making and discipleship. He does not seem to be the agent of the distribution of his benefits; it is as if his energy is dispersed into the processes of human "making sense" of Jesus. "'The risen Jesus,'" he remarks at the end of *Resurrection*, "only has clear content in the relation to the life of grace as experienced now. . . . Jesus' risenness and our risenness are visible only obliquely, in relation to each other."[92] Part of what is problematic here is a truncation of the biblical sequence of Jesus' exaltation, ending at resurrection rather than continuing through to his heavenly session and his exercise of his royal and prophetic offices. Jesus is resource—representable but not author of Christian representations, rather only their pattern. Do we not need to say more than "the Word become sign"?[93] Do we not need to say that Scripture requires us not so much to re-present Jesus under the pressure of his resourcefulness but simply to attend to him in his perfection?

This suggests a final thought. Is Williams's account of the processes of interpretation possessed of sufficient Christian specificity? He tends to subsume Scripture within a general cultural poetics and hermeneutics. But, if Scripture is the *viva vox Dei*, does not this require greater theological specification of the kinds of human acts that are fitting with respect to this text? Certainly

91. Williams 2000i: 172.
92. Williams 1982: 120.
93. Williams 2005a: 89.

Williams naturally gravitates toward the language of "learning," repentance, conversion, and so forth in order to emphasize the disturbance brought about by Scripture as a resource in the construal of Christ. Such language doubtless takes us far beyond the spiritual torpor of historical representation; but it may not quite suffice, because it is subsumed within an anthropology in which interpreting and "giving meaning"[94] have high priority. Of course, we want to say, there is interpretation; of course the Spirit gives life and sets the church to work on Scripture. But what kind of life and work? Those questions cannot be answered with sufficient determinacy unless there is a cutting back or relocation of the poetics of interpretation, a subsuming of all our reading acts under the rubric of *faith*.

From Augustine, Williams has learned the pervasiveness of the distinction between *uti* and *frui*: God alone is the end of desire, there can be no final meaning in time, there are only signs to push us beyond contingent satisfaction:

> The coming of the Word in flesh establishes, we might say, the nature of fleshly being as word, as sign, the all-pervasiveness of "use." That is to say, we live in a world of restless fluidities of meaning: all terms and all the objects they name are capable of opening out beyond themselves, coming to speak of a wider context, and so refusing to stay still under our attempts to comprehend or systematize or (for these go together) idolize.[95]

What Williams says about Scripture, we have seen, is an extension of what he finds there in Augustine: Scripture is difficult, irresolvably so; but the function of difficulty is to ensure that "learning from Scripture is a *process*—not a triumphant moment of penetration and mastery."[96] Alertness to "the threat of an idolatry of signs"[97] is the characteristic strength of Williams's theology as a whole and of what he has to say about the church's use of its canonical texts; it is also the point at which critical appraisal might begin.

94. Williams 2000j: 142.
95. Williams 1989b: 141.
96. Williams 1989b: 142.
97. Williams 1989b: 148.

8

The Normativity of Scripture and Tradition in Recent Catholic Theology

BENEDICT THOMAS VIVIANO, OP

"Is not my word like fire," says the LORD, "and like a hammer that breaks a rock in pieces?"

Jeremiah 23:29

The topic of this chapter is the normativity of Scripture and tradition in recent Roman Catholic theology and official documents. We should realize at the outset that in discussing this topic we are arguably committing a sin. We should rather be listening to and discussing a passage of Scripture itself. That is why I have begun with a passage from Jeremiah that asks whether God's word is not more powerful and interesting than any merely human word. But there is an undeniable interest in this topic, so I have agreed to address it.

M.-J. Lagrange and Pope Pius X

That said, let me begin with my hero, M.-J. Lagrange (1855–1938), founder of the French biblical and archaeological school in Jerusalem (1890). After being the "fair-haired boy" of Pope Leo XIII for thirteen years, he fell into disfavor in 1903 and remained so for the rest of his life. (He won posthumous victories in 1943 and 1965.) What had he said to upset church authorities? He began his new life in the Holy Land by walking around the Sinai desert, Bible in hand. He thus saw that the Exodus account could not be topographically sound in every detail. He was also confronted with the first publication of Hammurabi's Babylonian law code. He felt the need to analyze this code in comparison with the three law codes in the Pentateuch. Then there was the Gilgamesh flood narrative that needed to be studied with Genesis 6–10, Noah and the ark. Lagrange popularized his results in a little book, *The Old Testament and Historical Criticism* (1903). In its last chapter he wrote that students of the Bible, especially the Old Testament, needed to pay attention to the different literary genres used by the biblical authors. They did not always intend to write history in the sense of nineteenth-century positivistic historiography. They also wrote what he called primeval history, not to mention poetry. (In the background of his concerns there also lay the issue of different sources of the Pentateuch, as synthesized by Julius Wellhausen.)[1]

In this fateful year (1903) Leo XIII died, and Pius X was elected pope. Pius was guided in intellectual matters by several curial cardinals whose diplomatic goal was the restoration of the papal states to their full extent, in central Italy. This was no longer a realistic goal, but, in this pursuit, these cardinals (the best known are Rafael Merry del Val and Pietro Gasparri) felt that they must block all compromise with the modern world (the world created by the events of 1789). Because of his thesis on biblical literary genres, Lagrange became a suspected modernizer. His career in the church was stopped in its upward ascent. He barely escaped condemnation. He was saved by his own prudence, by his sense of loyalty to the church, and by a saintly protector, H. Cormier. Lagrange died in 1938, still under a cloud of official suspicion.

Divino Afflante Spiritu and the Bible's Literary Genres

By 1935 all the curial cardinals who enforced the rules of this period of theological suppression were dead. Catholic theology began to emerge from the cellar (Chenu, Congar, Mersch, Jungmann, Rahner, de Lubac, Daniélou, Bouyer). A group of French Catholic schoolteachers, led by Jean Guitton,[2] petitioned the elderly pope, Pius XI, that the question of the genre of Genesis 1–3 be reopened. He said that it was a difficult matter. He would leave it for his successor to tackle. The successor, Pius XII, took up the challenge. In 1943, in the middle of the war, he commissioned a Dominican, Jacques Voste, who had studied with Lagrange, and a Jesuit, Augustin Bea, to draft an encyclical letter that conceded the point about literary genres. The letter was called *Divino Afflante Spiritu* (1943). It was a posthumous vindication

1. Montagnes 2006.
2. Guitton 1992.

of Lagrange. His little book of 1903 was now officially accepted, forty years after it appeared and five years after Lagrange himself was safely dead. The encyclical said:

35. What is the literal sense of a passage is not always as obvious in the speeches and writings of the ancient authors of the East, as it is in the works of our own time. For what they wished to express is not to be determined by the rules of grammar and philology alone, nor solely by the context; the interpreter must, as it were, go back wholly in spirit to those remote centuries of the East and with the aid of history, archaeology, ethnology, and other sciences, accurately determine what *modes of writing*, so to speak, the authors of that ancient period would be likely to use, and in fact did use.

36. For the ancient peoples of the East, in order to express their ideas, did not always employ those *forms or kinds of speech* which we use today; but rather those used by the men of their times and countries. What those exactly were the commentator cannot determine as it were in advance, but only after a careful examination of the ancient literature of the East. The investigation, carried out, on this point, during the past forty or fifty years with greater care and diligence than ever before, has more clearly shown what *forms of expression* were used in those far off times, whether in poetic description or in the formulation of laws and rules of life or in recording the facts and events of history. The same inquiry has also shown the special preeminence of the people of Israel among all the other ancient nations of the East in their mode of compiling history, both by reason of its antiquity and by reasons of the faithful record of the events; qualities which may well be attributed to the gift of divine inspiration and to the peculiar religious purpose of biblical history.

37. Nevertheless no one who has a correct idea of biblical inspiration, will be surprised to find, even in the Sacred Writers, as in other ancient authors, *certain fixed ways of expounding and narrating*, certain definite idioms, especially of a kind peculiar to the Semitic tongues, so-called approximations, and certain hyperbolical *modes of expression*, nay, at times, even paradoxical, which even help to impress the ideas more deeply on the mind. For of *the modes of expression* which, among ancient peoples, and especially those of the East, human language used to express its thought, none is excluded from the Sacred Books, provided the way of speaking adopted in no wise contradicts the holiness and truth of God, as, with his customary wisdom, the Angelic Doctor already observed in these words: "In Scripture divine things are presented to us in the manner which is in common use amongst men." For as the substantial Word of God became like to men in all things, "except sin," so the words of God, expressed in human language, are made like to human speech in every respect, except error. In this consists that "condescension" of the God of providence, which St. John Chrysostom extolled with the highest praise and repeatedly declared to be found in the Sacred Books.

38. Hence the Catholic commentator, in order to comply with the present needs of biblical studies, in explaining the Sacred Scripture and in demonstrating and proving its immunity from all error, should also make a prudent use of

this means, determine, that is, to what extent *the manner of expression or the literary mode* adopted by the sacred writer may lead to a correct and genuine interpretation; and let him be convinced that this part of his office cannot be neglected without serious detriment to Catholic exegesis. Not infrequently—to mention only one instance—when some persons reproachfully charge the Sacred Writers with some historical error or inaccuracy in the recording of facts, on closer examination it turns out to be nothing else than those customary *modes of expression and narration* peculiar to the ancients, which used to be employed in the mutual dealings of social life and which in fact were sanctioned by common usage.

39. When then such *modes of expression* are met within the sacred text, which, being meant for men, is couched in human language, justice demands that they be no more taxed with error than when they occur in the ordinary intercourse of daily life. By this knowledge and exact appreciation of *the modes of speaking and writing* in use among the ancients can be solved many difficulties, which are raised against the veracity and historical value of the Divine Scriptures, and no less efficaciously does this study contribute to a fuller and more luminous understanding of the mind of the Sacred Writer.[3]

The main point of this text is the nine-times repeated affirmation that the interpreter must pay attention to the "forms or kinds of speech," the "modes of expression," used by the ancient biblical writers. This is Lagrange's idea of literary genres. But there are also some subsidiary points. (1) Six times "the East" is mentioned, especially in the phrase "going back wholly in spirit." These themes echo the romantic idea of history-writing that goes back to J. G. Herder, F. Schlegel, and F. D. Schleiermacher: the *Einfühlung* or feeling oneself into the past. They also reflect what Edward Said was later to label Orientalism, the idea that the Near Eastern mind is substantially different from the Western European mind.[4] (2) The passage also briefly mentions the genres of poetry, law, and history (see below). (3) It also says that the commentator cannot determine the genre "in advance." This is written against the a priori, deductive approach of systematicians such as Louis Billot who wanted to dispose of biblical criticism with a few Cartesian logical arguments. (4) At its close the passage alludes to the theological nerve point: the doctrine that the Bible must be inerrant in all matters, including scientific ones (see below, on Vatican II). This encyclical, for all its caution, was a great help to biblical scholars in the Roman Catholic Church. The issue of inerrancy would only be settled in 1965.

At this point let us pause to reflect for a moment on the fact of multiple genres in the Bible. For the Old Testament, it is clear that there are five main

3. The text of the encyclical is available at www.vatican.va/holy_father/pius_xii/encyclicals/documents/hf_p-xii_enc_30091943_divino-afflante-spiritu_en.html (italics added).

4. This is ill viewed nowadays, but that is not our main concern. On the theme of condescension (paragraph 37), see Dreyfus 1985. The reference to Thomas Aquinas, the Angelic Doctor, is found in his commentary on Hebrews, chapter 1, lectio 4, paragraph 64.

literary genres: (1) history and history-like narrative; (2) law; (3) prophecy; (4) wisdom; (5) praise. Often these genres are present within the same books. The Pentateuch, for example, contains elements of all five: Moses' story is told; he is presented as prophet and lawgiver (king), as a wise man or sage, who sings the praise of God. The danger is that we might privilege one of these genres to the exclusion of the others. Rather, ideally they should be maintained in a sane balance, in a mutually corrective dialectical dance. In reality, this is not so easy to bring off. Past experience has shown some of these errors. (1) In the nineteenth century, with its historicist positivistic obsessions, orthodox interpreters often felt that they had to defend the historicity of every detail—for example, Moses wrote the account of his own death (Deut. 34); Jonah stayed for days in the belly of the whale. The Bible thus was reduced to history and history only. (2) In reaction to Pauline Christianity, some forms of Judaism tended to concentrate on the detailed law of the Bible. (3) By concentrating on the phenomenon of prophecy, Thomas Aquinas gave the impression that the divine element in Scripture resided in the prophets (*Summa theologica* 2–2.171–178). (4) The Enlightenment reduced the Bible to rational wisdom, common sense, and natural law; the Jesus Seminar tends to see Jesus as a Cynic sage, without apocalyptic prophecy. (5) For the devout, the Bible is primarily a book of prayer, singing the praises of God in Psalms. (For aesthetes, the Bible is of interest as a series of *objets d'art* [e.g., parables].) Such selectivity impoverishes us. It cordons off parts of the biblical tradition for special privilege or for special neglect and thus prevents readers from receiving the Bible in all its rich variety.[5]

J. R. Geiselmann on Scripture and Tradition

This selective one-sidedness was provoked by real problems. (1) Once the idea became fixed in place that because the Bible is the inspired word of God, it must be free of error in every respect, the mind of the logician could push for wilder and wilder conclusions, further and further from the intention of the text. As the apologist labored to keep God free from the taint of evil, the hyperlogician fought to keep God free from the taint of error. Among the knights of consistent inerrancy were Louis Billot and James Montgomery. They argued that the honor of God required verbal inerrancy. (2) How should we understand Genesis 1–11? As history, as science, as myth, or as primordial history that includes elements of ancient science and myth? The last of these alternatives was Lagrange's response to Hermann Gunkel's challenge laid down in his *Creation and Chaos in the Primeval Era and the Eschaton* of 1895.[6] (3) Another big problem has been the right relation of Scripture and church tradition. In the wake of the Reformation criticism with its slogan "Scripture

5. Ricœur 1977 (reprinted in Ricœur 1980).
6. ET, Gunkel 2006. Lagrange's answer was accepted in 1948 by the Biblical Commission.

alone!" the Council of Trent responded with a "both . . . and." Divine revelation is to be found both in the Scriptures and in sacred traditions. This issue
became lively in the 1950s after Pope Pius XII made a dogma of the bodily
assumption of Mary into heaven. Oscar Cullmann, the Alsatian Lutheran,
weighed in with an important essay, to which Jean Daniélou responded.[7] Above
all, the publication of the debates behind Trent enabled J. R. Geiselmann
to free the interpretation of Trent from a view consciously rejected by the
council fathers. This view held that revelation was partly (*partim*) contained
in Scripture and partly (*partim*) contained in tradition, with the implication
that Scripture itself had been materially insufficient. That meant there were
doctrines to be believed that were necessary for salvation that were not contained in Scripture. Geiselmann could show that this view had been considered
by Trent (the *partim*s were in a draft) and freely set aside. That is, there are
no *partim*s in the final text of Trent, and the view that Scripture is materially
insufficient was not accepted as a dogma, although it was (and remains) a
tolerated theological opinion. Geiselmann went on to offer his own proposal
as to the right relationship between Scripture and tradition. Here is an English
translation of his conclusions:

> How is the relationship between the Holy Scriptures and the unwritten traditions
> to be determined? We have, by means of the proof from tradition that there is
> a material [i.e., content = *inhaltliche*] sufficiency of Holy Scripture as to what
> concerns faith, and that there is a material insufficiency as to what concerns
> *mores, consuetudines et leges* (morals, customs and laws) of the church; we have,
> I say, created the presupposition to be able to answer the question concerning the
> relationship between Scripture and tradition. As a result, it becomes apparent
> that this relationship cannot be determined unequivocally.
>
> With respect to faith, the Holy Scripture is materially sufficient [as to its
> contents]. But, thereby the Sola-Scriptura principle is not yet expressed. For the
> Holy Scripture is, with respect to the canon of the Scriptures, dependent upon
> tradition and upon the decision of the Church. For it was the Council of Trent
> which first definitively settled the canon of Holy Scripture. And with respect
> to the understanding of Holy Scriptures, it needs the clarifying tradition of the
> Fathers in matters of faith and morals. Tradition in these cases exercises the
> function of *traditio interpretativa*. Besides, the Holy Scripture is dependent
> upon the *sensus* which the church maintains and has always maintained, for the
> explanation of its contents which concern faith and morals.
>
> Here thus holds true with respect to faith the principle: *totum in sacra scrip-
> tura et iterum totum in traditione*, completely in Scripture and completely in
> tradition.
>
> The situation is otherwise with respect to the *mores et consuetudines* of the
> church. Here Scripture is insufficient and needs tradition for its completion in
> content. In these cases, tradition is *traditio constitutiva*.

7. Cullmann 1956; cf. Daniélou 1953.

> Here holds true with respect to the *mores et consuetudines* the principle: *partim in sacra scriptura, partim in sine scripto traditionibus*, partly in the Holy Scriptures, partly in tradition.[8]

So for Geiselmann, Scripture is sufficient in what is necessary for salvation, while tradition plays an important role in interpretation. This view has been supported in a thorough study by Yves Congar[9] and was not condemned at Vatican II, as some had expected. Thus it remains a permitted view within the Roman Catholic Church. It is not, however, embraced by all theologians, including some important ones.[10]

Other aspects of this issue of the relation of Scripture to interpretative tradition include that the Bible is not a good book of rubrics; it does not say how exactly one should celebrate the Lord's Supper, or whether one could baptize with wine or beer. More troublesome, it does not treat expressly the morality of nuclear weapons or the use of computers. Already at Nicea, the council fathers felt that they must use a nonscriptural word, *homoousion* ("of the same substance"), to save the scriptural doctrine about Jesus Christ from the wily Arians.[11] This is a significant test case, as is the question of who decides the limits of the biblical canon.

The Holy Spirit is not dead in the church or in the world (John 16:12–13). Besides new problems, new worlds are discovered: America, the Indians, other planets. This was the occasion for the Mormons to believe there was need of a further revelation. But the Bible does not contain the answers to every question or mention all cultures. It is concerned with sin and salvation and ethics. (See below on the Second Vatican Council.) The Great Church tradition tries to achieve a synthesis of biblical faith and reason, philosophy and theology, nature and grace, science and religion. The Bible itself absorbs many ancient cultures and pagan religions, but the challenges continue, especially with Islam and the Enlightenment. One could also add an eschatological limitation to the normativity of Scripture. For, if we believe that Jesus Christ will return in glory and will reign over the kingdom of God in its fullness on earth (as the Creed teaches), then it cannot be excluded in principle that, while reigning and judging, Christ will say something. That something would be new divine revelation from Christ.

8. Geiselmann 1962: 282.
9. Congar 1966.
10. Rahner and Ratzinger 1966; Ratzinger 1998. On the role of church authority in interpreting Scripture, see, among recent publications, Gilbert 2002 (he calculates that there are twelve biblical verses whose meaning has been defined, all done at Trent, all having to do with sacraments); Bieringer 2006. *Istina* 51 (2006): 225–330 presents a symposium on Catholic and Orthodox hermeneutics.
11. See Kelly 2006 (first edition, 1950): 213, 238–39, 286, 290, 294; Ayres 2006. See also Torrance in chapter 9 of the present volume.

The Contribution of Canon Criticism

This leads to fascinating and multifaceted issues of canon criticism, reception history of the canon, and the diversity of reading communities. Here I will make only a few remarks. First, regarding the deuterocanonical/apocryphal books of the Old Testament—that is, the longer canon of the Bible—I can only testify that in order to understand the New Testament I have found it helpful to have these additional books to fill in certain blanks. For example, John's reference to the Feast of Dedication (John 10:22) presupposes Maccabees. Romans 1 presupposes Wisdom 13–15. James 1:13–15 presupposes Sirach 15. If we are serious about the Bible as a history of salvation, we need to know what happened between Malachi (ca. 400 BC) and Jesus. Even understanding Daniel requires the Maccabees. My second remark concerns the importance of the dialectical mutual correction and balancing provided by different biblical books read in the same community of faith. For example, I find John ethically poorer than the Synoptic Gospels because he leaves out the love of enemies. John is better for its teaching on the person of Jesus, the Holy Spirit, and the sacraments; Matthew is better for its ethics (Sermon on the Mount). A balanced church needs both these voices.[12]

Dei Verbum and the Second Vatican Council

We come now to the Dogmatic Constitution on Divine Revelation (*Dei Verbum*) of the Second Vatican Council, voted on and approved with virtual unanimity by about 2,800 bishops and other delegates, 18 November 1965.[13] This document is not long, yet it was one with which the council wrestled till the last minute. Here I will try to offer the student a brief guide in six points, three major and three minor. The three key breakthrough paragraphs are 9, 11, and 19. The ninth paragraph treats the relation of Scripture and tradition.

> 9. Hence there exists a close connection and communication between sacred tradition and Sacred Scripture. For both of them, flowing from the same divine wellspring, in a certain way merge into a unity and tend toward the same end. For Sacred Scripture is the word of God inasmuch as it is consigned to writing under the inspiration of the divine Spirit, while sacred tradition takes the word of God entrusted by Christ the Lord and the Holy Spirit to the Apostles, and hands it on to their successors honestly, so that led by the light of the Spirit of truth, they may in proclaiming it preserve this word of God faithfully, explain it, and make it more widely known. Consequently it is not from Sacred Scripture alone that the Church draws her certainty about everything which has been

12. Sanders 1972; 1984; 1987; Childs 1992; McDonald and Sanders 2002; Söding 2006.
13. The text of *Dei Verbum* is available at www.vatican.va/archive/hist_councils/ii_vatican_council/documents/vat-ii_const_19651118_dei-verbum_en.html.

revealed. Therefore both sacred tradition and Sacred Scripture are to be accepted and venerated with the same sense of loyalty and reverence.

I have already treated this matter and need only to point out that the council affirms the roles of both Scripture and tradition. That is doing no more than stating a historical fact. The council does not try to explain their relationship. Thus, various theories that do try to work out their relationship are given free rein, including Geiselmann's. Further, the council teaches that Christian ministers have the duty to preach, explain, and spread the scriptural Word of God. Finally, borrowing an elegant turn of phrase from Trent, the council says that both Scripture and tradition are to be received with a like feeling (*affectu*) of piety. Reliable interpreters of Trent say that this phrase is only a rhetorical flourish, not to be pressed too closely, as though the council intended to say that Scripture and tradition were absolutely equal in value in every respect. A sympathetic interpreter can easily understand that the devout believer should normally revere both Scripture and the saintly heroes who suffered for the faith, such as Athanasius or Chrysostom, Justin or Irenaeus. But this does not mean that Athanasius never had a weak moment (he did). Nor does this phrase mean that we should not try to sift the abundance of church traditions for what is truer or more helpful in a given situation. Nor does it exclude further distinctions of tradition—for example, that Christ is the Tradition with a capital *T* (based on Matt. 11:27 and parallels), and that there are other traditions of varying weights. As a teacher of Scripture, I can attest that when interpreters past and present differ on a significant matter such as the sense of "the bread of life" in John 6, I find it helpful to know that the weight of tradition understands John 6:51–58 as referring to the Eucharist.

The real breakthrough at the council came in paragraph 11, which limits the inerrancy of Scripture to matters regarding our salvation; that is, Scripture can err in all other matters. As a line attributed to Galileo has it, "The Bible teaches us how to go to heaven, not how the heavens go."

11. Those divinely revealed realities which are contained and presented in Sacred Scripture have been committed to writing under the inspiration of the Holy Spirit. For holy mother Church, relying on the belief of the Apostles (see Jn. 20:31; 2 Tim. 3:16; 2 Pet. 1:19–20, 3:15–16), holds that the books of both the Old and New Testaments in their entirety, with all their parts, are sacred and canonical because written under the inspiration of the Holy Spirit, they have God as their author and have been handed on as such to the Church herself. In composing the sacred books, God chose men and while employed by Him they made use of their powers and abilities, so that with Him acting in them and through them, they, as true authors, consigned to writing everything and only those things which He wanted.

Therefore, since everything asserted by the inspired authors or sacred writers must be held to be asserted by the Holy Spirit, it follows that the books of Scripture must be acknowledged as teaching solidly, faithfully and without error that truth which God wanted put into sacred writings *for the sake of our salva-tion*. Therefore "all Scripture is divinely inspired and has its use for teaching the truth and refuting error, for reformation of manners and discipline in right living, so that everyone who belongs to God may be efficient and equipped for good work of every kind" (2 Tim. 3:16–17, Greek text) [italics added].

It took a century to arrive at the crucial phrase "truth . . . for the sake of our salvation." Cardinal Newman had taught that Scripture sometimes made *obiter dicta* ("incidental remarks"), without intending to affirm them with full authority. At the time, this solution was rejected by the pope. In making its restriction, the council returned to the teaching of Augustine and Thomas. After the council, some diehards tried to play with the Latin word *causa*, which can mean either the noun *cause* or the preposition *for the sake of*. This maneuver had to be put down, and it was.[14] This teaching on a qualified iner-rancy is important, but it remains on a very general level of truth. It does not address the issue of conflicting teachings on salvation within the Bible—for example, Matthew 5:17–20 versus Galatians 2–3. It is this particular conflict that gave us the Lutheran Reformation. Nor does it address the issue that faces the exegete every day: how to interpret the variants in parallel versions of the same incident in the Pentateuch or the Gospels, or successive rereadings or rewritings of the same tradition within the Bible.

The third major teaching of the council here concerns the specially qualified character of the history contained in the four canonical Gospels. It amounts to a cautious reception of the form criticism of the 1920s as propounded by K. L. Schmidt, Martin Dibelius, and Rudolf Bultmann. Paragraph 19 reads:

19. Holy Mother Church has firmly and with absolute constancy held, and continues to hold, that the four Gospels just named, whose historical character the Church unhesitatingly asserts, faithfully hand on what Jesus Christ, while living among men, really did and taught for their eternal salvation until the day He was taken up into heaven (see Acts 1:1). Indeed, after the Ascension of the Lord the Apostles handed on to their hearers what He had said and done. This they did with that clearer understanding which they enjoyed after they had been instructed by the glorious events of Christ's life and taught by the light of the Spirit of truth. The sacred authors wrote the four Gospels, selecting some things from the many which had been handed on by word of mouth or in writing, reducing some of them to a synthesis, explaining some things in view of the situation of their churches and preserving the form of proclamation but always in such fashion that they told us the honest truth about Jesus. For their intention in writing was that either from their own memory and recollections, or from the witness of those who themselves "from the beginning were eyewit-nesses and ministers of the Word" we might know "the truth" concerning those matters about which we have been instructed (see Lk. 1:2–4).

14. See Beretta 1999.

The main points to grasp are that for the council, the four Gospels contain the tradition about Jesus. The sacred writers wrote with the deeper understanding that they received after Easter, a particular emphasis (or admission) in John's Gospel (John 14:26; 16:13); so John is not just a videocassette recording of the historical Jesus, without theological reflection. The evangelists shaped their material through selection, condensation, and the style proper to preaching. (This point is the key concession to form criticism.) Finally, the council shares an apologetic concern to emphasize that the Gospel writers strove for honesty and truth (and did not intend to deceive). This paragraph builds on a key document of the Biblical Commission published only the year before (1964). We will look at this document a little later.

Three further contributions of the council can now be listed. The first concerns the issue of the canon within the canon. That is, granted the twenty-seven books that make up the New Testament, are some more important than others? Does the reader prefer one or two and tend to neglect the others? Does a believing community do something similar? Among Bible knowers, it is easy to position someone ideologically by what texts the other person quotes (and, by implication, neglects). Marcion wanted only an expurgated Luke and Paul in his canon. Luther cordoned off Hebrews, James, Jude, and Revelation as a ghetto of the unsound in his Bible. The Tübingen school of F. C. Baur had emphasized the conflicts within the New Testament canon (James versus Paul, with Luke-Acts and then John as harmonizers and reconcilers). Ernst Käsemann revived this model and led to its widespread discussion. The council's paragraph 18 teaches that the four Gospels enjoy pride of place because of their special witness to Jesus. After the Gospels come the letters and other writings of the New Testament (paragraph 20), and the whole Old Testament (paragraphs 14–16). This prioritizing is visible in the liturgy. The order of reading is Old Testament, Epistle, Gospel. The Gospel enjoys the climactic final position. Worshipers sit for the first two readings and stand for the Gospel, which may be accompanied by candles and incense. The reading of the Gospel is normally reserved for deacons and priests. It should be noted that the council does not address the issue of the relative merit of each Gospel in relation to the other three—for example, the relative ethical poverty of John or its spiritual superiority.[15]

The council also concedes an important point to Karl Barth in paragraph 10. There we read that the teaching authority of the church (the *magisterium*) is not above the Word of God but rather is at its service. I interpret this so: the church, pope, bishops, clergy, and devout lay readers of Scripture are not simply to sit in judgment on Scripture; they must not dictate to the Bible what it should or should not say. Rather, they should humbly submit to the purifying

15. On this matter, see the chapter on the canon in Viviano 2007: 270–89, and the literature there cited. See also Lienhard 1995; Neuhaus 1989.

lash of Scripture, as the great saints and reformers tried to realize (St. Francis of Assisi, St. Catherine of Siena, more quietly St. Benedict, less successfully Savonarola and many others). The Scriptures, especially the prophets and Jesus, instead sit in judgment on the church (and synagogue). The council adds that the church should listen to the Word carefully and lovingly, preserve the Bible (by handwritten copies or printed editions of the original texts, by memorization, and by interpretative study), expound it, and derive its message from it. And here there emerges an implicit, dangerous, yet inevitable qualification. No one can prepare a sermon without in some sense sitting in judgment on the biblical text, at least to select what to emphasize, to decide what it means for this audience at this time. Thus in reality there is a never-ending dialectic between text and interpreter, no matter how reverently it is done.

The third lesser point that has emerged in the reception of the conciliar text is a phrase that occurs in paragraph 12: "Sacred Scripture should be read and interpreted in the same spirit in which it was written." This apparently harmless phrase, derived from St. Jerome, has become a major arm in the war chest of the conservative backlash in the church. It is used as a club with which to beat the historical critics. It is taken to exclude any reading of the text that is not immediately devotional and edifying. It implies that the whole Bible must be taken as "spiritual reading," as if the whole Bible should read like the long prayer that is the letter to the Ephesians or some of the best loved psalms—for example, Psalm 23. But even the pearl of the Psalter, Psalm 139, contains cursing and hatred (vv. 19–22, often omitted in modern usage), as does Psalm 137 (v. 9). To the extent that this view prevails, it means the end of all critical scholarship within the church. Only the enemies of the faith would enjoy critical freedom. The church would be left defenseless and uninformed. This is a poisoned cup. The church is better served by intelligent scholarship, which presupposes a reasonable academic freedom.[16]

The Pontifical Biblical Commission

In our attempt to understand the normativity of Scripture and tradition in recent Catholic theology we turn now to a less solemn organ of Catholic thought on Scripture, the Pontifical Biblical Commission. Since its reform in the 1960s, this commission consists of twenty members, named by bishops' conferences and the pope. The members are from different regions of the world and meet annually during Easter. They work on a document over five years, on a problem proposed by the pope.

I will mention three of their documents plus one from the Commission for Dialogue with the Jews. The first dates from 1964. It concerns the nature of

16. See de la Potterie 1988; McGovern 1999; Lowe 2000; Levenson 1993.

the historical truth of the Gospels.[17] The "Instruction" helped prepare for the reception of form criticism at Vatican II, which we have already examined (*Dei Verbum*, paragraph 19). Here it is only necessary to mention its reception of the form-critical method's idea of the three *Sitze im Leben* (life settings) of the Gospel tradition. The instruction refers to these as three *tempora traditionis*, times or stages of the tradition: the time of Jesus, the time of the apostles and the oral transmission in the earliest church, and the time of the writing down of the Jesus story in the four Gospels by the four evangelists. This was a helpful developmental clarification.

In 1983 the Commission for Dialogue with the Jews issued an outstanding document on how to present the New Testament picture of the Jews, especially the Pharisees, in preaching and catechetics, without historical injustice, without contempt or hatred, without supersessionism. This last term refers to the idea that the revelation in the New Testament has simply replaced (superseded) the revelation in the Old Testament, that the church simply replaces the synagogue, that the Jews of today have no right to a continuing separate existence, that Jesus renders Moses superfluous. The document explains that polemics at the time of writing led Matthew and John to a harsher view of the Pharisees than was historically justified or than we find appropriate today.[18]

Starting around 1970 there occurred a methodological explosion in biblical studies. There was, for example, a narrative-aesthetic, ahistorical, reader-response literary method that became very popular in state universities. No Greek or Hebrew or ancient history was needed to apply it. Structuralist approaches came in from France, purely formal. The social sciences entered the field with an emphasis on the anthropology of honor and shame, not to mention liberation theology from Latin America. An analysis with the principles of ancient rhetoric was advocated. Feminists, psychologists, and fundamentalists joined in. (This list is not exhaustive.) This explosive manifold of methods led to student confusion. Professors who had invested in one option—for example, rhetorical analysis—felt frustrated that their choice was prevented by the competition from achieving a complete triumph. Rhetoric got lost in the shuffle. (Besides, rhetoric had already acquired a bad reputation in Plato's day. He rejected it as sophistry and style. Aristotle's *Rhetoric* took a calmer approach. Students still regard it with reserve.)

Into this lively, confusing debate the Biblical Commission entered in 1993 with a greatly appreciated document (130 pages) called *The Interpretation of the Bible in the Church*. We cannot enter into much detail here, so a few points must suffice. First, in reading the text, it is important to have an edition that provides the address of Pope John Paul II welcoming the document. There he

---

17. *Acta Apostolicae Sedis* 56 (1964) 712–18; an English translation is available in Fitzmyer 1982: 131–40.

18. "Notes on the Correct Way to Present the Jews and Judaism in Preaching and Catechesis in the Roman Catholic Church" (June 1985); available in English in Wigoder 1988: 149–59.

makes a crucial statement: "Catholic exegesis does not have its own exclusive method of interpretation, but, starting with the historico-critical basis (freed from its philosophical presuppositions or those contrary to the truth of our faith), it makes the most of all the current methods by seeking in each of them the 'seeds of the Word.'" This sentence makes three points. (1) The historical-critical method is the basic, normal method. Other methods are grafted on to it or otherwise assimilated to it. (It has been assimilating new methods since the eighteenth century: text, source, form, redaction criticisms.) (2) The church is open to new approaches and tests them for what is true and good in them (1 Thess. 5:21). (3) Methods come with philosophies or theologies. We may not share these—for example, an exclusion a priori of the possibility of miracles; or, the view that Scripture can never teach anything other than justification by faith alone.

The document itself then goes on to list, describe, and evaluate methods old and new, making a distinction between rigorous methods and mere "approaches." This may be too subtle, or unfair. A planned section on materialist (Marxist) exegesis was dropped after the fall of Communism in Eastern Europe. Feminists are warned not to grab for power, but why should they differ from other groups who do the same? Some scholars felt that the treatment of fundamentalist exegesis was not well informed.[19] Nevertheless, this first half of the document can be recommended to the student as a useful guide and survey.

When the document moves to larger hermeneutical issues—the role of philosophy, the different senses of Scripture, the relations between the two Testaments and between the different branches of theology, inculturation, the roles of patristic and rabbinic exegesis, the uses of the Bible in the church—the reader feels that the text is less successful. Nothing is false. It is simply that the issues are too complex to be sorted out in such a brief treatment. It is already a service to raise the issues, but they require further work.[20]

The Biblical Commission fully realized that more work needed to be done. Their next document was entitled *The Jewish People and Their Sacred Scriptures in the Christian Bible*.[21] In it the relation between the two Testaments is illustrated by examining nine themes that link them: creation, anthropology, the saving God, election, covenant, law, prayer, judgment, the promises to Abraham about a people and a land. Under this last theme are included the themes of the kingdom of God and the Messiah. So this document contains a pocket biblical theology. Besides this, the document powerfully resists all tendencies to a Marcionite rejection of the Hebrew Scriptures. It also addresses

19. For criticism, see Ayres and Fowl 1999.

20. There is a symposium on the document published by the Vatican: *L'interpretazione della Bibbia nella Chiesa*, with texts in English, German, and Italian (Pontifical Biblical Commission 2001).

21. Pontifical Biblical Commission 2002.

the problem of some apparently anti-Semitic texts within the New Testament (e.g., Matt. 23:13–36; 27:25; John 8:44; 1 Thess. 2:14–16). Jewish leaders were pleased by its affirmation that "the Jewish messianic wait is not in vain."

The Lectionary

More important by far for the daily life of believers and worshipers is the new liturgical lectionary, the selection of biblical readings for Sundays and weekdays. By designing a three-year Sunday lectionary, the liturgists ensured that the people who attended service would be exposed to a wide range of Scripture, especially the Gospels. Year A focuses on Matthew, Year B on Mark, Year C on Luke. John is used at Christmas and Eastertide and to fill out Mark's year, since Mark is so short. Many of the great texts of the Old Testament and the Epistles are also read to the people. It is a true feast of the Word of God. It also has major ecumenical implications. Many other Christian denominations have adopted this Sunday lectionary system to their own use. This means that on most Sundays, Christians of different denominations hear the same Gospel reading. This already contributes to a growing unity of Christian life. (The Church of England tried another system, emphasizing John, for ten years and then abandoned it.) This lectionary has been criticized by Christian anti-Semites for its abundant offering of the Hebrew Scriptures, but so far this has had little effect. Christian publishers are learning to market for the Year of Matthew, the Year of Mark, and so on. But that reflects the real objection to the lectionary: it is not easy to preach well each Sunday on such a rich variety of texts. It is hard work. That is the challenge in this blessing.

Conclusion

I have tried to show from official documents and theological construction that Holy Scripture remains supremely normative for Catholic theology in matters of faith and morals. One can therefore be a good Roman Catholic and live by a kind of *sola scriptura*, but with some qualifications. First, the Bible in question includes the deuterocanonical books. Second, tradition sometimes provides a dogmatically binding interpretative norm (e.g., the *homoousion* in the Nicene Creed). Third, there remains the freedom and, for those called, the necessity to interpret the Scriptures in the light of new knowledge (Hammurabi's Code, evolutionary theory) and new pastoral questions (e.g., nuclear warfare). In this endless process of reflection on and interpretation and application of Scripture, the teaching "officers" of the church (theologians, bishops, popes, councils) play a prominent, at times decisive, but not exclusive role. The Holy Spirit can work through any of the faithful, not only through the "professionals." Fourth, in practice a Roman Catholic who wants to remain faithful to divine revelation as contained in the Scriptures must accept that he or she will be living with believers for whom scriptural fidelity is not a high priority and who indulge in unscriptural beliefs and practices. So patience and charity remain necessary also in this most important area.

I conclude with a word of Scripture, Hebrews 4:12–13, delicious in its ambiguity. It is about the *Logos*, the Word of God, today commonly understood to refer to the Bible but which the church fathers understood to refer to the Word Incarnate, Jesus Christ.[22] Notice the shift in pronouns in the NRSV translation, here brought out with italics:

> Indeed, the word of God is living and active, sharper than any two-edged sword, piercing until it divides soul from spirit, joints from marrow; it is able to judge the thoughts and intentions of the heart. And before *him* no creature is hidden, but all are naked and laid bare to the eyes of the one to whom we must all render an account.

22. Swetnam 1981.

PART 3

Scripture and Theology

9

Can the Truth Be Learned?

Redressing the "Theologistic Fallacy" in Modern Biblical Scholarship

ALAN J. TORRANCE

It has become commonplace to hear theologians criticized for utilizing biblical resources with insufficient awareness of the relevant historical-critical debates, let alone the semantic and socioscientific tools necessary for academic engagement with the passages concerned. Too frequently such criticisms are justified. However, a parallel feature of some contemporary biblical scholarship also warrants comment: the apparent confidence with which the results of such scholarship can be regarded as constituting warrant for theological (and, indeed, ethical) claims—claims, that is, relating to the nature and purposes of God.

In *A Treatise of Human Nature* (1739–1740) David Hume complains of a move that G. E. Moore was later to refer to as "the naturalistic fallacy."

> In every system of morality, which I have hitherto met with, I have always remark'd, that the author proceeds for some time in the ordinary ways of reasoning . . . when all of a sudden I am surpriz'd to find, that instead of the usual copulations of propositions, *is*, and *is not*, I meet with no proposition that is

not connected with an *ought*, or an *ought not*. This change is imperceptible; but is however, of the last consequence. For as this *ought*, or *ought not*, expresses some new relation or affirmation, 'tis necessary that it shou'd be observ'd and explain'd; and at the same time that a reason should be given; for what seems altogether inconceivable, how this new relation can be a deduction from others, which are entirely different from it.[1]

With parallel regularity biblical scholars proceed in "ordinary ways of reasoning" when "all of a sudden" there occurs a change that is "imperceptible" but also "of the last consequence": the move from talk about god-talk to God-talk itself, from descriptions of biblical claims and their contexts to prescriptions as to how we ought to speak about God. In this chapter I wish to consider the conditions under which biblical and historical scholarship may make the move from saying "Mark, Luke, or Paul claim P about God" to "We ought (or ought not) to claim P about God." In short, the question I wish to consider concerns what are the conditions under which biblical scholarship can or should be conceived as a theological enterprise? The question at stake concerns the warrant for moves from the second-order (historical) study of the context of New Testament god-talk—what we might term "god-talk-talk"—to God-talk per se, that is, first-order claims about God.

If religious claims made by others (e.g., biblical authors) are to warrant first-order (contemporary) claims about God, then we are obliged to provide some account of what validates this move if we are not to commit what we might call the "theologistic fallacy"—what is, in effect, a form of the naturalistic fallacy. Clearly, some kind of ontological and epistemological framework must be assumed (and warranted, indeed) for any such move from indirect to direct statements about God.

One reason for the widespread failure to appreciate the radical and potentially fallacious nature of the move from second-order to first-order statements lies with the ambiguity attaching to the use of the word *theological*. To say that a claim is theological can mean two entirely different things. It may mean that the claim involves reference to the concept "god"—the claim is "theological." It may also mean, however, that the claim actually refers to "God"—it is "Theological." In the latter case, "Theological" functions within the context of a "success grammar" (in Gilbert Ryle's sense[2]) as a phrase that successfully refers to the concrete reality of God, where "God" functions as a kind of name and implies a (successful) demonstrative element.

This ambiguity means that if a claim described as theological meets certain formal criteria (i.e., that the concept utilized is "god," and there is no valid

---

1. Hume 1962: book 3, part 1, section 1.
2. Words such as *win* or *refute* are what Gilbert Ryle refers to as "achievement words" or "success words" with a success grammar (Ryle 1949: 143). See "Achievements" in Ryle 1949: 143–47; see also 211–12.

reason for supposing that the relevant claim fails to refer successfully to its referent), it is assumed that the claim is to be counted a "Theological" claim. It is as if an ethical presumption of innocence is assumed unless (ethical) guilt is proven.

This veils a subliminal argument of the following kind:

- Step 1: That god created men and women in his own image is an affirmation found in the Pentateuch.
- Step 2: This affirmation as it features in the Pentateuch is properly described as "theological," given that the subject of the statement is "god."
- Step 3: That we are created in the image of God is, therefore, a theological statement that refers to God.
- [Step 3b: Given that the affirmation meets certain important criteria— it can be universally affirmed, it is inclusive of persons, endorses those European moral/intellectual agendas to which modernity subscribes, is deeply entrenched in the ecumenical tradition and unfalsifiable by historico-critical research—there is no sufficient reason to question the success of its reference. Innocence may, indeed ought to, be assumed.]
- Step 4: It is appropriate, therefore, to affirm that God created us in his own image.
- Step 5: God created us in his own image.

Due perhaps to the subliminal impact of this kind of thinking, this text acquired almost incorrigible creedal status for a recent generation of liberal and liberationist theologians.[3] This canon within the canon too easily facilitated the following:

- Step 6: Whatever is deemed to be inclusive and affirmative of God's image is validly affirmed of God.
- Step 7: Anthropological affirmations constitute the grounds of theological affirmations.

Two Case Studies at the Roots of Contemporary British Biblical Scholarship

Here I will illustrate this concern with reference to two very different books that, though doubtless no longer "cutting-edge" in some of their aims and methods, served to define the parameters of theological engagement with the

---

3. This is also the case with conservative evangelicals, but less surprisingly so, given their commitment to the reliability of Scripture as a whole.

New Testament over the last three decades in the United Kingdom. The "slippery warrant" for the move from god-talk-talk to God-talk that they exhibit, far from being addressed by the guild over the intervening years, appears (with some notable exceptions such as Bockmuehl, Marshall, Thiselton, and Watson) to have been somewhat uncritically adopted.

Our first example is James Dunn's *Christology in the Making*. In his introduction to this immensely influential modern classic (first published in 1980, reprinted in 1989 with the same introduction but with an additional foreword), he writes, "The following study is simply *a historical investigation into how and in what terms the doctrine of the incarnation first came to expression*."[4] To stress that this is *all* that the study is seeking to accomplish, he places the relevant section in italics. In addition, he insists that the book "is not a philosophical essay on the concept of incarnation as such. . . . Nor is what follows an exercise in dogmatic theology."[5] His concern is "*to let the New Testament writers speak for themselves, to understand their words as they would have intended, to hear them as their first readers would have heard them*."[6] Again, he used italics to emphasize the limited goals in view. By the conclusion of the book, however, these modest aims have given way to extravagantly theological conclusions making a complex series of claims as to what it is that we celebrate at Christmas, Easter, and Pentecost, ending with a quotation from Kasper's *Jesus the Christ*: "In substance the trinitarian confession means that God in Jesus Christ has proved himself to be self-communicating love and that as such he is permanently among us in the Holy Spirit."[7] This is first-order God-talk—dogmatic theology, indeed, that bristles with philosophical assumptions vis-à-vis the concept of incarnation. All this reposes, ostensibly, on what was supposed to be a purely historical investigation of the god-talk of the New Testament writers. In short, the argument of the book rests on a less-than-subtle move from god-talk-talk to God-talk. Without that move, the book would not have been adopted so widely as an example of contemporary, sophisticated, historically responsible theological engagement with the biblical material.

Our second example concerns contributions to an earlier book (1977) edited by John Hick, entitled *The Myth of God Incarnate*.[8] The majority of the contributors saw themselves as New Testament scholars who, through their scholarship, felt obliged to deny the incarnation—that is, the concrete and unique ontological identification of God and the particular human Jesus

4. Dunn 1989: 10.
5. Dunn 1989: 9.
6. Dunn 1989: 9.
7. Dunn 1989: 268.
8. Hick 1977. This epitomized the kind of suspicion that has been cast on those within New Testament circles who seemed to be too well disposed toward Nicene orthodoxy over the three decades since.

of Nazareth. At the same time, however, they had no compunction about making a whole variety of "high" claims about the theological significance of Jesus. Frances Young, for example, seeks to deny the *homoousion* yet is happy to affirm: "I find salvation in Christ, because in him God is disclosed to me as a 'suffering God' . . . Jesus is the supreme disclosure which opens my eyes to God in the present";[9] or Maurice Wiles: "It may be claimed, it is supremely through Jesus that the self-giving love of God is most fully expressed and men can be caught up into the fullest response to him";[10] or Michael Goulder's "faith in the unity of activity of God and Jesus—*homopraxis*, if a Greek word is wanted rather than *homoousia*"[11]—a position to which he no longer holds; or Leslie Houlden's references to "the centrality of Jesus for all that concerns man's understanding of God" and "the deep and intimate involvement of God with the world" that is witnessed in and through Jesus.[12] All these statements are affirmed in the context of a book whose purpose is to dismiss the affirmation of the *homoousion* as a myth, indeed, as the thrust of Young's and Wiles's contributions implies, inconceivable, unwarranted, and ungrounded.

So how are we to understand the connection between New Testament interpretation and theological statement? Heikki Räisänen urges biblical scholars to move "beyond New Testament theology" (to cite the title of his monograph[13]) and not to confuse what a text meant with what a text means. This is consistent with the presuppositions ostensibly operative in much of the discipline since Wrede. What is striking about Räisänen's approach, however, is his commitment to avoiding any confusion between a historical, descriptive approach and a theological, normative approach. He summarizes his vision for the field by suggesting that "'New Testament theology' could be replaced . . . with two different projects: first, the 'history of early Christian thought' (or theology, if you like), evolving in the context of early Judaism; second, critical philosophical, ethical and/or theological 'reflection on the New Testament,' as well as on its influence on our history and its significance for contemporary life"; he continues, "My contention is not that these two tasks ought to be carried out separately, the one first and the other afterwards; that does not seem to be the way the human mind works. Nonetheless the two tasks ought to be kept distinct."[14] Christopher Tuckett summarizes Räisänen's approach still more succinctly:

9. Hick 1977: 38.
10. Hick 1977: 38.
11. Hick 1977: 62.
12. Hick 1977: 132.
13. Räisänen 1990 (second edition, 2000).
14. Räisänen 2000: 8.

There should be a distinction made between a "historical," "descriptive" approach, seeking to describe what the original authors said in their original historical contexts, and a "theological," "normative" approach in which the New Testament texts are exploited in the service of a contemporary Christian theology. . . . The task of the New Testament exegete . . . should be to seek to adopt the neutral role of the descriptive historian. The task of theologizing on the basis of the text is a logically separable, and logically secondary, activity.[15]

One question that this raises, of course, is whether there can ever be a theologically "neutral" option in dealing with such accounts. What should be clear is that such "neutrality" assumes that God is not, in any sense, an integral part of the equation. It is to determine in advance that God is not involved in this history, and that therefore reference to God cannot contribute to an "objective" account of what happened.

Semantic Continuity and Contemporary God-talk

It is often assumed that the fundamental challenge for constructive theological interaction with the biblical material is the problem of hermeneutical distance. Few in modern British biblical scholarship have engaged with this issue in greater depth than has Anthony Thiselton. In the first of his impressive analyses of the nature and task of biblical hermeneutics, *The Two Horizons* (1980), he integrated themes from Gadamer and Wittgenstein, arguing that in order for there to be valid interpretation of biblical texts, there must take place a *Horizontverschmelzung*—a *fusion of horizons* whereby we begin to "indwell" the world of the biblical authors, to share in their fields of reference and thereby become privy to the subliminal semantic rules and language games functioning in biblical material. This may indeed be regarded as the *conditio sine qua non* of understanding what they say—not least because, as Wittgenstein[16] (and also James Barr[17]) has shown, the meanings of terms and sentences are their use, and this cannot be abstracted from the contexts of their use, which, for Wittgenstein, means their public rules of use.[18] The question that we must ask here, however, is a further one: What *kind* of *Horizontverschmelzung* might facilitate our indwelling the theological statements of the New Testament writers in such a way that they might facilitate "first-order" theological statements?

This is emphatically not to play down the significance of Gadamer and Thiselton here. They rightly establish that a fusion (or *perichoresis?*) of

15. Tuckett 2007: 2.
16. Wittgenstein 1974: 20, 80–82.
17. Barr 1961.
18. The fact that there are "rules of use" is, perhaps, a factor insufficiently appreciated by Barr, as reflected in his general suspicion of lexicography.

horizons is a necessary condition for making theological statements that take seriously the significance of the history from which they stem. If the semantics of biblical statements is not to be "flattened," decontextualized, and crudely transported, then it is of the utmost importance that we come to indwell the "rules of use" that applied in the diverse contexts from which they emerged and in which they are located.

Scholarship in search of genuine semantic continuity cannot avoid becoming embroiled in a massively complex network or hierarchy of hermeneutical circularities interrelating diverse levels of inquiry. Archaeological study of texts and their contexts, involving research from the microscopic (genetic coding of animal skins to piece together ancient parchments) to macroscopic, sociohistorical research, not to mention analysis of redactive processes, literary forms, narrative styles as also the history of religious concepts, rituals, and so on, are all intrinsic to the task. To complicate matters further, most of these levels cannot be treated independently. In most instances, moreover, the lines of influence between levels of research are bidirectional. Indeed, disagreement between biblical scholars often reflects differences in how the relationships between suppositions operative at different levels are interpreted. What amounts to a diffuse maze of levels of syntactical, historical, socioscientific, and hermeneutical analysis is inescapable in the task of interpreting the semantic rules that apply within the further complex series of intratextual hermeneutical circularities that condition our interpretation of texts. There are, in sum, no shortcuts. These may be some of the necessary—though emphatically not, as is so often assumed, sufficient—conditions for biblically sourced God-talk.[19]

In this light, we can now articulate with greater specificity the issues that our question requires us to address:

1. The extent to which genuine theological perception on the part of biblical authors (if it exists) might constitute part of this complex hermeneutical matrix. If it does, then such theological perception clearly becomes intrinsic to the hermeneutical project constituting one of the interrelated levels of research requisite for making sense not only of the whole but also of other parts of the whole as well.
2. The extent to which participation in the very specific paradigm integral to such theological perception is necessary for understanding the "sense" of what is said.

19. They are not sufficient conditions per se because scholars who are maximally accomplished in all the relevant fields may still be unwarranted in their theological conclusions because they lack a necessary condition, which a humble reader of Scripture might conceivably possess: whatever is meant by "eyes to see" or discernment "according to the Spirit," or what is, for Kierkegaard, the redemption of their reason.

3. How it is that hermeneutical inquiry might take due cognizance of any such level of perception/meaning, given that, as we will see, theological perception is bound to a paradigm of a very specific kind if it is to be veridical.

4. How we are to conceive theologically of the conditions of our being privy to any such theological insight together with the unique paradigm within which such insight is couched.

Clearly, by the phrase "theological insight" I mean something very different from any "neutral" entertaining of religious ideas. I mean the perception of God together with the disclosive "success" of any derivative theological affirmations. To reiterate: we are concerned with *whatever it is that is being assumed* when a scholar appeals appropriately to a biblical text as warrant for God-talk (i.e., as constituting God-talk that we can reiterate in a first-order manner) as opposed to warranting simply further reflection on the god-talk of the time (i.e., god-talk-talk).[20]

If the affirmation of theological statements (of the kind described in the two case studies above) is not to be conceived as merely coincidentally related to the biblical material but, rather, is and requires to be in "semantic continuity" with it, then we must be willing and able to provide reasons why semantic continuity with the writings of biblical material is theologically relevant and, further, how shared participation in their theologically "veridical" paradigms is possible. These requirements, it will become clear, suggest that a three-dimensional *Horizontverschmelzung* becomes the necessary condition of hermeneutical interpretation.

Athanasius on Mythology versus Theology

It was these concerns that Athanasius was addressing when he articulated the grounds of the patristic conception of the *ekklēsiastikon phronēma* (the "mind of the church"). Here I am drawing on work by Heron, Florovsky, and T. F. Torrance.[21] Given, moreover, the concern over recent decades to distinguish theological from mythological statements—that is, statements

20. Clearly, my argument assumes that if there is veridical (successful) theological insight attaching to any or some biblical statements, then this is of relevance to the hermeneutical task. I am assuming, in other words, that it is relevant to the task of interpreting an author's statements whether there is any impetus, objective control, or irreducibly theological criteria informing what the author is saying and that transcends her or his cultural context. This is surely not controversial, as it is relevant for interpreting the meaning of any book to distinguish between the kinds of truth claims made—whether the writing is surreal antirealism, speculative science fiction, faction, or informed biography, for example. It is also relevant whether the author, thinking to be engaged in one, is in fact engaged in another.

21. These include Torrance 1975; Heron 1981; Florovsky 1962.

that validly refer to the divine from those that simply project culture-specific, anthropomorphic categories onto the divine—it is equally pertinent to observe that it was precisely this distinction (between *theologein* and *mythologein*) that stands at the heart of Athanasius's arguments vis-à-vis the epistemological necessity of the *homoousion*. Athanasius's primary concern was to ask about the conditions of our distinguishing (in the task of interpretation [*hermeneuein*]) between mythological projection of human conceptual constructs onto God (*mythopoiēsis*) and warranted theological affirmation (*theologein*) that was true.[22]

The background to his concerns was, of course, the gnostic/Origenist disjunction between the divine and the human realms—the traditional Greek gulf or dichotomy (*chōrismos*) between the realm of intellectual knowing (*kosmos noētos*) and the realm of experience (*kosmos aisthētos*), between the eternal transcendent realm of ideas and ideals and the spatiotemporal realm of contingent human history and fleeting creaturely experience.[23] Operating within this dichotomy, the Arians affirmed that the Son of God must belong to the created order as the first creature (*prōton ktisma*). As one who was begotten, he belonged to the spatiotemporal side of this gulf. There was, therefore, a "qualitative" distinction to be made (denoting an unbridgeable epistemic gulf) between the being of God and the person of the incarnate Son and *Logos*.

The hermeneutical consequences of such a dichotomy were unambiguously clear to Athanasius. There was no sense in which the *Logos* could mediate knowledge of God. Any views that he might have vis-à-vis the divine were, like the rest of ours, mere *epinoiai*—creaturely opinions projected across an epistemically unspannable gulf that deprived the church of any warrant for assuming that they could be correlated with the being of God. How could the *Logos*, conceived in these terms, be perceived as constituting a control upon, or justification for, theological statement? On this view, theological statements by creatures (including the *Logos*) can be expressions of little more than creaturely *agnōsis*. For Athanasius, christologically informed statements interpreted in these terms, constitute *mythologein*. As Heron comments,

> By a curious irony, on which Athanasius was not slow to remark, Arius seemed to possess a good deal of privileged information. But where had he got it from? Athanasius was in no doubt about the source: the Arians had fabricated this concept of the divine being out of their own minds, thus making their own

22. The question as to whether a theological statement is true (*alēthōs*) and, if so, on what grounds was of significantly greater concern for the church fathers than for academic theology in a postmodern world, which is shy of this concept.

23. For a discussion of the influence of this Platonic dichotomy on early Christianity, see Wytzes 1957; 1960.

intellects the measure of ultimate reality, and assigning to Christ, the Word-made-flesh, the place which their minds could make for him.[24]

To confuse the projected constructs of our creaturely minds with God-talk is delusional (*mania*).

As Athanasius saw with such clarity, the possibility that the New Testament claims have any objective theological value or warrant whatsoever reposes on an internally consistent dynamic wherein God discloses himself within the contingent order as the person of the incarnate *Logos* becoming, thereby, the *skopos* of Scripture and the *topos* ("place") or reference point for our understanding God's dealings with humanity. In and through this God gives himself to be spoken of in and through the one perceived as "Immanuel"— God concretely and specifically (and, one might add, inclusively) present with and for humanity in space and time. On such an account, through the person of the *Logos* our human concepts (*noiai*) are given to refer to the divine in a manner that affords genuine cognitive access (*kata dianoian*[25]) to God in and through the *ana*-logical event of faith. This contrasts dramatically with the only conceivable alternative option: theology is mythmaking (*mythologein*) driven by arbitrary human opinion (*kat' epinoian*), which, devoid of reference, is ultimately no more than the self-deceiving opinions of those who, on their own terms, possess *agnōsis*. To confuse such *mythoplastia* with *theologein* is, again, delusion.

The affirmation of the *homoousion* of the Son—that is, of the *Logos Theou*—was therefore seen to be the *conditio sine qua non* of theological statement. Contrary to popular supposition, however, this did not constitute for Athanasius a sufficient condition for God-talk, *theologein*. A hermeneutical gap still remains—a gap between our own alienated minds and the *Logos*, with whom God is ontologically identified; between our own confused paradigms and the objective givenness of God as Word. In the background of Athanasius's thinking here stood the Pauline insight that human beings are alienated or hostile in their capacity to think through to the reality of God (*echthroi tē dianoia*), that their mindset, judgments, or paradigms (*phronein*) are of the flesh. For Athanasius, therefore, a transformation of our understanding (*noein*)—paralleling the New Testament meta*noia* of our *noein* by grace—was necessary for veridical perception of the *Logos*. The subjective condition of this was the creative presence of the Holy Spirit. By the Spirit, what we might refer to in modern parlance as our "paradigms" are reconciled and transformed such that we are given eyes to see and ears to hear what we

24. Heron 1981: 70.
25. This is where human concepts (*noiai*) are given to penetrate through (*dia*) to the reality of God. This contrasts with mere human opinions (*epinoiai*) about the divine that characterize the mythological projection or fabrication with which we are left if the twofold *homoousion* is no longer to be affirmed.

could not otherwise appropriate. For Athanasius, affirming the *homoousion* of the Spirit as the subjective condition of theological reference is the second, necessary condition of *theologein*—an argument articulated extensively in his *Letters to Serapion*.[26]

This raises the question as to whether there can be a theological New Testament hermeneutic of any kind if we deny God's free presence with humanity, first as the incarnate Son/*Logos*, and second as the Holy Spirit, who constitutes the subjective condition of our perception of the former, and where each is affirmed as "of one being with the Father" (*homoousios tō patri*). For the Nicene fathers, the twofold *homoousion* constitutes the necessary condition by which our contemporary understanding can participate in the "apostolic mind," enabling semantic continuity with the theological paradigms of the apostles. Through the Spirit, our *phronein* is given to share in the mind of the body of Christ (*to ekklēsiastikon phronēma*). What has taken place, in effect, is a theological fusion of horizons—participation in a reconciled continuity of mind and, thereby, of reference between the authors of the New Testament and the contemporary church. The condition of this is what we are calling that "third Horizon" made possible alone on the grounds that not only the incarnate *Logos* but also the Holy Spirit is *homoousion tō patri*.[27]

The Hellenizing of Hermeneutics in the Enlightenment and Modernity

Despite the fact that the supporters of Athanasius may have won the day at Nicea, Hellenic idealism, with its associated *chōrismoi* (gulfs, dualisms), has continued to mold the hermeneutic agenda right through to modernity. G. E. Lessing epitomized the suppositions so influential in hermeneutics by integrating the key principles from two of the giants of European philosophy: (1) the epistemology of Leibniz, with its sharp distinction between necessary truths of reason (demonstrable on a priori grounds) and contingent truths (which are known by sense perception)[28]—a dichotomy that echoes that between the *kosmos noētos* and the *kosmos aisthētos*; (2) the thesis of Spinoza's *Tractatus Theologico-Politicus*, that the truth of a historical narrative, however certain, cannot give us knowledge of God, the latter being derivable only from general

26. See Shapland 1951.

27. What place do tradition and the history of reception (*Wirkungsgeschichte*) possess on this account? If *Wirkungsgeschichte* is not to become simply *Kulturgeschichte*, and if tradition is to be defined as handing down God's self-disclosure as God's *eph' hapax* ("once for all") Word to humanity, then both require the category of the "ecclesial mind." If this ecclesial mind is not to be conceived in Heraclitean terms, as in a process of arbitrary flux or as the voice of the culture of the day, then it will require to be interpreted along Athanasian lines, as J. H. Newman saw in his discussion of Athanasius and Scripture (see Newman 1903).

28. See Leibniz 1989.

ideas that are indubitably known.[29] Spinoza was, of course, the major influence on the hermeneutics of D. F. Strauss, ostensibly the founder of myth theory in New Testament scholarship.

These convictions generated Lessing's repristination of the Greek *chōrismos*. His "big ugly ditch" reposed on the principle that "'accidental' truths of history can never become the proof of necessary truths of reason."[30] History and its claims can never proffer theological truth—on a priori grounds. Any "leap" from the contingent truths of history to the necessary truths of divine revelation is "intellectually impossible."[31] The impact of Lessing's resulting immanentism can be seen in the systematic idealism of Hegel.

The giant of the nineteenth century who took up the cudgels from Athanasius and rearticulated the central issues for those seduced by the Enlightenment's Hellenizing of Christianity was Søren Kierkegaard. He set out to demonstrate the radical formal incompatibility between a hermeneutic that assumes that we possess the conditions by which to evaluate New Testament claims and a hermeneutic framed by the radically different theological horizon of the New Testament writers that suggests that those "conditions" are given in and through God's reconciling self-disclosure in Christ. It is to this that we must now turn, albeit briefly.

Kierkegaard opens *Philosophical Fragments* by articulating the central question at the heart of the hermeneutic debate: "Can the truth be learned?" The problems stemming from the attempt to answer this question in the affirmative led Socrates (together with all forms of idealism ever since) to answer negatively and adopt the view that knowledge must necessarily be a form of remembering that which is immanent within our minds in some way. What Kierkegaard refers to as the "pugnacious proposition" of Plato's *Meno* is quite simply the proposition that the truth cannot be learned anew—we cannot learn what we do not actually know already. The problem is quite simple: "A person cannot possibly seek what he knows, and, just as impossibly, he cannot seek what he does not know, for what he knows he cannot seek, since he knows it, and what he does not know he cannot seek, because, after all, he does not even know what he is supposed to seek."[32] The idealist's answer is quite simply to affirm that one must always already know what one is seeking; otherwise, one could never "re-cognize" it to be true. Immanent within us and complete in advance of every hermeneutical inquiry lies the totality of theological knowledge—the ideas, the ideals, the concepts of God, and so on—that the scholar will distill in any analysis of any text. Not only is it the case that nothing new *is* learned, but also that nothing new *can be* learned. The so-called discovery of anything that we come to know about God necessarily

29. See the helpful discussion in Chadwick 1967.
30. Lessing 1956: 53.
31. Chadwick 1967.
32. Kierkegaard 1985: 9.

amounts to no more than a process of anamnesis. For Socrates, therefore, the true philosopher is no more than a midwife, and the highest form of teaching is simply facilitating the birthing of that knowledge already immanent within the learner (*maieuesthai*)—helping to deliver those religious ideas and ideals that lie within us and that we already know. In parallel, the highest function that any text can achieve is to facilitate our recalling those eternal, timeless, ethical, and transcendent ideas (and ideals) immanent within us. The message, therefore, to the hermeneutical scholar is the same message that the gods gave Socrates at Delphi: *gnōthi seauton*—"Know thyself!" It is self-knowledge that alone leads us and alone *can* lead us into all truth.

What follows from this? As Kierkegaard points out, "Viewed Socratically, any point of departure in time is *eo ipso* something accidental, a vanishing point, an occasion."[33] And both the occasion and the teacher (whoever that may be) can only be incidental and insignificant.[34]

The implications of the Socratic for "Bible and theology" are clear. Neither the Bible, nor its authors and their horizons, nor the person of Christ can have any particular, let alone decisive, significance for apprehending God or any truth whatsoever about God or, indeed, about humanity. At best, they possess a maieutic function serving to prompt and remind us of what we already know.[35] When this purpose is served, the means of that prompting or reminding (be it Jesus Christ or the church or Scripture) must disappear from view and must not in any sense claim an essentially mediatorial role. To the extent that it is suggested that there is any necessary or ongoing connection between our being in relation to the Truth and our being related to Christ or the church, our relationship to the Truth (to the eternal and to the divine) is necessarily distorted and eclipsed. The relation of the learner to the eternal, to the divine, is undermined and obstructed to the extent that the learner fallaciously and

33. Kierkegaard 1985: 11.

34. The teacher (or text) who seeks to draw attention to self as important does not give but rather takes away. The teacher (or text) who places self where the eternal truths alone should be detracts from the truth. The teacher who is true to the eternal ideals, therefore, must fade away, become nothing—a mere vanishing point or occasion of a relationship that is much greater: the relationship between the mind and the nonhistorical, nonpersonal, eternal ideas or ideals that are the true objects of contemplation.

Socrates would therefore draw shapes in the sand in order to aid in the process of anamnesis. He would then quietly disappear, not wishing to attract attention to himself in any way.

As Kierkegaard (1985: 13) summarizes the Socratic position: "The temporal point of departure is a nothing, because in the same moment I discover that I have known the truth from eternity without knowing it, in the same instant that moment is hidden in the eternal, assimilated into it in such a way that I, so to speak, still cannot find it even if I were to look for it, because there is no Here and no There, but only an *ubique et nusquam* [everywhere and nowhere]."

35. The verb *maieuesthai* means "to be a midwife"—that is, to facilitate the birthing of something that is already present (immanent) within one and to which the midwife in no way adds or contributes.

destructively confuses the timeless and the universal with the historical and the particular. To the extent, moreover, that other texts or persons serve to facilitate our "remembering" what we already know of the divine, they are equally significant, whatever form they take. In short, the success or truth of religious claims is determined by the extent to which they facilitate our own self-discovery.

Kierkegaard then has the agnostic Climacus consider how the situation must look if it is to be otherwise. He writes, "If the situation is to be different," and if the moment in time or the occasion or the teacher by means of which we come to the truth is not to be of arbitrary or contingent significance, then the only alternative is that it be of real, and hence, "decisive significance."[36] If that is to be the case (and we do not go with the Socratic), then there must be an intrinsic connection between the occasion or the teacher and the truth or the message, such that "for no moment will I be able to forget this occasion," because it is constitutive of the real relation between the self and the eternal.[37] If this is the case, then the moment or occasion or teacher cannot be forgotten and yet the truth be retained, since the reality of the truth and the occasion or teacher must be intrinsically and not arbitrarily related.

He then pursues the implications of the occasion's being of decisive significance. If it is, then until this occasion takes place, the learner is in error. The learner can possess neither the truth in embryo nor the conditions for remembering or recognizing it.[38] The learner is simply without the truth in these respects. What does this mean? If "the learner is to obtain the truth, the teacher must bring it to her, but not only that. Along with it, the teacher must provide her with the condition for understanding it, for if the learner were herself the condition for understanding the truth, then she merely needs to recollect, because . . . the condition and the question contain the conditioned and the answer."[39]

So if the teacher and historical occasion are to be of decisive significance then, Climacus argues, the teacher is no longer merely a midwife and thus incidental; rather, the teacher actually gives birth to the truth, creates anew a state in the hearer that was not tacitly there. In sum, the teacher "gives the condition" and thereby "gives the truth." Kierkegaard does not hesitate to draw out the implications of this through Climacus: such a teacher would be required to be regarded as a "savior" for the teacher saves "the learner from unfreedom," from a state of truthlessness, of error. The teacher is also a "deliverer" in that

36. A related point is made in an important essay by Stewart Sutherland, when he argues that the concept of revelation necessarily implies the discovery of that which is new and not already known (see Sutherland 1989: 43).

37. Kierkegaard 1985: 13, 15, 16, 19.

38. To possess the conditions of the recognition of the truth is, for Kierkegaard, to possess the truth in embryonic form.

39. Kierkegaard 1985: 14.

the teacher delivers "the person from the self-imprisonment" that is the vain attempt to find truth solely and exclusively in and through oneself. Still further, such a teacher is also a "reconciler" and, finally, the moment that is filled with the eternal that he suggests we call "the fullness of time."[40]

In sum, what Kierkegaard offers over against the Socratic or idealist approach is an affirmation of precisely that which Athanasius was insisting upon in affirming the epistemological necessity for the Christian faith of the twofold *homoousion*. The theological conditions of God-talk are that the *Logos*, who makes himself present to us in an event of the reconciliation of our minds in Christ, is in the most concrete sense God from God, and that the Holy Spirit, the subjective condition of our perception or recognition of that same *Logos*, is also God from God. Without this, theological hermeneutics can never be more than the expression of our immanent self-understandings, wherein we utilize the biblical texts simply to illustrate our prior, subjective values, orientations, and religious affinities. If the latter is the case, what conceivable theological value could accrue from a "fusion of horizons"? It becomes superfluous; if anything, it detracts from the truth rather than offering a means of access to it. Moreover, there is every reason to suppose that no other horizon can provide profounder access to eternal truths and ideals than our own. There can be no reason why *gnōthi seauton* is going to be particularly well served by engagement with the horizons of members of a Jewish sect who lived in an ancient prescientific period of history any more than with those of any other contemporary religious thinker, be they Anglican, Moonie, Branch Davidian, or Scottish Presbyterian.

Contemporary Hermeneutical Implications

It was Karl Barth who rearticulated the Athanasian option and the radical incompatibility of Hellenic idealism with the gospel and the existence of the church. The idealism that he opposed took the form of the Marburg neo-Kantianism in which he was raised (and from which Bultmann's program of demythologization never departed) and immanentism, in the form of German *Kulturprotestantismus*. Only the affirmation of the twofold *homoousion* obviated a theological approach to biblical interpretation in which we ceased simply to reiterate our own prior agendas in a loud voice. The Christian claim that God is given to be known through the witness of the Bible and that it is thus theologically relevant lies with the fact that God is not only the revealer but also the revelation and the "revealedness." God is the incarnate Word and the active condition of the perception of that revelation.[41] This is not, of course, to question the fact that God is veiled by the human form of his

40. Kierkegaard 1985: 17–18.
41. Barth 1975b: 295.

revelation—indeed, for Barth, God is only revealed to humanity because of this veiling.

In short, if there is to be a *Horizontverschmelzung* that facilitates God-talk, then there need to be three horizons, not two. There is the horizon of the people and culture of the biblical period; then there is our horizon in the twenty-first century. But there also has to be another human horizon, through which God is present by the Spirit and which facilitates the transformative integration of these two horizons—what we might call the "mind of Christ." The New Testament bears witness to the beginnings of a *Horizontverschmelzung* in which through the incarnate *Logos* (Immanuel), and through the creative, reconciling presence of the Holy Spirit, a new humanity is created that participates *en Christō* constituted as his body and sharing in his mind. Its members are reconstituted "from above" and have eyes to see and ears to hear what their culture and natural capacities cannot provide. This is not something that historical inquiry of even the most sophisticated kind or any hermeneutical methodology could ever deliver. (That it could is the naïve assumption of "methodological naturalism," as C. S. Evans has argued so effectively.[42])

Where does this leave us? It presents us with a straight "either . . . or . . ."—a choice, that is, between incipient idealism where theological hermeneutics does not actually perceive the otherness of *this* text as theologically significant but simply uses biblical texts to illustrate those prior religious ideas and ethical principles (or, indeed, the agnosticism) that we already possess. The alternative is a theological hermeneutic that is grounded in the perception that these texts witness uniquely to an occasion of decisive significance and where the conditions of its God-talk are given in and through this occasion. For this *tertium datum*, the impetus for God-talk and the control upon it repose in this particular event, and the condition for the interpreter's perception of this resides in the reconciling presence of God as the Holy Spirit.

It is precisely here, however, that we are faced with unavoidable implications—implications that are exclusive and hence carry the potential for offense. These concern the fact that there is an essential "intrinsicity," constitutive of Christian faith and understanding. Given that we cannot supply the condition for that form of perception that is the *sine qua non* of a non-Socratic theological hermeneutic, there is no possibility of our arguing to it from commonly endorsable foundational principles or grounds internal to our natural constitution. There is no possibility even of establishing by any independent, external means that such a dimension is integral to the hermeneutical task in this case. The reason for this relates to the nature of the hermeneutical paradigms integral to theological perception—an issue that Francis Watson engaged admirably in his book *Text, Church and World*, and that Markus Bockmuehl addresses with great insight in the context of his exposé of the "methodological

42. Evans 1999.

and substantive malaise observable in late-twentieth-century New Testament scholarship, with its deeply corrosive consequences for agreement about the nature of argument and even the very subject of study."[43]

A Question of Paradigms

An implication of what I have said is that the fusion of horizons that alone can lead to semantic continuity with the writers of the New Testament involves a divinely conditioned transformation and reconstitution of our interpretive paradigms. But what is the nature of such a *metanoia*, and to what extent may it be regarded as a hermeneutical goal?

Any such *metanoia* requires, as Murray Rae argues, to be conceived as revolutionary rather than evolutionary. Theological perception neither develops nor can develop by virtue of any hermeneutical program; it is not the end result of any "continuous evolutionary advancement."[44] As Thomas Kuhn has shown, such is the character of the really significant discoveries in science and is not unique, therefore, to theological discovery. As Kuhn argues in *The Structure of Scientific Revolutions*, the paradigm shifts involved are "a reconstruction of the field from new fundamentals, a reconstruction that changes some of the field's most elementary theoretical generalizations as well as many of its paradigm methods and applications."[45] What takes place is a discontinuous, qualitative leap. What this means, as Rae says, is that

> there is nothing to be done within the old paradigm which may be a propae-deutic for the new. By the standard of the new paradigm those who continue to operate within the old exist in untruth and employ structures of understanding which compel them to dismiss the claims of those who have undergone a paradigmatic transition.[46]

This is not dissimilar to Hans Urs von Balthasar's characterization of the difference between Simon and the unanticipatable discovery and perception

43. Bockmuehl 2006: 24. One would have to look hard to find a more subtle integration of theological and historical insight than that which Bockmuehl accomplishes in his essay "Resurrection" in *The Cambridge Companion to Jesus* (Bockmuehl 2001: 102–18).

44. Rae 1997: 113–19.

45. Kuhn 1970: 85.

46. Rae 1997: 119. The point is that we should not assume any continuity between paradigms reposing on Western concepts of (the canons of) reason or experience or culture and the paradigm that results from the presence of the Spirit liberating us to discover in the biblical material a witness to the *eph' hapax* presence of God with us in the human Jesus. It is for these reasons that the publication of Barth's *Römerbrief* (Barth 1922 [ET, Barth 1933]) constituted a sea change in the context of the *Kulturprotestantismus* of the time; he was arguing that Romans was required to be interpreted within a paradigm that was intrinsically incompatible with the culturally conditioned hermeneutical agendas of the time.

constitutive of Peter—a similar analogy can be drawn in the distinction between the pre-Christian and the Christian Paul.[47] If there are useful analogies with paradigm shifts in science, it remains the case that, as Eberhard Jüngel argues, "theology has to do with a paradigm change *sui generis*: the existential change in human understanding conveyed in the phrases *ta tēs sarkos phronein* and *ta tou pneumatos phronein* (Rom. 8:5)."[48] The creative heuristic discontinuity (or leap) that takes place when the concrete "theological dimension," to which the New Testament bears witness, comes into operation is not the result of any heuristic capacity on our part. Its epistemic condition is the concrete and dynamic presence of God and God's creative reconciling of our minds.

A whole host of New Testament metaphors strive together to articulate this: being born from above, being born again, being given eyes to see and ears to hear, the renewal of our minds, the reconciliation of our minds, *metanoia*, the new creation, the new humanity, participation in the mind of Christ, the analogy of faith, and, as we have seen, judgment in accordance with the Spirit contrasted with judgment according to the flesh. Our tendency, of course, is to translate these into the language of ethics, thereby making recourse to universal, immanent ethical categories and agendas.

The offense to academe that emerges is that if this is the case, then the perception of its being the case must be irreducibly bound up with the kind of perception given within the context of such a unique paradigm shift. The hermeneutical *metanoia* that, I am arguing, constitutes the condition of a theological hermeneutics is not an enhancement or perfection of prior, immanent hermeneutical conditions nor indeed some kind of optional *Gestalt* switch;[49] rather, it constitutes a unique form of paradigm shift that interprets the old paradigm as a form of alienation from which one is delivered and where the new paradigm is given by grace. The "mind" that was in Christ Jesus is manifest in us by the creative presence of the Spirit such that we are given the eyes to discern God's presence in otherwise inconceivable ways—rather as if an intellectual "faculty" were enabled to function anew, as Alvin Plantinga suggests.[50]

47. Von Balthasar 1986.

48. Jüngel 1989: 297–98 (cited in Rae 1997: 130). The primary difference is that the paradigm shifts integral to major scientific advances discussed by Kuhn are the results of imaginative heuristic leaps. Michael Polanyi describes the conditions of these as relating to the operations of our tacit dimension whereby pressure on our subliminal ordering of experiences engenders an unanticipatable leap. The creativity is ours.

49. That is, where a shape can be glimpsed as a rabbit at one moment and a duck the next, and where one can direct one's perception of the shape to oscillate between the two.

50. See Plantinga 2000: 175–76. The obvious question that emerges here is whether this model allows for verification, falsification, or even adjudication. Does it not, moreover, preclude the possibility of self-criticism? To express the concerns more bluntly: it would seem either that this does not amount to a great deal in practice or that if it does, it appears quasi-gnostic at best and dangerous at worst.

The suggestion that a condition of recognizing God's presence is being given "the eyes to see" does not mean that those who do believe that they glimpse God's purposive presence in

What this means is that there can be no simple appeal to "reason." Reason cannot be the means by which an old paradigm is abandoned and a new one adopted, as Murray Rae's interpretation of Kierkegaard makes so clear.[51] Any appeal to reason to justify the new paradigm must necessarily take place within the new paradigm itself. This means that there will inevitably be perceived to be a degree of circularity in all our thinking. There is a *sui generis* circularity that applies specifically within Christian thought and that involves the "intrinsicity" to which I referred above: perceiving a revelational event to be what it is can occur only from within the sphere of that event. This perception, one might say, is intrinsic to the event of disclosure.

Four potential rejoinders require brief consideration.

1. Does this suggest an individualistic approach to the hermeneutical task implying the equivalent of a private language? This was the telling criticism that Thiselton, using Wittgenstein's "beetle in a box" analogy, leveled at Bultmann's advocacy of an esoteric, hermeneutical paradigm appealing to "deeper levels of meaning."[52] Where meaning is accessed privately by the self with exclusive reference to the self's existential self-understanding, it is difficult to see how one can avoid Wittgenstein's arguments on the incoherence (meaninglessness) of "private language."[53] Thiselton observes, "If with Bultmann we substitute an emphasis on the other-worldly and 'my' existential experience in place of the public tradition of Old Testament history, the problem of hermeneutics becomes insoluble."[54]

As Athanasius saw so clearly, the theological paradigm that underpins a theological approach is irreducibly bound up with the life of the community

---

the history of Jesus are justified in attaching some kind of inerrant infallibility to their interpretations. What one does see will inevitably be seen "through a mirror dimly" and will be a form of perception only completed in the eschaton. However, just as some are given the ears to hear the beauty of Brahms and others less so, discerning God's presence is a "gift" and not purely the result of human endeavor. To pursue the analogy further: to appreciate Brahms does not mean that one immediately possesses an "in depth" grasp of his use of harmony or the strategies inherent in his approach to orchestration, nor does it mean that such musicological scholarship is not immensely significant and could serve to enhance one's understanding and appreciation of Brahms's symphonies. The point is that if one is tone deaf, it is unlikely that one will appreciate fully the nature of the music. To the extent that this is the case, one cannot but fail to appreciate the significance of a great deal of what scholarly studies of his music aim to enhance: an understanding of the nature of the music.

Being given the "eyes to see" would, on this model, enhance (albeit incompletely) one's understanding of the nature of the history of Jesus Christ—something that can only play into one's interpretation of every facet of that history.

For an analysis of the significance of viewing New Testament history theologically, see Rae 2007.

51. Rae 1997: 113–19, 123, and passim.
52. Thiselton 1980: 379–85.
53. Wittgenstein 2001.
54. Thiselton 1980: 382.

of the body of Christ. There is no dichotomy between having that mind which was in Christ Jesus and participating in the body of Christ. This constitutes a theological counterpart to the Wittgensteinian insight that there is no such thing as a private language. The paradigm with which we operate is what the church fathers referred to as the *ekklēsiastikon phronēma*.[55]

2. Does this mean that the theologian can ignore the diverse forms of academic scholarship applied to Christian resources as irrelevant to a theological hermeneutic? Again, the answer is a negative one with one qualification. When scholarship goes beyond its remit and draws "theological" conclusions from prior incompatible paradigms such as naturalism or Enlightenment humanism, then that scholarship must recognize itself for what it is: irreducibly incompatible with there being any theological insight in the relevant texts. To the extent that biblical scholars (Christian and non-Christian) are being truly "scientific" and allowing their conclusions to be conditioned by the objects of their inquiry, the relationship should be mutually constructive and dialogical. Such scholarship should serve the integration of the levels of scholarship intrinsic to the *Horizontverschmelzung* discussed above. Without scholarship of this kind, a theological hermeneutic is impossible.[56]

Further, it should be remembered that no theological paradigm is static. Engaging with the results of scholarship at all levels is relevant to theological paradigms that remain *semper reformanda* (always in need of reform). That having been said, it is the nature of the case that the conditions of the *Horizontverschmelzung* that facilitate God-talk are not ultimately attributable to scholarship of any kind.

3. Is such a position not ultimately an exclusive one? Every truth claim is necessarily (logically) exclusive of contrary truth claims. All "inclusivist" positions are themselves inherently exclusive. Consequently, the endorsement of inclusivism is incompatible with itself. The theological dynamic to which I am referring as underpinning a theological hermeneutic is exclusive precisely for the sake of that radically inclusive divine love and communion that alone can constitute humanly affirmative and transformative community.

4. Nevertheless, given these kinds of criticism, may it not be that the idealist paradigm offers the least academically offensive way forward? The appeal of the Socratic is substantial: it enables the academic biblical scholar (whether belonging to a majority group or, indeed, to a marginalized minority) to operate as a Platonic philosopher-king (to use Richard Rorty's expression) who confidently "knows what everyone else is really doing whether *they* know it or not, because he knows about the ultimate context (the Forms, the Mind,

---

55. This participates in the one who, by the Spirit, is the Self-authenticating *Logos*—the *Autologos*.

56. Unfortunately, given that theological neutrality is never an option and atheistic suppositions are not theologically neutral, this will occur more often than we might choose or wish to admit.

Language) within which they are doing it."[57] To such approaches we must reiterate Karl Barth's "Nein!" and with all the vehemence of his opposition to the "higher" cultural ideals of the German Christians. Or, with Kierkegaard, "Better well-hanged than ill-wed"![58]

The question that all biblical scholars have to address is whether they endorse an immanentist/Socratic approach to the texts as defining the grounds of rational, academic theology or whether, with Athanasius, they see it as deluded. What Kierkegaard has served to show is that we look in vain for middle ground.

57. Cited in Watson 1997: 129.
58. Kierkegaard 1985: 3.

10

The Moral Authority of Scripture

OLIVER O'DONOVAN

"There is no authority except from God," said the apostle Paul (Rom. 13:1).[1] That is to say, nothing can command our free obedience unless God has sent it. We are, of course, self-moving beings. But we do not have our end in ourselves, so that the possibility of meaningful self-movement, directed to a purpose fit for us, depends on God's engagement with us. What we call "authority"—by whatever medium it comes to us—encounters us from God. And if nothing comes to us in that way, our freedom remains unrealized, mere undeveloped potential. But there are many media by which the authority of God may encounter us. Some belong to the structures of creation. We may become aware of the authority of God through angels or demons; we may become aware of it through the relations in which we stand to others—through parents and family, through compatriots, through teachers. We may become aware of the authority of God through death, as it says to us in his name, "Return to dust, you children of men!" But authority mediated in this way does not encounter us directly from God, and that is how the possibility arises of corrupt "rulers and authorities" of this world, as the New Testament calls them, which will in the end direct our freedom onto self-destructive paths. And it is because of that possibility that the gospel instructs us to look to another authority, that of

1. Scripture quotations throughout this chapter are the author's translation.

God's Son, that overrides the voices of the elements of the world, instructing our freedom to be truly free. So Christian moral reasoning begins not with the authority of created structures but rather with the authority of Christ. He is the "Last Adam," the sovereign Lord of creaturely authorities, appointed to bring them to their goal in the purposes of God.

But when we have mentioned the authority of Christ, we have made a beginning—only a beginning. For his authority, too, authorizes. The crucial thing to understand about all authority is that it is self-communicating. When commanded, we are made free; when we are free, we command. In a verse from Matthew's Gospel the centurion at Capernaum says to Jesus, "I am a man under authority," and then he goes on, "I say to one 'Go!' and he goes, and to another 'Come!' and he comes" (Matt. 8:9). Jesus recognized in this a mark of his faith. To be under authority is to be in a chain of command that authorizes. When the centurion says, "Go!" or "Come!" he exercises the authority that he stands under. And so it is that Jesus' triumph over the rulers and authorities of this fallen world authorizes those who stand under his authority. And from speaking directly of Jesus' authority, we are bound to speak of the authorities that his authority authorizes. What are these? In the broadest sense, we are speaking of the authority of the church. But we must be careful here: the church has many roles within it; it is a complex organism, as Paul describes it, like a body. There are different authorities to do and say and command different things. "When he ascended on high, he led captivity captive," says the apostle to the Ephesians, "and he gave gifts to men. And his gifts were that some should be apostles, some prophets . . ." (Eph. 4:8, 11). And then follow evangelists, pastors, teachers, and so on through the offices of the church. Apostles and prophets stand at the head of this list, and we know that they occupy a special place. The church, says the same apostle, is "built upon the foundation of the apostles and prophets, Christ Jesus himself being the cornerstone" (Eph. 2:20). Who, then, are these first authorities within the church, flanking Christ as the foundations of a wall flank the cornerstone? They are, it is clear, the authors of the New and Old Testaments.

Talk about the authority of Scripture has been made horribly difficult by the Fundamentalist Controversy (or, if you prefer, the Modernist Controversy), which tortured the church for over a hundred years and is only now fading into memory. But it is all the more important that we should talk about the authority of Scripture now, and so, before getting into aspects of the question on which a moral theologian may shed some special light, I offer a thumbnail dogmatic sketch.

1. Scripture is set apart from every other literary corpus simply by its function in the saving purposes of God; it is a literary corpus that is, to use

John Webster's term, "sanctified" to its task.[2] But that task is of a piece with the saving purposes of God to call out Israel and to anoint Christ for the salvation of the world. The specialness of Scripture belongs to its connection with Israel and Christ.

2. Holy Scripture is a part of God's own self-attestation in deed and word. It is not a secondary reflection on it, which, had it not occurred, would have left God's message about himself intact. In speaking of Scripture, then, we properly speak of the voice of God as well as of the voice of its human authors.

3. The authors of the books of Scripture were called to perform human tasks in God's service, just as Israel was. Their specialness does not consist in some unique superhuman activity, as though writing a Gospel was different from writing anything else. They are special because of their place in the redeeming work of God. Nothing in the humanity of the authors implies an imperfection in their work; nothing in their election to divine service authorizes us to attribute to them any other perfection than the one relevant perfection: God attests himself through them.

4. The faith demanded of the reader of Scripture is faith in the saving work of God attested there, which is therefore a faith in Scripture too. It implies willingness to accept the testimony of Scripture without presuming to improve upon it—by excision, by correction, or by privileging a canon within the canon—but instead simply seeking to understand it in fidelity and obedience, without presuppositions or conditions.

5. Every element of Scripture contributes to the testimony of the whole, but the different contributions are not uniform. The right understanding of any given element of Scripture is determined by its relation to the whole; but that means by its relation to the historical shape of the event that Scripture attests, the calling of Israel fulfilled in the coming of the Christ.

6. The church's role in determining the canon was in the first place an act of recognition, discerning and acknowledging the unity and authority that belonged to this literature by virtue of its sanctification by God. At the same time, secondarily, it was, like the framing of the creeds themselves, an exercise of its authority to teach. The ARCIC report *The Gift of Authority* said well, "It was at the same time an act of obedience and authority."[3]

---

2. Webster 2003.

3. ARCIC (Anglican/Roman Catholic International Commission) 1998: paragraph 22. See also Webster 2001.

The church maintains its obedient relation to Holy Scripture by reading it (in particular as the foundational act of the liturgy) and by expounding it, seeking to make the sense of the text understood. However, understanding Scripture is not a goal that can be pursued in isolation from obedience to what is understood.

Here, then, we come to the point at which the interaction of text and moral judgment must occur. There are two conjoined intellectual tasks, for neither of which can there be secure rules, two "discernments" that simply have to be made and that may possibly be made wrongly with serious consequences. There is the task of discerning what the text means, on the one hand, and there is the task of discerning ourselves and our position as agents in relation to the text, on the other hand. The first discernment is *of* the text; the second discernment is *out of* the text, *of* our situation. In the first discernment the text is before us: we read of David, of Peter, of Jesus and decide what it is that is said of them. In the second discernment the text is behind us: we do not read of ourselves in the way we read of David, Peter, and Jesus. Yet what it says of them sheds light upon us. It provides us with the categories and analogies that we need for questioning our position and coming to practical resolutions. The Scripture tells me not to bear false witness against my neighbor, but whether a particular ambiguous statement that I have in mind will be false or merely discreet is something that the Scripture will never tell me; I must judge that for myself under the Holy Spirit's guidance. Yet everything that the Scripture does tell me about truth and falsehood will contribute to making that judgment possible.

The most mysterious question that anyone has to face is not "What does Scripture mean?" but rather "What does the situation that I am facing mean?" If we have even begun to appreciate the nature of this question, and how easily a wrong answer may lead us to destruction, we will be on our guard against any proposal to reverse the sequence of discernments—starting with our own situation and turning back to Scripture to look for something there to fit it—for that would presuppose that we already knew the answer. Such proposals are often heard in theological discussion, sometimes with a liberal slant, sometimes with a conservative one. Either way, the mistake is to think that there is a concrete moral truth immediately and categorically known to everyone, a peremptory and unchallengeable moral certainty, and that we can negotiate the relation of this certainty to what we find in Scripture. This fails to allow for moral danger. All our action is exposed to danger: we may act on false assumptions about the facts, we may misunderstand the situation, we may form an inadequate conception of the task, we may fail to envisage the good to be pursued, and so on. Nothing except perpetual vigilance can arm us against such mistakes.

A discipline of biblical "hermeneutics," of interpretation, has no point unless it is undertaken out of a sense of need and unless we are resolved to be obedient. That will serve as a summary of where we have come so far. There is, however, another side to it. Obedience is a duty that needs serious hermeneutic reflection if it is to be carried through. We cannot obey in a vacuum of understanding.

In what follows I am pursuing a disagreement with Karl Barth, who (in many places, but especially in the memorable II/2 of *Church Dogmatics*) undertook to refound ethics in contradiction to Kantian "universalism," as he understood it, on the basis of the divine command. The question of what makes the divine command superior in authority to all other forms of ethical conception was answered in a number of ways; one recurring answer was that it was "concrete" and "definite," by which Barth meant something like this: it is focused upon the immediate situation in which it is given. It concerns, as he liked to say, the *hic et nunc*. "We must divest ourselves of the fixed idea that only a universally valid rule can be a command. We must realize that in reality a rule of this kind is not a command."[4] The Bible, Barth thought, was remarkable for its lack of anything like a universal rule; it is "replete with ethics," he tells us rather riddlingly, "except that what is usually understood by 'command' and 'ethics,' namely universally valid rules, is not to be found there. . . . Nothing can be made of these commands if we try to generalize and transform them into universally valid principles. Their content is purely concrete and related to this or that particular man in this or that particular situation."[5] We may say that for Barth, the divine command in the Bible is, like the burning bush, a wonder that at certain unrepeatable points in history has unexpectedly invaded and taken control of the life of some agent, leaving only the choice to obey or to rebel. Our moral experience has, in some measure, to be like that historical wonder and related to it.

To get a purchase on this point, let us consider what we sometimes call *implicit* obedience. That epithet suggests that there is no room to stop to think; the reflective content of obedience seems to be squeezed right out. The command is barked out, and the troops leap to it, like when the drill sergeant says, "When I say 'Jump!' you jump and ask 'How high?' on the way up." Is this not, after all, the right model for obedience to God? The story of Abraham's sacrifice of Isaac would hardly make sense if there were nothing laudable about simply doing what God commands, all questions aside. Yet even implicit obedience demands a measure of understanding. There is a well-worn joke about a desperate man who decided to seek guidance from the Bible by randomly flipping it open and pointing to a verse. On his first attempt he landed on Matthew 27:5, which says that Judas went and hanged himself. Trying again, he landed on Luke 10:37: "Go and do likewise." It is not a particularly funny joke, but a joke it is, not a tragedy. What makes it

4. Barth 1957: 673 (§38.2).
5. Barth 1957: 672.

a joke? Jokes are about fools, and the hero of this joke is a ripe fool. He did not understand something elementary about commanding and being commanded. Commands are events that occur within a relationship. They are given *by* someone *to* someone at a particular juncture. The order barked out at the new recruits by the drill sergeant requires a parade ground. There must be an understood relation between barker and barked-at. Otherwise, it cannot be obeyed. Imagine walking quietly down the street and hearing a voice mysteriously borne to you through the air: "Present arms!" What are you to do? Probably, you think, you have overheard something from a nearby barracks not intended for your ears. Alternatively, you may think that it was the voice of an angel sent to warn or command you in some way—although, you will have to give your mind very seriously to interpreting what the angel meant by it. The one thing that you cannot possibly do is simply present arms. You do not have any arms, only an umbrella. The recruits can obey "implicitly," but you cannot. They can obey because they know that they are recruits in training, that they are standing on a parade ground, that the loud-voiced man is their drill sergeant, and so on.

Implicit obedience needs a frame of reference. Even Abraham had to reckon that this was Yahweh speaking to him, the same Yahweh whose promise had led him out of Mesopotamia to the land that his descendants were to occupy, who could bring his purposes to bear in the teeth of seeming contradiction. The point is emphasized by the writer to the Hebrews: "Abraham considered that God was able even to raise people from the dead" (Heb. 11:19). The page-flipping fool in the joke does not know how to relate himself to the commands that he reads. The problem lies not in the Bible but rather in a failure of practical reason in himself. We may be tempted to call him "literal-minded," but that does not quite identify the problem. The biblical texts that he selected make perfectly good sense when read literally, on their own terms; he would have achieved no further clarity by trying to read them figuratively or allegorically. But he is unable to read them on their own terms at all. Preoccupied with finding a reference to himself, he diverts their literal sense out of its proper context and thus arrives at a conclusion that they never intended, literally or figuratively or in any other way.

Commands are acts, and acts are performed at certain times and in certain circumstances for certain definite purposes. Divine commands are acts of God, exerting their claim upon their own historical context primarily, on those to whom they are directly addressed. But because any act has a certain intelligibility in its context, and the context of God's acts is his will to bless and redeem the world, God's commands will always have some implications for other times and circumstances. The Decalogue was not of interest only to a barbarous people gathered at the foot of a mountain in Arabia; we have our own analogous ways of honoring our father and our mother and of not coveting our neighbor's goods. But in order to judge their bearing on other times and circumstances, we have to observe their place in their historical context first. If we say, "That applies to us too," we are already engaged in moral reasoning.

Karl Barth asked us, in order to "assure ourselves of the specific character of the divine command," to distinguish two facts: "(1) that the divine law in the Bible is always a concrete command; and (2) that this concrete commanding to be found in the Bible must be understood as a divine command relevant to ourselves who are not directly addressed by it."[6] What content can Barth give to that "relevance"? We will see how he tried to answer that question, but first we must make a distinction that Barth failed to make. The commands in the Bible do not all display the same kind of concreteness. All emerge from some particular situation, a moment in narrative history to which they belong; however, not all are "bare" commands, focused in principle on the immediate *hic et nunc* of the situation that they address. There is not only the burning bush to consider as a model of the divine command; there is also, and surely more suitable as a paradigm, the command to Adam and Eve in Eden: "You may freely eat of every tree of the garden, but of the tree of the knowledge of good and evil you shall not eat" (Gen. 2:16). This command is notable for all the features that Barth found most suspicious: it is formal, doing little more, in effect, than separating a sphere of permission from a sphere of prohibition; it is universally and continually valid, not confined to any here and now; and it is given in and with the order of creation, the world as a human dwelling, represented to us by the garden.

Some of the commands that we read in the Bible are very "bare" indeed, free of wider implications and wholly defined by their historical situation, so that they could never be obeyed more than once, even analogously. "Go into the village opposite you," Jesus told his disciples, "and immediately you will find an ass tied, and a colt with her; untie them and bring them to me" (Matt. 21:2). It might be an edifying liturgical innovation if one Palm Sunday a village congregation walked across the fields to meet its neighbors and was presented there with a suitably domesticated horse for the minister to ride back on, everyone waving palms and singing, "All glory, laud, and honor!" But not on even the widest construction could this be considered obedience to the command that Jesus gave his disciples. That command cannot be obeyed now. On the other hand, there are commands whose content makes it clear that they are meant to be obeyed whenever they are relevant. Consider the passage in the Sermon on the Mount where Jesus says, "You have heard that it was said . . . but I say to you . . . : Be reconciled to your brother. . . . If your right hand causes you to sin, cut it off. . . . Do not swear. . . . Do not resist one who is evil. . . . Love your enemies" (Matt. 5:21–48). These are not at all like

6. Barth 1957: 672.

"Untie the colt." They claim to direct our action in kinds of situations that arise occasionally or frequently.

In explaining how a concrete biblical command can be relevant to us too and not only to its original addressees, Barth is in something of an embarrassment: "In its capacity as witness," he writes, the Bible "claims not only our recognition of facts, but also our faith, not merely our appreciation of the past events which it attests but also our realization that matters are still the same here and now, and that as and what God commanded and forbade others, He now commands and forbids us. The Bible wills that we should be contemporaneous with and of the same mind as those other men in regard to the divine command."[7] There are, in fact, two different explanations given here, which seem to turn in contrary directions. According to one of them, the command has a reach that goes beyond the limits of its original point of utterance and extends to our time. Whether "matters are still the same here and now" may, of course, be discussed—sometimes they are, sometimes they are not—but it is true, at least, that the generic command addresses types of situations that *may* be instantiated, perhaps in analogical form, here and now as well as there and then. According to the other, we must, in faith, be part of the scene on Mount Sinai when the command was first addressed. Whatever validity such a conception may have in describing believers' participation in saving events—Kierkegaard's "contemporaneity with Christ" comes to mind—it seems rather heavy stage machinery to negotiate a commonplace moral communication. We do not need to travel back to the tenth century BC in order to grasp the relevance of a condemnation of adultery.

But again these generic commands divide into at least two types: moral rules and public laws. The moral rules in the Sermon on the Mount are concerned with dispositional attitudes: conciliatoriness, self-discipline, restraint, forgiveness, and so on. They are radically and surprisingly expressed, without much interest in whether we will find them easy to obey or not. They have nothing much to say to dilemmas of practical casuistry such as "What if my brother refuses to be reconciled unless I join him in a solemn oath of undying hatred to our enemy?" Such questions are left, as it were, for later. As a result, these moral rules are capable of directing our conduct in a wide variety of circumstances and producing a varied style of performance. By contrast, public laws are designed to be straightforward and easy to keep with a degree of uniformity in performance. We have an outstanding example of a legal code in Deuteronomy 14–25. Shaped, very evidently, out of preexisting legal traditions, it aims to maintain a practical continuity with these while achieving certain reforming aims. It chooses its topics apparently randomly, in the light of questions that have come up and legal rulings that are at hand. It has a lot to say about detailed dilemmas, but comparatively little (though not nothing)

7. Barth 1957: 700.

about underlying attitudes. Moral rules and public laws look different, and they do different jobs. In a very obvious way moral rules are more "portable," more easily applied to changing situations, than public laws can be.[8] We still have brothers and sisters to be reconciled to, even if there is no temple to leave our gift in. We would have considerable difficulty in obeying the Deuteronomic law of slavery, however much we might sympathize with its intentions.

These two types of generic moral instruction, as they appear in the Bible, share a common feature: they are framed by a narrative context. The metaphor of "framing" is, perhaps, misleading. A picture frame is designed to display the picture, and it can be removed or changed. Narrative, however, is a constituent element in the text's moral claim on us. The legal code of Deuteronomy 14–25 is preceded by twelve chapters of mixed narrative and exhortation, explaining how this law code originated in the birth of the nation and the ministry of Moses, and why a code originating in Israel's nomadic past should have authority over a settled agricultural society governed by monarchy and other civil institutions. This setting is continually relevant for understanding the point of the commands as they arise. When told that we must leave the gleanings of the grape harvest for the stranger passing by, we are reminded that God heard our cry when we were strangers in the land of Egypt (Deut. 24:22). Similarly, the Sermon on the Mount is situated in Matthew's Gospel as a prelude to the account of the ministry of Jesus and a climax to the account of his birth and commissioning. And this, equally, is not irrelevant to those who come to this text for guidance. When we are told not to resist evil, we are prepared to hear how Jesus refused to enlist the aid of legions of angels to resist arrest in Gethsemane. The difference in the content of the two texts corresponds to the difference in the narrative that supports them: on the one hand, a narrative about the founding of a holy nation; on the other hand, a narrative about the fulfillment of history and the redemption of the world. Neither is "timeless" in the sense of being indifferent to historical context. If we call the Sermon on the Mount "timeless," and contrast it with Deuteronomy, what we mean is simply what we mean when we speak of Jesus of Nazareth as the Savior of the world: here is the point at which the particular history of a nation with which God dealt is taken up into God's all-embracing act of redemption; here is the event in which we are all directly involved, and here are the commands that belong to that event. At the center of the biblical message is an announcement about what God has done in history: "When the time had fully come, God sent forth his Son" (Gal. 4:4). In that message all the authority of the biblical texts finds its source. Biblical commands speak with authority to us because that deed of God in history speaks with authority to us. Let us sum it up like this: it is not the commands that the Bible contains that we obey; rather, it is

8. See, in chapter 4 of the present volume, N. T. Wright on doctrines as "portable stories" (pp. 62–65).

the purposes of God that those commands, set in their context, reveal to us. The purpose of God is the ultimate reason why anything at all is good or evil to do. The Bible is authoritative for ethics because it speaks to us of those purposes and demonstrates them in the acts of God in history.

We have begun from commands simply because they form a kind of limit case. The question about "implicit" obedience is raised most sharply by them. But there are other forms of moral instruction in the Scriptures. Moral teaching is given in exhortation, parables, lists of virtues, and so on. Narrative, command, prediction, and invocation (i.e., prayer and praise) all teach us how to direct our ways pleasingly to God. We can learn of the wrong of adultery from the story of David and Bathsheba, not only from the seventh commandment of the Decalogue. But of every other type of moral communication the same must be said as was said about the commands: it claims its authority on the basis of what God has done.

There are occasions on which nothing but implicit obedience will do. But even recognizing those occasions depends on the general presumption that we have to think through what is required of us patiently and reflectively. And when the church is at sea over how to read the message of the Gospels, only patient attention to reading, interpretation, and obedient thought will do. A shrill call for implicit obedience never substitutes for careful exploration of what it is that must be obeyed. And in that exploration there has to be *hermeneutic distance*. What that term refers to is a gap between the reader and the text, a gap that understanding has to overcome. This distance is often understood as a historical one, but that particular turn in hermeneutic theory led, in my view, into a blind alley. There is no reason why I should find the gap any wider in reading Plato than in reading Emmanuel Levinas. The distance that we have to insist on, rather, arises from the objective standing of the text, especially any text that claims to speak to us in the name of God. The distance between the text and ourselves can never be, and should never be supposed to be, swallowed up by our understanding of it. Whatever it may be that I have concluded from reading the Scriptures, that conclusion must be open to fresh interrogation, since the Scriptures themselves will be its judge. If, after reading the Bible faithfully, I am confident enough to make some ringing declaration, this does not mean that my declaration is as good as contained within the Bible. In a faithful dogmatic formulation there is, of course, a proper authority. There are times and places where that authority allows for, or requires, a ringing declaration. Yet the question of whether the dogmatic formulation has in fact faithfully expressed the Scriptures' emphasis is always worth discussing, even if the outcome of the discussion is affirmative every time. The question "What does the Bible mean, and how does it affect us?" can never be out of order in the church, as though the giving of well-founded answers in the past could make the whole question of merely antiquarian interest.

We must not, then, in the supposed interest of a "biblical" ethic, try to close down moral issues prescriptively, announcing that we already know what the Bible teaches and guarding against wrong answers by forbidding further examination. The church's leading institutions may, of course, properly resolve that it is inappropriate for *them* to invest further time and effort in study of a matter that may be considered closed for all practical purposes. But what the leading institutions may quite properly resolve not to undertake, the Spirit in the church may prompt other believers to undertake, for the word *authority* means, quite simply, that we have to go on looking back to this source if we are to keep on the right track.

Why should we find this difficult to accept? The truth is that we resist admitting indeterminacy in our understanding of the text. Once such an admission is made, we fear, "anything goes." A host of false prophets will take advantage of our respectful distance; they will rush forward to wrest Scripture out of its plain sense, force it into authorizing what cannot be authorized. And of course in the short run, at least, this fear is likely to prove all too well grounded. False prophets are, and always will be, legion. We must simply expect to hear abominations and absurdities put forward in the confident claim that such are compatible with or authorized by Scripture. To this intense annoyance we, like generations of faithful believers before us, are called. The question is this: What sacrifice of our faith would we make if, to avoid the annoyance for ourselves and the disturbance for the church, we closed down on the reading and interpretation of Holy Scripture, declared that there was nothing to discuss? To our fears we have to put the question in return of whether the Spirit of the living God is a match for the perversity of humankind, whether Jesus' promise about the gates of hell being unable to prevail is seriously enough meant to be trusted.

Obedience must be thoughtful obedience. This "must" is, in the end, a logical necessity, not merely an obligation. Moral instruction is directed to what we "do," but nobody "does" anything without thinking. If obedience is what we are called to, thought is what we are called to, thought about how we may frame our action in conformity to the demand. Thoughtful obedience does not exclude immediate encounter with the commanding God. Moments of fear and trembling before God will befall us, but these are not an alternative to reflective and considered thinking, the "rational worship" by which our minds are renewed to "appreciate distinctions" (Rom. 12:1–2). It is another way of saying that the obedience required of us is the *obedience of faith*—no less!

11

The Fourfold Pattern of Christian Moral Reasoning according to the New Testament

BERND WANNENWETSCH

The Circular Pattern of Moral Reasoning

The following considerations explore the nature of reflective ethos from within the scriptural witness of the Christian communities. In highlighting four practices that I take to be essential for this phenomenon (perceiving, discerning, judging, and giving of account), I am, however, not suggesting a straightforward methodology of Christian moral reasoning. Contrasting the purism of neo-Kantian ethics (and its distillation of ethical thought and practice into ever more narrow and isolated principles such as the categorical imperative), I wish to draw attention to a plurality of reflective and deliberative practices that together constitute what I take to be the circle of reflective ethos as it is suggested by a conceptually alert reading of the New Testament.

With this attempt, I do not see myself competing in the traditional field of "New Testament ethics," in either its more historically geared version (ethics *in* the New Testament) or its more applied version (ethics *of* the New Testament). It is certainly legitimate to read the New Testament in pursuit of its most basic moral principles, such as "love" or "justice," or, as Richard Hays has suggested, to read it in pursuit of a series of "focal images," such as cross, community, and new creation.[1] Yet my interest in this contribution differs from such attempts in that I wish to explore the core practices that constitute Christian ethics—the art of moral reasoning in a theological vein.

To put the same difference in Aristotelian terms: The four core elements that I suggest (perceiving, discerning, judging, and giving of account) represent theoretical virtues rather than practical ones, although we must certainly grant that the programmatic communal nature of these practices in their Christian version tends to discourage an all-too-strict separation between the two types of virtues. While these practices, as intellectual activities, do not directly fall under the rubric of "moral acts," they are directed to such acts in a teleological way. And the way in which these practices engage the human being as a whole, embracing all its faculties, suggests another reason for not separating them from moral action in a categorical way by relegating them to a mere preliminary status. For this reason, I have chosen to refer to these intellectual virtues as belonging to the "reflective ethos" of the church in no less a constitutive way than the disposition to act and concrete ways of acting that characterize this community.

In identifying a number of discursive, reflective, and deliberative practices, my proposal may appear similar to what Hays suggested under the heading of "the four-fold task of NT ethics."[2] He suggests a sequence of (1) descriptive, (2) synthetic, (3) hermeneutical, and (4) pragmatic operations, while I think of (1) perception, (2) discernment, (3) judgment, and (4) giving of account. Leaving aside for a moment the difference in the way each of us formulates the individual tasks, a generic difference between the two proposals should be noted at this point. Whereas Hays's operational steps are derived from the tradition of moral philosophy, my interest is in exploring a set of activities that I find suggested and characterized in the New Testament tradition itself. Strange world: where the New Testament scholar borrows from a philosophical-ethical framework, the moral theologian borrows his conceptual framework from the New Testament.

Of course, nowhere in the Scriptures are we presented with precisely such a list or system of intellectual practices, nor can one be easily distilled from a synoptic reading of the books of Scripture. My suggestion remains the attempt of the moral theologian to read the Christian Scriptures with a conceptual curiosity as to whether the practices that constitute Christian ethics are to be conceived and elaborated independently from Scripture or rather within Scripture's own flow. Although the suggested sequence of four intellectual practices may not be totally exhaustive, I do think it fairly comprehensive and "rounded." In speaking of their rounded comprehensiveness, what I have in

1. Hays 1996.
2. Hays 1996: 3.

mind is that these four practices can be envisioned as forming a cycle in which each move presupposes the previous one and calls forth the next.

Although we should not expect to find the complete cycle represented or alluded to in any one biblical passage, we have clear indicators that biblical authors such as Paul not only envisioned the individual practices as they appear on my list but also attended to the way in which, for example, judgment and accountability interlock. Another point is associated with the proposed cyclical nature of the scheme: unlike a linear construal, circularity allows for teleology but disallows hegemony. Speaking of a "cycle" of practices, the quest for one central or even overarching practice or any other sort of priority becomes meaningless. As each practice can be said to flow from another and into yet another, a teleological relationship between the individual practices must be assumed, but the circularity of the pattern prevents this teleology from grounding hegemonic relations. Even "judgment," with its inner sense of arrival and finality, does not constitute a case for such hegemony. Nor does the rendering of an account of what one has done mark the end of the process of moral reasoning. Rather than putting an end to the sequence, genuine accountability will provoke renewed perception, thereby prompting the circular pattern to start anew: when our actions and judgments are exposed to the judgment of others as in our giving of account, they trigger a self-critical reapprehension of our actions that may lead to a revision of our judgment, thereby provoking an eventual renewal of the categorical framework of our perception.

At this early point I wish to rule out a possible misunderstanding. Speaking of a cyclical motion does not imply the principled denial of progression. Although such a motion will not amount to "progress," there is room for a nonlinear (though always vulnerable) "progression" in terms of the gradual refinement of the process of moral reasoning that may, like a helix, gain depth every time the circle comes around.

Think of the way a newborn develops: a baby's (visual) perception is highly schematic at first, distinguishing only contrast of light; it then progresses toward the identification of real schemes, contours such as the shape of the mother, and from there to the discernment of faces, first of mother and father, then of others. We experience from the beginning of our life how refined sensory perception gives way to discernment, discrimination, and judgment. Or as Hebrews 5:14 describes the progress of maturing precisely in terms of the refinement of the believers' perception by training toward the capacity of moral discernment, "Solid food is for the mature, who by constant use have trained their sense of perception to distinguish good from evil [*dia tēn hexin ta aisthētēria gegymnasmena echontōn pros diakrisin kalou te kai kakou*]" (my translation).

With these preliminary clarifications done, we can now turn to a more detailed analysis of the four individual practices and their inner relatedness.

Perception (*aesthesis*)

Situation and Moral Description / Moral Notions

Why start with perception or even sensory perception? Is perception not actually a premoral faculty, a spontaneous impression that falls outside of the realm of moral responsibility? It is true: the widely shared assumption that ethics is essentially about decision-making does not accommodate perception as morally relevant. It rather assumes that decision-making consists of the dual task of (1) identifying the appropriate moral principles or imperatives and (2) finding ways of how they can be applied in a given situation. In this vein, the situation itself tends to be presumed as a given, a "material condition" to be dealt with, a matter of sheer factuality, awaiting its moral evaluation. Yet, as common as this fact-value distinction is in moral theories, it hardly lives up to the reality of human life.[3]

Contrary to such a portrayal, a situation is never simply "out there," determining our place in it as a matter of external circumstance; rather, the way in which we conceive of a situation is already a constitutive part of the situation that we are in. Often our judgments are prefigured by the way in which we describe the situation. The language that we use is a case in point. Are we aware of the moral emphasis that our chosen terminology carries? The application of so-called moral notions already reveals something about our perception. It makes a difference morally whether we speak of "abortion" or "termination of pregnancy," of "dying" on the battlefield or of "being killed" there, of an "embryo" or of "embryonic material." Formulas such as "the situation demands," "the situation leaves no choice," and the like usually only indicate anticipated judgment that grounds our perception and description of a situation. Yet even a case in which a situation is presented as a matter of options or choices might be far from being truthful perception.

Let us take an example. Imagine a pregnant seventeen-year-old going for counseling, and the counselor, trying to display the empathy learned in training, opens the conversation by saying, "I understand that you are now in a situation in which you are asking yourself, 'Should I keep the baby or not?'" Yet, is this a genuine perception of the situation "teenage pregnancy"? Or, rather, is the counselor perhaps imposing a "decision" on the young woman where, in fact, there is no decision for her to make? Suppose the girl has been brought up in a family in which not having and keeping the baby is not an option, and she has come to the counselor only to learn about the institutional support that she might be entitled to? A situation is always more than a set of external circumstances; it embraces the agent's (or the observer's) personal convictions, beliefs, and dispositions.[4]

3. See Pincoffs 1986.
4. See McClendon and Smith 1975.

If it is thus understood that perception plays an important role in the shaping of a moral character, both individually and communally, we must now turn to the two basic dimensions of perception: the sensory-affective and the intellectual-conceptual; both perceptive dimensions (*kardia* and *nous*) are addressed in the New Testament with regard to their moral significance. We first turn to the conceptual dimension.

Conceptual Perception: The Renewal of the nous (Rom. 12)

In a condensed formulation Paul addresses the congregation in Romans 12:2–5:

> Do not be conformed to this world time but be transformed by the renewing of your perception, so that you may discern what is the will of God—what is good and acceptable and perfect. For by the grace given to me I say to every one among you not to think of yourself more highly than you ought to think . . . because we, though many, are one body in Christ, and individually members one of another. (my translation)

Paul summons the community to a transformation that entails the abdication of the schemata of this world as a result of the renewal of the mind. *Nous* refers to the mind in a specific sense, addressing its faculty to comprehend reality as it is especially associated with the ability to conceptualize, the grasping of reality in its generic aspects. In Aristotle's philosophy of mind, the *nous* occupies the central position between *sophia* (the immediate vision of the ends) and *phronēsis* (the means-to-end rationality) as the conceptualizing faculty of the mind. In Paul's view, the renewal of the mind is necessary, given the schematizing power that the *aiōn* holds—*mē syschēmatizesthe*: "do not be conformed to this world"; literally, "do not be made one with the schemata of this eon" (my translation). Here, the passive voice is no less in place than it is in the subsequent call to be transformed: "let yourselves be transformed."[5]

The latter case is certainly a grammatical "divine passive": the transformation cannot be a mere "rethinking" of things as resulting from an intensified effort by the human mind itself; a new mind can only be a gift, part and parcel of the *kainē ktisis*, God's creation of a new humanity, so that the imperative can only mean that it is necessary to watch out for God's activity of renewing. Yet, the initial call, *mē syschēmatizesthe*, has a passive voice too, which indicates, as James Dunn puts it, the "recognition of a power or force to mould character and conduct and which 'this age' exercises."[6] Mainstream patterns of thought are so ubiquitous and powerful that we do not even recognize their influence; they have become a sort of second skin to us.

---

5. For a fuller account of this, see Wannenwetsch 2002.
6. Dunn 1988: 2.712. Dunn opts for the passive voice rather than the middle voice.

Yet, how does the Spirit break through this second skin and help people to unlearn the schemata of the age? The example that Paul himself gives is related to the church as body of Christ. What the envisioned transformation is meant to overcome is "disordered" thinking about the relationship of members to each other and to the whole body. Through the *hyperphronein* ("think too highly of oneself") Paul wants, presumably, to highlight and reject the classical idea of the political sphere as an arena for the striving for excellence at the cost of others. From this classical perspective, place and status in society are seen as a "natural claim" by virtue of heritage or personal achievement. Paul's call to transcend this pattern of thought recalls Jesus' response to the competition over greatness between his disciples as recorded in Luke 22:24–27 and parallels.

There, the schema of rule in the secular world ("the rulers of the nations lord it over them, and those in authority are called benefactors"), in which "natural authority"—the authority of means—dictates status, is confronted ("but not so with you") with a new way of understanding and exercising authority: "The greatest among you must become like the youngest, and the leader like one who serves." Most significant within the framework of our inquiry is that Jesus' claim "not so with you" is not in an egalitarian fashion doing away with the notion of authority and greatness altogether; rather, it aims at a *reconceptualization* of what it means to be great: from my striving to excel over others, which aims to let them appear smaller in my presence, toward a notion of service or ministry that marks out a greatness that makes others grow rather than diminish in my presence.

In sum: Christian moral reasoning is concerned not simply with moral imperatives ("do not think highly of yourself") but rather with a renewed conceptuality that grounds these imperatives, such as, in our example, the redefinition of greatness in the light of Christ's service.

Sensory-affective Perception: The "Seeing Heart" (Luke 10; Phil. 1:9)

So much for the conceptual side of perception—the *nous*—in its constant need of renewal in the light of the gospel. Yet there is also a sensory-affective side that the biblical tradition addresses. For this, we turn to Luke 10 and the parable of the good Samaritan. This parable demonstrates that sensory perception like "seeing" does matter morally. Ethics is not about mere acting, acting blindly perhaps; Christian moral reasoning is geared toward acting with open eyes. At stake is truthful perception that sees things as they really are instead of seeing them as we would like them to be and declaring this, and ourselves, "aright." As with Paul's emphasis on the liberation from the schemata of the age, Christian moral reasoning cares for sensory perception precisely as it recognizes a human tendency to deception and self-deception. This is why the prophetic tradition, as it is reflected in the New Testament, has put great emphasis on the signs of the messianic age in terms of the recovery of sensory perception: the blind will regain their eyesight, and the deaf will have their hearing restored. *Ephphatha*: open up! (Mark 7:34). Jesus' liberating ministry is one of creating eyes that really see and ears that really hear and listen.

This becomes evident in the story that Jesus tells of the three men who went from Jericho to Jerusalem (Luke 10:25–37), all of whom are said to have "seen" the wounded victim lying there. Yet while the Samaritan has seen a human being in misery, the other two must have perceived something else: a source of potential danger—an ambush perhaps—or at least a source of unacceptable delay of their journey. Their seeing really makes the difference; all parties in the parable are acting out what they have perceived. When the parable addresses the perception of the protagonists, the Greek employs a participial construction, which points us to another essential feature.

Whereas it is said of both the priest and the Levite that "seeing the man, he passed by [*idōn antiparēlthen*]," in the case of the Samaritan, the Greek has "seeing him, he felt compassion [*idōn esplanchnisthē*] and went to him and bandaged his wounds" (my translation). The Samaritan's eyes were, so to speak, connected to his heart, which was "torn open"—"compassion" is perhaps too weak a translation for what the Greek verb connotes. The Latin translation for "compassion," *misericordia*, however, does illuminate the point of the plot well, as it literally means "to have the heart with the poor."

What we have in the semantic subtlety of the narrative is a moral anthropology in a nutshell, where the affections are seen as a sort of transmission belt between our sensual perception and will-guided action. By "transmission," we do not mean another "step" in the process but rather the simultaneity of seeing and feeling suggested by the Greek participial construction: in seeing him, he felt compassion; the heart was "in" the eye, so to speak.[7] As Luke 10 makes clear for us, there need not always be a moment of reflection *between* perception and action, a so-called deliberation. In facing a factual situation, we do not always have to pause and reflect on what to do, much less ponder a range of alternatives before finally settling for the most appropriate one. Acting is not always and necessarily a function of a decision-making process.[8]

The language of our narrative seems to employ a different logic that assumes a transmitter role of the affection within a given simultaneity of perception and action-impulse. So when our sensual perception is oriented appropriately as a matter of a "seeing or listening heart," the right action can be expected to "flow" from it by engaging our mind and will accordingly. At times, "eth-

---

7. For a fuller account of a theological pan-aesthetics, the way in which all sensory perception can coincide in faith, see Wannenwetsch 2000.

8. Alasdair MacIntyre points out that in the classical concept of the practical syllogism in Aristotle, what results from the appropriate perception of the highest good and the wise pondering of its realization in a given circumstance via *phronēsis* is action itself. "There is no logical space for something else to intervene: a decision, for example" (MacIntyre 1988: 140).

ics" as we know it—the cycle of reflection and deliberation—can in fact even function as a surrogate for the lack of or deficiency in sensory or affective perception.

We may even find the modern syllogistic account to be part of the story, if we allow for some imaginative or even slightly speculative interpretation. If we ask what it might have been that prevented the priest and the Levite from turning to the victim, we can at least imagine them as caught up in a syllogistic pattern of thought similar to the modern account. They might actually have reflected about the situation (and most likely not without moral considerations that for them perhaps came down to a weighting of competing goods): the congregation in the temple waiting for them to arrive and celebrate an important feast; the compulsion that they felt from the Torah to avoid corpse contamination by approaching or even touching a "half dead" (Luke 10:30), which would render them unfit for ritual duties;[9] the weighing-up of the good of the many righteous members of God's people versus this one man's need; the prudent anticipating of the likelihood of an ambush or of another helper to arrive soon with more time, more medical expertise, and so forth. All this is not, of course, to suggest that our reading of Luke 10 advocates an emotivist ethics in which reflection and deliberation are outplayed by the overwhelming role of affective perception. We need to remind ourselves that the emphasis on the latter is to be understood *within* the cycle of the four patterns, not outside of it. Within this cycle and its educative significance, we are to reckon with affective perception that is shaped by the experiences in the other three practices just as much as it is felt to be "immediate."

In an exciting passage in the beginning of the Epistle to the Philippians, Paul connects both aspects of the moral meaning of perception, the conceptual and the affective, when he binds them both to love. The apostle writes in Philippians 1:9,

> And this is my prayer, that your love may abound more and more in knowledge [epignōsis: insight, cognition] and depth of perception [aisthēsis]. (my translation)

Here, conceptual and affective perceptions are conceived as distinct spheres in which love (agapē) should come to flourish. As much as Paul stresses love as something that should be neither blind nor blinding but rather bound up with truthful perception of reality, he also insists that perception needs to become a sphere and indeed an occasion of the enactment and growth of love, lest cognition and perception shrink to what has been described as the cold gaze of modernity, the gaze that freezes everything in the glacier of sheer factuality. In the light of our fourfold pattern, it is also noteworthy that in this passage

---

9. See Bauckham 1998a; Bockmuehl 2003: 31, and passim.

Paul not only demonstrates both perceptive practices, *epignōsis* and *aisthēsis*, simultaneously by binding them to love; he also marks them out as constitutive features of the practice of moral discernment when he adds the consecutive phrase "so that you can discern and prove that which makes a difference [*eis to dokimazein hymas ta diapheronta*]" (Phil. 1:10 my translation). And to discernment we now turn.

Probing, Testing, Discerning (*dokimazein*)

The term *dokimazein* as it appears in the biblical tradition is particularly multifaceted. Originally drawn from the process of probing metal for its purity over the fire, the image conjured up is one of a variety of meanings and possible objects. *Dokimazein* comprises the testing of humans by God, as in the "God who tests our hearts" (the Septuagint translation of Jer. 11:20 in 1 Thess. 2:4), and God's eternal judgment of human action through the fire (1 Cor. 3:13). Yet the term also conveys a sense of the self-testing of believers (1 Cor. 11:28), the testing of the spirits (1 John 4:1) to determine whether they are from God, and even the testing of "everything": "test everything [*panta dokimazesthe*] and keep the good" (1 Thess. 5:21 my translation). The ultimate purpose of this activity, however, is the exploring of the will of God (Rom. 12:2) in order to prove what pleases the Lord (Eph. 5:10).[10] What may be perceived as a perplexing multiplicity of usages is actually theologically significant.

Transitive and Intransitive: Probing God's Will by Proving Ourselves in It

The grammar of the term *dokimazein* combines transitive and intransitive usage: our testing *of* a case cannot be separated from the proving of ourselves *in* the case as either worthy (*dokimos*) or unworthy (*adokimos*) of the gospel. In the biblical usage *dokimazein* is construed in this tellingly comprehensive sense, integrating the transitive and intransitive meanings of "probing" and "testing." Our probing of God's will is not separable from God's probing of our hearts (1 Thess. 2:4) and deeds (1 Cor. 3:13). Therefore, the translation of "discerning" aims at more than a purely intellectual operation and must assume a specifically moral meaning wherein the discernment of God's will is identical with the discovery of the "good and acceptable and perfect" (Rom. 12:2 ESV).

What is at stake in *dokimazein* is not disengaged reasoning *about* God's will but rather the exploring *of* this will from within any concrete situation. In this vein we may say, for example, the following with regard to marriage: in their sexual lives, Christians are not setting out to test and probe (the institution of) marriage or a (concrete) partner but rather are testing themselves

10. See Schunack 1992.

in what it means to be a faithful partner *in* marriage; and they expect their understanding and appreciation of this social institution to grow through that probing of themselves within the institution.

Community of Discernment

In all its biblical comprehensiveness, as a simultaneously transitive and intransitive activity, discerning/probing is marked as a communal and discursive task: Paul addresses the church in Rome as a community of *dokimazein* in the *pluralis ecclesiasticus* ("ecclesial plural"): "so that you [plural: *hymas*] can discern the will of God" (Rom. 12:2 my translation). As regards the commonality of the task, we understand that, on the one hand, discerning needs to engage a multitude of voices, moral debate, and arguing, as well as patient listening to the perception of others. On the other hand, probing and exploring cannot be an endless roundabout journey without a final destination. It is bound to arrive somewhere at its given time, and this arrival we call judgment. If perception addresses the question "What is the case?" and discernment is organized around the question "What is the heart of the matter?" judgment is what settles both questions by ruling "This case is a matter of X and not of Y."

Judgment (*diakrinein*)

The verb *diakrinein* literally means "to cut asunder, to lay apart." Judgment lays a substance matter apart, not only analytically (as in discerning) but also synthetically. In the process of the laying apart of the different aspects and components of a situation, a new combination becomes visible: "This, being a matter of X [analytical], belongs here [synthetical], while that, being a matter of Y, belongs there." If the will of God is the core object of this inquiry, the fundamental form that a judgment in Christian moral reasoning assumes will be "This is a matter in accord with God's will, while that is not (it is against his will, or perhaps is merely a matter of preference, etc.)."

Judging often appears as a subdiscipline of logic: reaching syllogistic conclusions, moving from maxims to derivations of various degrees, and so on. Yet while syllogistic reasoning is an important dimension of the activity of judging, it is by no means the whole of the matter. When all is said and done, a judgment cannot be constructed like a mathematical operation, with all relations between terms precise and linear. Rather than being constructed or achieved by following a strict method, moral judgment "emerges" from the soil of perception and discernment in a way that is open for illumination. Theologically speaking, judgment cannot defy the *illuminatio spiritus sancti*, as it is the Spirit of truth that empowers the discernment of the spirits (1 Cor. 12:10), which leads to proper judgment. Or, as the letter described the decision taken in the apostles' council, "It seemed good to the Holy Spirit and to us" (Acts 15:28 my translation).

This latter quotation reinforces the communal nature of judgment as a task performed by the body as a whole, which again indicates that moral judgment is more than a result of paying attention to the technicalities of a procedure. The alertness of the community as a whole is required in order to discern when a judgment is "ripe" or when judgment would be the premature interruption of the discernment process.[11] Yet, if and when the time is ripe, judgment must be ventured. It can be boldly ventured precisely under the biblical recognition that every judgment must eventually expose itself to God's final judgment. It is from this final judgment that any temporal human judgment receives its empowerment and dignity—as provisional judgment that nevertheless can and must be ventured as definite action.[12]

Giving of Account (*logon didonai*)

In 1 Peter 3:15 we read,

> Always be ready to give an account of your deeds [make your defense] to any-one who demands from you an accounting for the hope that is in you. (my translation)

Although an act of judgment completes and ends a process of moral de-liberation or reflection and literally cuts off further considerations or other possible directions, no human judgment can be considered irrevocable. This difference between definiteness and irrevocability is often overlooked, and weakness in judgment is easily confused with tolerance, whereas an apodictic judgmental habit, on the other hand, is mistaken for strength of judgment.

Liberated Accountability

The justification that arises from God's merciful judgment on sinners liber-ates them both to judge boldly and to revise a wrong judgment. The freedom to venture judgment, as it arises from the *iustitia aliena* of divine justifica-tion, comes to occupy exactly the location that is otherwise held by the urge to self-justification. Self-justification is the attempt to absorb and anticipate the judgment that others (including God) might have on our own deeds by

11. On the political significance of this distinction, see my argument about the "conciliar obligation" of the church to arrive at a consensus in elemental questions (Wannenwetsch 2004: 298–317).

12. See Oliver O'Donovan's considerations on the "imperfectability" of human judgment that needs both to distinguish itself from God's judgment and to imitate it in a certain way (O'Donovan 2005: 13–30).

providing an irresistible justificatory account of "what really happened" in a course of action and "what it really was about."[13]

In contrast to this, it is a clear sign of liberated accountability if one is willing and able to expose oneself, one's action and one's judgment, to others and their judgment (1 Cor. 14:29). Here we can use a maritime metaphor. In navigating our ship of moral reasoning after it has left the haven of prejudices and sailed the open sea, where it is exposed to the winds of probing and testing, and has arrived at a safe haven of judgment, we must be willing still to weigh anchor again by exposing our judgment to the judgment of others by the giving of account. Otherwise, our port of judgment, even if it was totally right at the time it was reached, becomes just another haven of future prejudices. In this vein, the giving of account within the cycle of Christian moral reasoning is categorically different from the recently emerging culture of "accountability" in which the managerialist imperative of benchmarking and controlling that has conquered most of our public institutions teaches people to present themselves and what they have done in the best possible, if not deceptive, light.[14]

My description of the fourfold task of Christian ethics has focused on the reflective-deliberative moments and not on the performance of actions as such. Yet, as we have noted, the discrimination is analytically necessary but not absolute. This is clear when we look at how judging and action are related: since acting is not simply impulse-driven behavior but rather is intentional activity, it can be stipulated that every action embodies a particular judgment. That is the reason why the agent can be held accountable for it. It is not that I judge first and then transform a judgment into action. That would be a simplification. Rather, my particular course of action is an implicit account of the way in which I perceive reality as I have learned to discern alternatives and to judge types of action. Although sometimes the action speaks louder than the words, the implicit nature of action as embodied judgment typically calls for a moment of *logon didonai*—giving reasons.

The Narrative Structure of Witness

Although the situation envisioned in 1 Peter 3:15, quoted above, is apologetic, to counter false accusations, it expresses the logic of witness in general: it is expected that action—Christian action in the world—will arouse curiosity about the judgments on life, death, and so on that underlie it. As Jesus puts it in the Sermon on the Mount, "Let your light so shine before men, that they may see your good works and give glory to your Father who is in heaven" (Matt. 5:16 RSV). The power of witness is to live in such a way as to stir up

13. On the distinction between subjective accounts of any human action and its objective purpose, the actual "object of the act," see Wannenwetsch 1998.
14. See Wannenwetsch 2005.

such curiosity that demands an account of the hope expressed in those good works.

As philosophers such as Alasdair MacIntyre[15] and theologians such as Stanley Hauerwas and L. Gregory Jones[16] have reminded us, the giving of such an account typically will take on a narrative format if it is to be transparent to its sources. If the questioner demands, it will have to go into detail about the underlying judgments, distinctions, and perceptions—all the way backward in the described cycle of moral reasoning, as it were. And it may happen in the process of giving an account of our judgments and actions that our own perception is challenged to transformation so that we are to start afresh the cycle of intellective-affective practices that marks the reflective ethos of the Christian community.

Conclusion

In contrast to the frequent habit of immediately focusing on the substantive characteristics of Christian ethics as they can be found in the New Testament (such as the concept of love) and being rather blurry when it comes to the precise way in which these are applied to various circumstances, my inquiry has aimed at an analytical account of the distinctive reflective and deliberative practices that together characterize Christian moral reasoning according to the New Testament. In spite of the more formal focus, I hope that it has become clear that the idea of a cycle of reflective-deliberative practices does not suggest a "methodology," a mere technical array of functional patterns that can be abstracted from the substantive framework of doctrinal and ecclesial patterns that make moral reasoning theological and Christian in the first place: faith, hope, and love.

As the individual analysis of the four features will have indicated, each of them can be appropriately understood only as rooted in or geared toward (one of) the three theological virtues.

1. The discussion of the significance of perception for the moral life had to be specified in terms of a sort of *agapeic aesthetics*: perception rooted in *love* (Phil. 1:9).
2. Discernment had to be specified as the distinguishing of spirits, geared toward the discerning of God's will: the good, the pleasing, and perfect (Rom. 12:1–2).
3. Judgment had to be qualified as being rooted in God's judgment that is appropriated in eucharistic *faith*. The appropriateness or inappropriateness

15. See his chapter "The Virtues, Unity of a Human Life and the Concept of a Tradition" (MacIntyre 1981: 204–25).
16. Hauerwas and Jones 1989.

of human deeds is measured in terms of their "fittingness" with the sacramental practice of the church: "You cannot drink the cup of the Lord and the cup of demons. You cannot partake in the table of the Lord and the table of demons" (1 Cor. 10:21). In this light, the Eucharist can be seen as a "form of judgment"[17] in its own right. God is not punishing the evildoers in that he adds a penalty to their deeds. It is rather the nonfittingness of their deeds with the Eucharist that equals judgment: "For anyone who eats and drinks without discerning the body eats and drinks judgment upon himself" (1 Cor. 11:29 ESV). In a similar fashion, Paul makes baptism the moral unit of measure of the lives of believers when he speaks of the body as the "temple of the holy Spirit" (1 Cor. 6:19 ESV) in the context of discussing sexual sins, the logic of dispossession of one's own self being essentially a baptismal one: "Do you not know that all of us who have been baptized into Christ Jesus were baptized into his death? . . . No longer present your members to sin as instruments of wickedness, but present yourselves to God as those who have been brought from death to life, and present your members to God as instruments of righteousness" (Rom. 6:3, 13 NIV, slightly revised).

4. The giving of account had to be understood as a matter of witness: its gaze is not fixated on one's own works and their defense in a self-justificatory fashion but rather is looking forward to God's eventual vindication, so that giving an account of our works is no different from giving an account of the *hope* that is in us.

---

17. For a fuller account of the sacraments as a form of action and judgment, see Wannenwetsch, forthcoming.

12

The Apostolic Discourse and Its Developments

KEVIN J. VANHOOZER

Introduction: A Challenge, Gambit, and Construal

"Much in every way." (Rom. 3:2)

Paul's estimation of the advantage of the Jew comes close to serving as a response to our set question—"To what extent is the New Testament authoritative, and how does it shape and prescribe Christian theology?"—but ultimately may say too much. Not everything that readers may extract or infer from the New Testament is necessarily normative for all times and places: etymologies of Greek terms; sources that may have been used in the process of textual composition; background cultural practices; assumptions about botanical phenomena.[1]

David Kelsey challenges theologians to go beyond mere professions of biblical authority in order to specify exactly how one is to use the Bible

---

1. It should be acknowledged that it is not always easy to judge what counts, say, as an incidental, nonauthoritative background cultural practice and what counts as a binding practice for disciples in other cultural contexts. For one attempt to formulate criteria for distinguishing the authoritative from the nonauthoritative, see Webb 2001.

authoritatively to formulate doctrine. His *Proving Doctrine: The Uses of Scripture in Modern Theology* (1999) contains three relevant lessons: (1) the way Scripture functions authoritatively in theology is inseparable from a view of God, an inseparability that I call "first theology"; (2) one's first theology invariably involves an "imaginative construal," a decision to take the Bible *as* something or other based on our discernment of how God relates to the community of readers via Scripture; (3) all the theologians whom Kelsey examines construe the Bible singularly, as one type of thing only.[2] It is far from obvious, however, that the New Testament's diverse historical, narrative, ethical, and other statements can be subsumed under a single systematic construal.[3]

Paul Ricœur pursues first theology without theologians. His gambit involves sacrificing not a pawn, or a bishop, but the queen of the sciences. He wagers that he will come to a fuller understanding of the biblical text by attending to the ways in which its diverse literary forms (the "originary language of faith") reconfigure existence, and by excluding systematic theologians from the conversation. Ricœur prefers to have the exegete as his dialogue partner because systematic theologians, in their haste to arrive at the clarity and closedness of concepts, run roughshod over the *textuality* of faith's expression.[4]

While no systematic theologian to date has taken up Ricœur's suggestion that understanding Scripture's subject matter requires attention to the diverse literary forms in which it is presented, this is precisely one of the purposes of the present chapter: to appropriate certain Ricœurian insights for the sake of my own imaginative construal of Scripture as *discourse*.[5]

My own exegetical dialogue partner, C. H. Dodd, in his *The Apostolic Preaching and Its Developments* (1936), discovered in the recorded sermons of Acts a core *kerygma* that appears in Paul's letters and undergirds Mark's Gospel like a theme with variations. In contrast to Bultmann, who stressed the event of preaching, Dodd focused on the content: "a proclamation of the facts of the death and resurrection of Christ in an eschatological setting

---

2. For example, Warfield construes the Bible as doctrine and thus views its authority in terms of the propositions conveyed, whereas Bultmann construes the Bible as myth and authority in terms of the self-understanding of human existence expressed therein.

3. This question leads to another: "Which discipline, New Testament studies or systematic theology, is in the best position to construe Scripture theologically and thus to reap a harvest of textual meaning by separating the theological wheat from the cultural and historical chaff?" The answer of the present chapter is "Both, if they can work together."

4. See Ricœur 1974: 482.

5. Ricœur's own answer to our guiding question would be "the biblical imagination" (see his essay "The Bible and the Imagination" [Ricœur 1995: 144–66]). His hermeneutical philosophy correlates the world projected by the biblical text with the perennial questions of human existence.

which gives significance to the facts."[6] In short, Dodd construes Scripture as *kerygma*.[7]

A Thesis (and Some Correctives)

The Definition of Discourse

Dodd probably exaggerates the distinction between the church's preaching (*kerygma*) and teaching (*didachē*). Such a distinction owes less to differences in the substance of the message than to the diverse settings of the communicators.[8] Furthermore, the form critic in Dodd is overly concerned with reconstructing the shape of the earliest *kerygma* rather than exploring the *kerygma* that we have. I therefore propose the following modification of Dodd's title and to let it also serve as my answer to our guiding question: not *kerygma* but *discourse*—"something someone says to someone about something in some way."[9] What New Testament studies should study, and what is also authoritative for theology, is nothing less than the apostolic discourse and its development.

The Variety of Discourse

An immediate benefit of this proposal appears in contrast to that of Kelsey, for whom one's imaginative construal involves the decision to read all of the Bible as a single kind of speech or literary genre. "Discourse" admits of many varieties and saves us from having to construe the Bible narrowly in terms of one thing only.[10]

A brief statement of my own first theology is now perhaps in order. Once upon a time, if asked what in the New Testament was authoritative, I would have replied, "Revelation." (On this point, Thomists, evangelicals, and Barthians all agree, though they parse "revelation" differently.) Theology's task,

6. Dodd 1936a: 18.

7. What I find helpful in Dodd is his deep commitment to treating the New Testament as history, literature, and theology; his conviction that the beginning of Christian theology is in the New Testament's use of the Old Testament; his passion for discerning patterns of ideas and actions alike (cf. Rom. 6:17: "But thanks be to God, that you . . . have become obedient from the heart to the standard of teaching [*typon didachēs*] to which you were committed"). See Markus Bockmuehl's related "discussion" with Dodd in Bockmuehl 2006: 27–74. Bockmuehl is particularly struck by Dodd's silence with regard to the role of the reader in New Testament interpretation.

8. So McDonald 1980: 5.

9. See Ricœur 1976: 30.

10. Kelsey himself thinks that what makes the Bible Christian Scripture derives not from what it says but rather from what it does; he thinks of biblical authority in functional terms, as a matter of "shaping Christian identity." Viewing the New Testament texts as discourse exposes Kelsey's crucial shortcoming here too: because discourse pertains to what a person *does* with words, there is no need to contrast God saying with God doing.

I thought, was the extraction of propositional revelation or truth content from Scripture and its consequent organization into a consistent conceptual system. Two pictures—one of Scripture as revelation and one of theology as a two-stage process, from descriptive exegesis ("what it meant") to normative dogmatics ("what it means")—held me captive.[11]

There is a more compelling picture. Exegesis and theology are not in a relay race but rather in a dance: an exegetical-theological two-step in which the interpreter, like the nimble Mr. Fezziwig, advances and retires, holds hands with his partner, then "cuts so deftly" that he appears to wink with his legs, making it impossible to say which partner is leading, biblical studies or systematics.[12]

The Drama of Discourse

Scripture is not simply a propositional shaft to be exegetically mined and theologically refined like so much textual dross to be purified into systems of philosophy or morality. On the contrary, both the form and content of the New Testament are elements in the divine drama of revelation and redemption (i.e., focusing on the triune missions of Word and Spirit, what God says and does on the stage of redemptive history). It follows that theological interpretation of the New Testament must attend to yet another kind of context alongside the grammatical-historical, literary, and canonical: the theodramatic.

Theology facilitates the church's participation in the ongoing evangelical action by helping us to understand the New Testament as the church's authoritative script that, as covenant document, both records what God has said or done and solicits our fitting response.[13] Doctrine, as direction for fitting participation in the already-finished-yet-ongoing drama of redemption whose center and climax is Jesus Christ, is both theology's product and a part of the interpretative process. And what norms doctrine is precisely the apostolic discourse and its developments.

The present chapter pursues two primary goals and advances two theses.

The first goal: Clarify the concept of apostolic discourse, especially with regard to the woefully neglected aspect of its manifold forms ("in some way"). The corresponding thesis: Attending to these literary forms is conducive to theodramatic understanding. "The very form of the text shapes responses in us that make it hard to become a mere spectator or a mere moralist."[14]

The second goal: Negotiate a settlement between authorial discourse-oriented and canon-oriented theological interpreters of Scripture. The corresponding thesis: Attending to the forms, small and large, of apostolic discourse is the

11. For a fuller description and a critique of this hermeneutical two-step, see Gilbertson 2003: 21–31.

12. From Charles Dickens, A Christmas Carol, Stave II.

13. See Vanhoozer 2005b.

14. Peterson 2005: 182.

best way to make the authorial discourse lion lie down with the canonical lamb and thus to realize the promise of a combined linguistic-canonical (or, canonical-linguistic) approach.[15]

And so to an extended exegesis of my definition of discourse: "something someone says to someone about something in some way."

The Elements of Discourse

"Something": The Sense of Discourse

It is appropriate that we begin with the "what," or sense, of discourse (*something* someone says), for propositional content has preoccupied Western theology for much of its history, and most interpretative disagreements are over *what* texts are actually saying—their verbal-textual meaning.

To construe texts as discourse is to claim that they have determinate meaning: saying *something* is markedly different from saying *anything, everything,* or *nothing.* Modern New Testament scholars hold that we cannot determine the content of the text, or the meaning of its configuration, without first establishing its context. To establish the "what" of discourse we therefore need also to ask, "Where?" "When?" and perhaps "Why?" Such questions tend to relocate decisions about the sense of the text to the world *behind* the text. Discourse does indeed involve such contextual matters, but the central, and more encompassing question, is "Who?" Who is actualizing the potential meaning of words and using them to say something to someone?

"Someone": The Subject of Discourse

The point in highlighting apostolic discourse is neither to demean the role of the reading community nor to lessen the significance of the canon but rather to situate them theologically.[16] The recent dispute between discourse-oriented and canon-oriented approaches to the theological interpretation of Scripture is much to be regretted.[17] There is little to be gained in pitting an author-centered hermeneutic against a text-centered one[18] or in forcing the vague notion of "canonical intentionality" to do authorial work. Interpreters have no recourse

15. I also have two secondary goals: (1) aid and abet theological interpretation of Scripture by nurturing the emerging discussion between systematic theology and New Testament studies; (2) respond to my critics (and to confine these occasional skirmishes to the footnotes).

16. When readers impose their own sense on the New Testament texts, they do to the apostles what Feuerbach says theologians do to God: project their own ideas. This way interpretative idolatry lies.

17. The criticism flows in both directions. Carl Henry (1990) attacks Brevard Childs for having a weak notion of inspired authorship, and Brevard Childs (2005) attacks Nicholas Wolterstorff for imposing "an imaginative philosophical construct" (see especially p. 385).

18. Chapman 2006: 186.

but to imagine what a string of words would mean were they uttered in such and such a context by such and such a person. The question "Which sense?" thus shades into another: "Whose intentionality?"[19]

Apostolic Discourse

In response to this last question, we do well to recall Kierkegaard's essay "On the Difference between a Genius and an Apostle" (1847). The genius speaks of what she is the first to know thanks to her greater powers of ratiocination. By contrast, the apostle speaks either because he has seen or because he has been told. Equally important is the element of commissioning. An apostle is one sent out with a message, one "set apart for the gospel" (Rom. 1:1–2) by having seen and been commissioned by the risen Lord (Acts 9:15; 22:21; 26:16; 1 Cor. 15:7–8).[20] Intrinsic in the notion of "apostolic," then, is the "who" of discourse. And because testimony is a speech-act that "asks to be trusted,"[21] *who* is testifying makes all the difference.

The actual authors of the New Testament may not have been eyewitnesses themselves, yet Richard Bauckham contends that the Gospel texts "are much closer to the form in which the eyewitnesses told their stories or passed on their traditions than is commonly envisaged in current scholarship."[22] He also notes that in the ancient world, "the historian himself should have been a participant in the events he narrates."[23] From a somewhat different vantage point, Francis Watson depicts the evangelists as actors whose authorial speech was a kind of reading (of the Old Testament and, in the case of Matthew and Luke, of Mark) that improved or "improvised" on what proceeded.[24] In

19. I agree with Stephen Chapman that "a canonical account of inspiration keeps the theological interpretation of Scripture focused where it should be—on the text" (Chapman 2006: 200), with the proviso that we need to construe the text as apostolic (and ultimately divine) discourse. Chapman (2006: 186) appeals to Sandra Schneiders's account of the "ideal meaning" produced by the interaction between (1) what the text says about something, (2) the genre in which it is said, and (3) the personal style of the author. This account ascribes communicative agency to an impersonal text; authors here have only stylistic, not substantial, significance. Chapman believes that the concept of authorial discourse cannot by itself do justice to the process of canon formation. Everything depends on what we mean by "author," however. For my own part, I understand the author to be the person or persons responsible for the final form of the text and hence its concomitant illocutions (e.g., meaning), and I understand inspiration to ascribe authorship to God as well as to the apostles, his proximate human agents.

20. Jesus was the first "apostle": God the Father sent Jesus, who was the Word, *as* his message (Mark 9:37; cf. Heb 3:1); Jesus in turn sends out his apostles with the message to spread the word (Mark 3:14; cf. 1 Thess. 2:6). See Barnett 1993.

21. Bauckham 2006: 5. See p. 475, where Bauckham cites Coady's landmark philosophical study of testimony: "When we believe testimony we believe what is said because we trust the witness" (Coady 1992: 46).

22. Bauckham 2006: 6.

23. Bauckham 2006: 9.

24. Watson 2006: 121.

various ways, then, we may say that the apostles participate in the economy of triune communicative action. Accordingly, I have a slight revision to our definition: apostolic discourse concerns "something someone says in some way to someone about something *that one saw for oneself or was told by someone else* (not least, the Holy Spirit)."

DIVINE DISCOURSE

In churches the world over ministers conclude the weekly reading of the apostolic discourse by saying, "The word of the Lord." The congregation responds, "Thanks be to God." These theologically laden utterances call for deeper reflection than we have space for here. Suffice it to say that the church has taken the apostolic discourse as authoritative precisely because it communicates the word of God.

Scripture repeatedly depicts God as speaking, and the creeds confess that the Spirit of God *locutus est per prophetas*.[25] It is precisely this emphasis on discourse that saves an author-oriented approach from the sting of Barth's criticism that the traditional view freezes the Word of God in a text, thereby caging the "bird in flight" in the prison house of language. Discourse is realized in the event of speaking and hearing/reading, and God is Lord of both events. The external testimony of the apostles is fixed; the internal testimony of the Spirit is free. In brief: we can affirm the Bible as God's speech in a way that preserves God's sovereign freedom (i.e., the authorial activity of God as speaking subject), precisely by doing justice to the notion of texts as written discourse as opposed to texts as simply containers of propositional revelation.

Brevard Childs worries that Nicholas Wolterstorff's call for a "second hermeneutic," one that reads for the divine discourse, implies that God is committing new illocutionary acts with old verbal wineskins, thus ignoring or violating

---

25. The operative term is "inspiration" (*theopneustos* [2 Tim. 3:16]). Although some attempt to reduce the notion of God's speaking to divine dictation, it would be a mistake to equate divine discourse with that caricature. The human authors were not simply passive scribes; on the contrary, they actively did things with words, performing various illocutionary acts. Stephen Chapman notes that the concept of inspiration arose in the early church to account for the unity of the two Testaments, not to say "that God was somehow responsible for the literary authorship of the Bible" (Chapman 2006: 185). But how, one wonders, does invoking the language of divine inspiration make the case for the unity of the Old and New Testaments except by implying that God really was their ultimate author? The church fathers had no compunction in using phrases such as "the Holy Spirit saith" or in referring to *ta logia* of God. Irenaeus states that the "Scriptures are perfect, inasmuch as they were uttered by the Word of God and His Spirit" (*Against Heresies* 2.28.2). For a comprehensive listing and discussion of the relevant patristic evidence, see Westcott 1895: 417–56. Perhaps one reason for the lack of early creedal statements regarding divine authorship was that there was no need: their divine origin was everywhere assumed. J. N. D. Kelly comments, "It goes without saying that the fathers envisaged the whole of the Bible as inspired" (Kelly 1978: 61; see Kelly's broader discussion of the meaning of inspiration on pp. 61–64).

the human meaning.[26] The remedy is to view divine authorship in theodramatic terms. It is the Holy Spirit who inspires—prompts and directs—the apostolic discourse in all its diversity. God speaks through apostolic discourse as a playwright speaks through the various characters in a play, all of whose voices, in their particular registers, are needed to achieve the total communicative effect. If God says more than do the human authors, this best comes to light in view of the whole canonical script, at which point the meaning and christological focus of the theodrama is best seen and most fully appreciated. Instead of a "second hermeneutic," then, there is only a single hermeneutic with multiple levels of description including, at the most encompassing level, the theodramatic context that brings to light what we may call the *plain canonical* meaning.

DOMINICAL DISCOURSE

The apostolic discourse is testimony commissioned by the risen Christ.[27] The divine discourse is the *dominical* discourse. Scripture is the visible/audible representation of the lordship of Jesus Christ, a vital ingredient in his communicative self-presentation. We see this in the Lukan writings, where the career of Jesus in Luke is mirrored, and continued, by the career of the "word" (*logos*) in Acts.[28] The Spirit who accompanies and ministers the word of God is also the Spirit of Christ (John 16:13, 14; 1 Pet. 1:11; cf. Rev. 19:10). The apostolic discourse is ultimately a function of the Son's prophetic office.[29]

"Says": The Predicate of Discourse

To the extent that apostolic discourse is under the lordship of Christ, we may go even further and suggest that it includes Christ's kingly and priestly offices as well, for the word of the Lord not only informs but also rules and mediates. To repeat: *saying* something must not be reduced to *stating* something. On the contrary, *saying* is a form of *doing*, and many things may be done with words. The "predicate" of discourse thus refers to the various things that authors do as communicative agents: illocutionary acts.[30] The apostolic discourse involves more, but not less, than propositional proclamation. Authors can say/do more than one thing at a time: one can bear witness to the

---

26. "By performing an illocutionary act with the noematic content of the human discourse, God can say something entirely different" (Childs 2005: 387).

27. So Webster 2007.

28. "The parallels between the portrayal of Jesus in Luke and the word in Acts affirm the narrative unity of the two works" (Pao 2002: 253).

29. Cf. Karl Barth's depiction of Jesus as the active agent in our knowledge of him: "For in this [biblical] attestation He Himself lives. . . . He Himself lives only in the form which He has in the picture. . . . It is the picture which He Himself has created and impressed upon His witnesses" (CD IV/3).

30. For more on the illocutionary dimension of discourse, see Vanhoozer 2002: 172–77.

Christ and narrate a story and allude to the Old Testament and encourage someone, all in a single discourse.

"To Someone": The Indirect Object of Discourse

The event of discourse is in one sense incomplete until it achieves what Ricœur refers to as its interlocutionary or "allocutionary" act—its address *to someone*.[31] Here too the essentially dialogical and dramatic nature of discourse comes to the fore. Every discourse is an initiative in language that expects some kind of answering response: "To assert something is to expect agreement, just as to give an order is to expect obedience."[32]

New Testament scholars understand the importance of establishing the identity, and ethnicity, of the original addressees. Yet Scripture was intended for future generations as well. The apostle Paul says that the things that happened to Israel in the wilderness "were written down for our instruction" (1 Cor. 10:11). To whom, exactly, does "our" refer? We have seen the reader, and he is *us*! The contemporary church is in the same situation, eschatologically speaking, as the primitive church: between the times, between the first and second advents of Christ.

Markus Bockmuehl thus rightly calls for New Testament studies to focus on the implied or ideal reader, the reader envisaged by the discourse itself, for the ideal reader is a disciple, one "drawn into an act of reading that involves an active part on stage."[33] This aspect of discourse brings a new figure into the spotlight of theological interpretation of Scripture: the *implied canonical reader*. The person or community to whom the apostolic discourse is ultimately addressed is one who is able to see Christ in the Old Testament and the church as the new Israel, thus able faithfully to enact the script.

"About Something": The Referent of Discourse

The referent of apostolic discourse is not simply the world "behind" the New Testament text but also the world "of" and "in front of" it: what God is doing in Christ through the Spirit (cf. 2 Cor. 5:19) to restore Israel and to renew creation.

In a word: the apostolic discourse is about the gospel. This gospel centers on Jesus Christ, though Paul can also identify himself as an apostle "set apart for the gospel of God" (Rom. 1:1).[34] This is the same gospel that is "the power

---

31. Ricœur 1976: 14.
32. Ricœur 1976: 15.
33. Bockmuehl 2006: 72.
34. The Pauline letters contain seven references to "gospel of God" and ten to "gospel of Christ." I take these phrases as objective genitives, indicating the content of the gospel. However, I am not averse to taking them as subjective genitives, in which case the emphasis falls on divine authorship.

of God" (Rom. 1:16), the same gospel in which is revealed "the righteousness of God" (Rom. 1:17). The revelation of God's righteousness is accomplished not in a statement but rather in an eschatologically freighted theodrama in which God has to demonstrate that he can remain godly while establishing right relations with the ungodly (Rom. 3:21–26). To the extent that apostolic discourse is about "righteousness of God," then, it is not simply theological discourse, but *theodicean* discourse.[35]

"In Some Way": The Form of Discourse

Each of my three dialogue partners has, in his own way, prompted me to focus on this single neglected aspect of discourse.[36] Kelsey, for example, proposes that ultimately it is the patterns (not the content) in Scripture that make it normative for theology, but he fails adequately to relate these patterns to the forms of apostolic discourse.[37] Instead, he argues that the decision imaginatively to construe the Bible as having a certain kind of pattern is determined not by exegesis but rather by something "pre-textual." He thus overlooks the embedded patterns in Scripture intrinsic to its forms of discourse and literary genres.

Indeed, as far as I know, no systematic theologian has focused on the significance of Scripture's diverse literary forms to the extent that exegetes and hermeneutic philosophers have, and this in spite of, for example, official Vatican pronouncements since *Divino Afflante Spiritu* about the importance of the Bible's literary genres. What we do see is theologians reading *all* of Scripture as if it were only one kind of genre, so that everything becomes apocalyptic (Pannenberg), or wisdom (Bultmann), or narrative (Barth), or doctrine (Hodge): "entire theological constructs have gravitated toward certain genres as their linchpin."[38]

POETIC ANALYSIS

To take the apostolic discourse as normative for theology, one must do more than read it as direct communication—that is, as a straightforward teaching of revealed truths. Theologians must do more (but not less!) than "narrow" analysis that simply distills clear propositions from texts in order to assess their cogency. This kind of analysis—"the dissection of sentence structures and investigation of language as the best means of investigating concepts"[39]—yields

---

35. I will return to the theme of "theodicy" in the conclusion.
36. Dodd 1936b: 37. Ricœur has practiced what Dodd preached, producing several seminal studies on the cognitive significance of the Bible's literary forms for understanding revelation, time, and the name of God. See, for example, his essays "Biblical Time" and "Naming God" (Ricœur 1995: 167–80; 217–35).
37. Kelsey 1999: 192–97.
38. Martens 2005: 97n51.
39. Harris and Insole 2005: 2–3.

only thin textual descriptions that overlook the cognitive significance of larger forms of discourse, such as literary genres. The conceptual tools of the Anglo-American analytic trade seem better suited to sentence-long discourse than to larger discursive forms. In this connection, we may note Ben Ollenburger's criticism of Nicholas Wolterstorff: "Among my puzzlements in reading *Divine Discourse* is its almost exclusive attention to sentences."[40]

Wilbur Howell insists that Englishmen of the sixteenth and seventeenth centuries considered poetry "to be the third great form of communication, open and popular but not fully explained by rhetoric, concise and lean but not fully explained by logic," containing instead "both characteristics at once."[41] If "the defining principle of literature is that meaning is communicated through form,"[42] then New Testament scholars and systematic theologians would do well to meet on the fertile ground of poetics—"the systematic working or study of literature as such"[43]—and to cultivate literary-poetic as well as linguistic-analytic competence.

THE DRAMATICS OF BIBLICAL LITERATURE

As a fourteen-year-old, I read *Pride and Prejudice* but failed to understand it. I grasped the propositional content but missed Austen's voice; I caught the story but missed the satire. Something similar occurs when readers get the Bible's propositional content but fail to hear the voice of God. The New Testament is more than literature, but not less. Abraham Kuyper offered this answer to the question of why there are so many literary forms in the Bible: so that all the cords of the human soul, and not the intellect only, could be touched.[44]

Fully to attend to apostolic discourse calls for *dramatics*—the systematic working or study of drama as such, including its dialogical forms. Theodrama is, I submit, the "form of forms" in which other biblical speech and literary genres live and move and have their being. More to the theological point: the form of drama confronts the reader not only with words that describe divine communicative action but also with voices that are themselves ingredient in that action—voices that draw the reader into the action, eliciting various kinds of response.

How does imaginatively indwelling the discursive forms of the Bible help us discern the theologically normative from the culturally relative, core beliefs about

---

40. Ollenburger 2006: 50. Although speech-act philosophers themselves have not attended to literary forms, others have (against Stanley Porter, in Marshall, Vanhoozer, and Porter 2004: 117). There are now significant works that employ the concept of illocution, for example, to account for features of narrative and drama (e.g., Pratt 1977; Lanser 1981; et al.).

41. Howell 1961: 4.

42. Ryken 2005: 457.

43. So Sternberg 1985: 2.

44. Kuyper 1954: 520.

God from incidental remnants of obsolete worldviews? It does so by enabling us to keep our eye on the theodramatic action and on the task of moving it forward. The historical scenes and the cultural props may vary; not so what God is doing in Christ to form his church and renew creation. Each form of apostolic discourse contributes to the church's ability to understand and participate in this divine missionary work. Some situations call for a rehearsal of the gospel narrative to remind us who and where we are in the theodrama; others call for a good dose of apocalyptic, and still others a parabolic wise saying.

"And Its Developments": The Life of Discourse

CANONICAL DEVELOPMENTS

What is doctrinally normative in the New Testament is *canonical discourse*—that is, the apostolic discourse in canonical context, viewed as part of what is ultimately a unified work.[45] We may now pose the crucial question: "Whose work is it?" Canonical approaches to interpretation, to the extent that they require interpreters to read the text as a unified work, need to be underwritten by a premise either of divine authorship or of some collective communal intent. I have dealt with the phenomenon of intracanonical development elsewhere and have argued that the New Testament, and Jesus himself, works a singular kind of divine improvisation on the Old Testament.[46] Here I want to reflect further on the role of the risen Christ in incorporating the apostolic discourse into the canon.

David Pao argues that Luke bases his account of the Acts of the Apostles on the Isaianic "new exodus" motif, and that the "word of the Lord" is the main actor or central character in the book of Acts.[47] Where previous scholarship focused on the content of the apostolic discourse, Pao examines the "pattern" of the word's journey from Jerusalem to Rome. The journey is actually a conquest narrative: despite opposition, the word of the Lord "grew and multiplied" (Acts 12:24), advancing through Samaria to Corinth and Ephesus and beyond.[48]

There is nothing in Pao's account of the conquest narrative of the word of the Lord that pertains directly to the process of canonization. Nevertheless, Pao identifies the goal of the word's journey into the far country as "the construction of the community of the word."[49] It is significant that

45. "To authorize a sequence of words *as a work* is to declare that one wants one's readers to read it as a totality" (Wolterstorff 2004: 226).

46. See Vanhoozer 2005b: 388.

47. Pao 2002.

48. Pao employs the term *hypostatization* of the word to describe the way in which Luke speaks of it as having power and agency, noting that the word is "the main actor of the conquest" (Pao 2002: 155).

49. Pao 2002. As the Mosaic law and covenant formed a community, so the gospel too is a community-forming word.

Acts treats the two themes—the power of the word and the formation of the community—together. The word "conquers" only in the sense that, together with the Spirit, it convicts and persuades hearers/readers of its truth, thereby forming a community of obedient interpreters. If the event of God's revelation in Jesus includes its own reception, and if the Spirit who is the Lord of the hearing (Barth) is also the Spirit of Jesus Christ, then may we not conclude that the prophetic activity of Jesus includes the reception of the apostolic testimony that he also commissioned? If so, may this not respond, at least in part, to what Childs names as the most fundamental flaw in authorial discourse interpretation: "the failure to understand the role of the church in collecting, shaping and interpreting the Bible, which is the issue of canon"?[50] The process of the church's gradual recognition of certain texts as apostolic, which from a historical perspective appears both tainted and arbitrary, makes good theological sense when viewed in christological perspective. The proper dogmatic location of the canon may well be the prophetic office of Jesus Christ: "You have heard that it was said. . . . But I say to you . . ." (Matt. 5:21–44).

POSTCANONICAL DEVELOPMENTS

New Testament scholars and systematic theologians do well to attend to the history of reception of the apostolic discourse, but one should not be too quick to equate "effective history" with faithful continuation or with truth. The history of the New Testament's so-called effects include beatific as well as horrific visions—slavery, the Inquisition, and the Holocaust, to name but a few. The *drama* of doctrine stems from the church's having to make decisions about what to say and do in new situations that correspond to what is said and done in the apostolic discourse—hence the importance of learning good canonical judgment. But how?

Robert Gundry, noting the diversity in the New Testament, even in regard to the way the various evangelists identify Jesus as the Christ, asks whether their canonization means that they should be synthesized or allowed to stand next to, or even in tension with, one another.[51] Does the canon call for and enable a systematizing view of Jesus, or does it delimit a space within which a thousand (well, at least four or five) Christologies may bloom? Does the canonical form itself privilege the work of the theologian or of the exegete? For his part, Gundry calls attention to the occasional nature of the documents and opts for preserving the canon's biblio-diversity.[52]

50. Childs 2005: 380.
51. Gundry 2005.
52. Diversity of apostolic discourse is a pastoral strength: "For postcanonical churches find themselves in circumstances similar to those for which biblical books were variously tailored, and tailored not for the sake of suprahistorical comprehensiveness (producing a unifiedly systematic theology) but for the sake of intrahistorical pertinence" (Gundry 2005: 17).

Gundry's points are both sobering and salutary to aspiring systematic theologians. He is right to remind us of the occasional and diverse nature of the texts, and to delimit hermeneutical freedom by textual fidelity. Indeed, his comments are entirely in keeping with the recent emphasis on theology as a form of *sapientia* that takes particular situations into account.[53] What matters most for this approach are not the particular words or concepts that the apostles employed but rather their patterns of judgment.

Jesus himself exercises a special kind of patterned judgment when he understands himself to be the fulfillment of the Scriptures (Luke 24:27). Typological interpretation is ultimately a form of theodramatic judgment whereby one understands oneself and one's church community as caught up in the same basic action (though in a new scene) as the primitive church.

How may we learn to form judgments that display creative apostolic understanding? The short answer: by becoming members of the "society" of biblical literature. We acquire habits of apostolic judgment when we imaginatively indwell the diverse literary forms of the New Testament, letting them serve as interpretative frameworks, as modes of cognition and experience.[54] It is within the canonical galaxy of the various worlds of the biblical texts that "we learn to think accurately, behave morally, preach passionately, sing joyfully, pray honestly, obey faithfully."[55]

Crosswords, Theological Discourse, and the Christospective Conscience of the Canonical Text

The challenge of theological interpretation of Scripture is to render judgments concerning what is "meet and right"[56] to say and do as disciples of Jesus Christ in light of the apostolic discourse.

"MEET": FITTINGNESS

Something is meet if it is fitting or befits. The apostolic discourse that gives voice to the theodramatic action is the Christian's ultimate criterion for discerning the true, the good, and the beautiful. These are all functions of fittingness, and what is fitting is ultimately a matter of what befits the gospel: the theodramatic form of Jesus Christ.[57]

---

53. See Treier 2006.

54. Or, to use Michael Polanyi's terminology: the "focal" point is Christ, but the canonical forms are enabling "tacit" perspectives.

55. Peterson 2005: 182.

56. Phrase taken from the 1662 *Book of Common Prayer*. Compare the corresponding phrase in the Latin Mass: *Dignum et justum est* ("It is right and fitting").

57. What we say and do must also befit the particular situation. The New Testament remains the norm, but the contemporary context affects how one stages or performs the apostolic script (see Vanhoozer 2005b: 325).

The apostolic discourse opens up a window onto what we could call "the strange new ontology" of the Bible: an account not of being-in-general but of being-in-Christ (2 Cor. 5:17). What is normative for Christian doctrine is not some scientifically outmoded·worldview, but the strange newworld view of the Bible, rendered in and through a variety of word views (i.e., literary genres). Historical narrative is fine for describing the past, but we need apocalyptic to depict the end of history. Scientific discourse is fine (though not exhaustive) for explaining the causal regularities observed in nature, but we need wisdom discourse if we are to discern a deeper dimension, the created order, underneath the surface phenomena. The various forms of apostolic discourse provide "training in Christianity" (Kierkegaard) by discipling and directing our imaginations to discern diverse theodramatic patterns, all of which ultimately originate and end "in Christ."

"RIGHT": RIGHTEOUSNESS

The New Testament is not only profitable but also authoritative for training in rightness: for speaking, thinking, and acting fittingly with regard to the truth, goodness, and beauty made known in Jesus Christ.[58] Theological interpretation of the Bible involves right (i.e., developed apostolic) judgments about rightness and, ultimately, the righteousness of God. "For in these last days he has spoken to us by a Son" (Heb. 1:2), the one whose life and work is the very substance of theodrama, the one who embodies God's right-doing. God's right-doing is the heart of the gospel, the revelation of God's righteousness (Rom. 1:17) that climaxes in God's justifying the ungodly by means of Christ's cross.[59] God's right-doing also features prominently in what is perhaps the most controversial issue in the philosophy of religion, the problem of evil, inasmuch as it forces us to choose between God's power and his goodness/righteousness.

Does the apostolic discourse of the cross "answer" the problem of evil? The prior question, of course, is whether one ought to be seeking such answers, or even whether evil constitutes a "problem" that admits of a solution. According to Terrence Tilley, "theodicy" is not an apostolic form of discourse but rather a modern one that warps the way biblical texts are read.[60] A theodicy is a monological, theoretical discourse that does not solve but instead inadvertently contributes further to the problem of evil by failing to deal with real evils. Its key declarative assertion—"the World is as well as it could be

---

58. To say that something—an assertion, a friend, love, a square—is "true" is to say that it measures up "in being or excellence, to whatever way is operative in the context" (Wolterstorff 2006: 42). Something similar holds, I believe, for goodness and beauty. We may thus define the "right" as what is in keeping with something's metaphysical, ethical, or aesthetic purpose.

59. I take the phrase "righteousness of God" as indicating in the first instance God's own being and action, especially as these pertain to his upholding his covenant relationship with Israel.

60. Tilley 2000: 1.

made by infinite *Power* and *Goodness*"[61]—cannot be sustained in the face of ongoing sin, suffering, and evil. Theodicies cross the fine line between uttering true propositions ("You will get your reward in heaven") and administering verbal opiates.[62]

Tilley's study is essentially a plea to recognize the need for a variety of speech-acts and forms of discourse, not just assertives, to deal with evil. But this is precisely what we find in the New Testament: in contrast to the standard discourse of analytic philosophy of religion, the apostolic theodicean discourse not only declares but also warns, exhorts, consoles. And, as concerns evil, a little apocalyptic discourse goes a long way. The point is that God's right-doing revealed in Jesus' death on the cross requires several forms of discourse in order fully to articulate it.[63] It is just these forms of cognition and experience that ought to form, inform, and transform theological judgment. When they do, we get not an "answer" to the problem of evil but rather a way of perceiving (and responding to) evil: as temporary, as defeated, yet nevertheless as something we ought to oppose. We also get a precious insight into suffering from the perspective not only of eternity but also of the theodrama (Rom. 8:18).

What Eugene Peterson says about Leviticus applies equally to apostolic discourse: "Leviticus is an extended schooling for training our imaginations to grasp that virtually everything that we do has to do with God but requires God's action to make it (us) fit for God."[64] Everything depends on using the New Testament to train right theological judgment, especially about the rightness of God revealed in the gospel.

Conclusion: Toward Theological Understanding

The apostolic discourse, received in faith, is normative for theological understanding. But what is understanding? It has to do with grasping the whole, and our place in it, and it requires not only reason but also imagination—not that idolatrous projection of man-made images but rather that synthetic power which discerns and discovers patterns that are truly there, in history and in the text. Steven Millhauser's novel *Martin Dressler: The Tale of an American Dreamer* depicts such understanding when the main character, after exploring a hotel from top to bottom and interrogating everyone from bookkeepers to chambermaids, grasps how its various parts fit together: "The details interested him . . . but they had no meaning until they were connected to the larger design.

---

61. Cited in Tilley 2000: 85.

62. Tilley 2000: 4.

63. As with metaphors that describe the saving significance of Jesus' death, these larger forms of discourse are ultimately irreducible to theoretical discourse, even though it is often expedient to provide monological distillations: "We believe. . . ."

64. Peterson 2005: 204.

Then he grasped them, then he held them in place and felt a deep and almost physical satisfaction—and . . . realized . . . that the [hotel] itself was part of a block of buildings, and all the blocks went repeating themselves, rectangle by rectangle, in every direction, until they formed a city."[65]

The project of theological interpretation of Scripture has nothing to do with hotels, of course. It does, however, have to do with the Father's house, in which there are many rooms (John 14:2). It takes imagination to grasp that edifice too. In exercising authority over and training our imaginations, the apostolic discourse helps us both to understand and to fit into the holy structure of which Jesus Christ is the cornerstone (Eph. 2:20–22). Indeed, in the mouths of its ministers and in the power of the Spirit, the apostolic discourse (and its theological interpretation) is, to use Kierkegaard's phrase, "upbuilding" discourse—the indispensable and chief means of the church's edification.[66]

---

65. Millhauser 1997: 58.

66. In saying this, I take nothing away from the role of baptism and the Eucharist. These two dominical ordinances are also forms of communicative action that require the apostolic discourse in order to be intelligible. See Vanhoozer 2005b: 407–13.

Contributors

Markus Bockmuehl is a Fellow of Keble College and professor of biblical and early Christian studies at the University of Oxford, having previously taught at the Universities of Cambridge and St. Andrews. Among his books are *The Epistle to the Philippians* (Hendrickson, 1998); *Jewish Law in Gentile Churches: Halakhah and the Beginning of Christian Public Ethics* (Baker Academic, 2003); and *Seeing the Word: Refocusing New Testament Study* (Baker Academic, 2006).

James Carleton Paget is senior lecturer in New Testament studies at the University of Cambridge and Fellow and tutor of Peterhouse. His publications include *The Epistle of Barnabas: Outlook and Background* (Mohr Siebeck, 1994) and a number of articles on subjects related to early Christianity and its origins.

R. W. L. Moberly is professor of theology and biblical interpretation at Durham University. His publications include *The Old Testament of the Old Testament* (Fortress, 1992; reprint, Wipf & Stock, 2001); *The Bible, Theology, and Faith: A Study of Abraham and Jesus* (Cambridge University Press, 2000); and *Prophecy and Discernment* (Cambridge University Press, 2006).

Jan Muis is professor of systematic theology and biblical theology at the Protestant Theological University in Utrecht. He is the author of *Openbaring en Interpretatie* (Boekencentrum, 1989), on Barth's and Miskotte's understanding of Holy Scripture; *Credo in Creatorem*, on Christian thought about God as creator (Utrecht Faculteit der Godgeleerdheid, 1998); and a number of articles on the doctrine of God and on theological epistemology.

Oliver O'Donovan, FBA, an Anglican priest, was Regius Professor of Moral and Pastoral Theology and canon of Christ Church at the University of Oxford from 1982 to 2006, and since then he has been professor of Christian ethics and practical theology at the University of Edinburgh. His writings include *Resurrection and Moral Order: An Outline for Evangelical Ethics* (Apollos, 1986; 2nd ed., 1992); *The Desire of the Nations: An Outline for Political Theology* (Cambridge University Press, 1996); *The Just War Revisited* (Cambridge University Press, 1996); *The Ways of Judgment* (Eerdmans, 2005); and *From Irenaeus to Grotius: A Sourcebook in Christian Political Thought* (Eerdmans, 1999), co-edited with his wife, Joan Lockwood O'Donovan.

Alan J. Torrance is professor of systematic theology at the University of St. Andrews. Previously, he taught at Kings College London and at the Universities of Otago, Aberdeen, and Erlangen. Among his publications are *Persons in Communion* (T&T Clark, 1996), several edited and coedited volumes (including most recently *The Doctrine of God and Theological Ethics*, T&T Clark, 2006), and a number of articles on Christian dogmatics and philosophical theology.

Kevin J. Vanhoozer is research professor of systematic theology at Trinity Evangelical Divinity School. Previously he taught for eight years at the University of Edinburgh. He is the author of *Biblical Narrative in the Philosophy of Paul Ricœur: A Study in Hermeneutics and Theology* (Cambridge University Press, 1990); *Is There a Meaning in This Text? The Bible, the Reader, and the Morality of Literary Knowledge* (Zondervan, 1998); and *The Drama of Doctrine: A Canonical-Linguistic Approach to Christian Theology* (Westminster/John Knox, 2005). He is also the editor of *The Cambridge Companion to Postmodern Theology* (Cambridge University Press, 2003); *Dictionary for Theological Interpretation of the Bible* (SPCK and Baker Academic, 2005); and a co-editor of *Everyday Theology: How to Read Cultural Texts and Influence Trends* (Baker Academic, 2007).

Benedict Thomas Viviano, OP, is professor of New Testament at the University of Fribourg in Switzerland. He is the author of "Matthew," in *New Jerome Biblical Commentary* (Prentice-Hall, 1990); *The Kingdom of God in History* (Wipf & Stock, 1998); *Trinity-Kingdom-Church: Essays in Biblical Theology* (Fribourg Academic Press and Vandenhoeck & Ruprecht, 2001); and *Matthew and His World: The Gospel of the Open Jewish Christians* (Fribourg Academic Press and Vandenhoeck & Ruprecht, 2007). He also is a contributor to *Judaïsme, anti-judaïsme, et christianisme* (Saint-Augustin, 2000) and *Marie Madeleine: Appropriations contemporaines* (Sainte Baume, 2007) and is co-editor of *Le dialogue interreligieux* (Fribourg Academic Press, 2007).

J. Ross Wagner is associate professor of New Testament at Princeton Theological Seminary. He is the author of *Heralds of the Good News: Paul and Isaiah in Concert in the Letter to the Romans* (Brill, 2002) and of a number of articles on topics pertaining to the New Testament and to the Septuagint.

Bernd Wannenwetsch is university lecturer in ethics at the University of Oxford and Fellow of Harris Manchester College. He formerly taught systematic theology and ethics at the Universities of Erlangen-Nuremberg and Mainz. His publications include *Die Freiheit der Ehe: Das Zusammenleben von Frau und Mann in der Wahrnehmung evangelischer Ethik* (Neukirchener Verlag, 1993); *Gottesdienst als Lebensform: Ethik für Christenbürger* (Kohlhammer, 1997), in English as *Political Worship: Ethics for Christian Citizens* (Oxford University Press, 2004).

John Webster is professor of systematic theology at the University of Aberdeen. His publications include several books on the theology of Barth and works in dogmatic theology such as *Word and Church: Essays in Church Dogmatics* (T&T Clark, 2001); *Holiness* (SCM Press, 2003); *Holy Scripture: A Dogmatic Sketch* (Cambridge University Press, 2003); and *Confessing God: Essays in Christian Dogmatics II* (T&T Clark, 2005).

N. T. Wright is Bishop of Durham (England). He taught New Testament studies for twenty years at the University of Cambridge, McGill University, and the University of Oxford. He has been visiting professor at the Hebrew University in Jerusalem, Harvard Divinity School, and the Gregorian University in Rome. He has published over forty books, including *The Climax of the Covenant* (T&T Clark, 1991), the multivolume *Christian Origins and the Question of God* (SPCK and Fortress, 1992–), and the "Everyone" commentaries on the New Testament (SPCK and Westminster/John Knox, 2001–).

Works Cited

Aejmelaeus, Anneli. 2006a. "Faith, Hope, and Interpretation: A Lexical and Semantic Study of the Semantic Field of Hope in the Greek Psalter." In *Studies in the Hebrew Bible, Qumran, and the Septuagint: Essays Presented to Eugene Ulrich on the Occasion of his Sixty-Fifth Birthday*, ed. P. W. Flint, E. Tov, and J. V. VanderKam, 360–76. Supplements to Vetus Testamentum 101. Leiden: Brill.

———. 2006b. "Von Sprache zur Theologie: Methodologische Überlegungen zur Theologie der Septuaginta." In *The Septuagint and Messianism*, ed. M. A. Knibb, 21–48. Bibliotheca Ephemeridum Theologicarum Lovaniensium 195. Leuven: Leuven University Press.

———. Forthcoming. "Levels of Interpretation: Tracing the Trail of the Septuagint Translators." *COLLeGIUM*. http://www.helsinki.fi/collegium/e-series/.

ARCIC (Anglican/Roman Catholic International Commission). 1998. *The Gift of Authority: Authority in the Church III*. http://www.ewtn.com/library/Theology/Arcicgf3.htm.

Ashton, John, ed. 1997. *The Interpretation of John*. Studies in New Testament Interpretation. 2nd ed. Edinburgh: T&T Clark.

Ayres, Lewis. 2006. *Nicaea and Its Legacy: An Approach to Fourth-Century Trinitarian Theology*. Oxford: Oxford University Press.

Ayres, Lewis, and Stephen E. Fowl. 1999. "(Mis)Reading the Face of God: The Interpretation of the Bible in the Church." *Theological Studies* 60: 513–28.

Bächli, Otto. 1987. *Das Alte Testament in der Kirchlichen Dogmatik von Karl Barth*. Neukirchen-Vluyn: Neukirchener Verlag.

Baer, David A. 2001. *When We All Go Home: Translation and Theology in LXX Isaiah 56–66.* Journal for the Study of the Old Testament: Supplement Series 318. Sheffield: Sheffield Academic Press.

Barnes, Michael. 2002. *Theology and the Dialogue of Religions.* Cambridge Studies in Christian Doctrine. Cambridge: Cambridge University Press.

Barnett, Paul W. 1993. "Apostle." In *Dictionary of Paul and His Letters*, ed. G. F. Hawthorne and R. P. Martin, 45–51. Downers Grove, IL: InterVarsity Press.

Barr, James. 1961. *The Semantics of Biblical Language.* Oxford: Oxford University Press.

———. 1999. *The Concept of Biblical Theology: An Old Testament Perspective.* Minneapolis: Fortress.

Barsam, Ara Paul. 2001. "Reverence for Life: Albert Schweitzer's Mystical Theology and Ethics." DPhil thesis, Oxford University.

———. 2007. *Reverence for Life: Albert Schweitzer's Great Contribution to Ethical Thought.* Oxford: Oxford University Press.

Barth, Karl. 1922. *Der Römerbrief.* 2nd ed. Munich: Kaiser.

———. 1933. *The Epistle to the Romans.* Trans. E. C. Hoskyns. London: Oxford University Press.

———. 1957. *Church Dogmatics.* Trans. G. W. Bromiley and T. F. Torrance. Vol. II/2. Edinburgh: T&T Clark.

———. 1974. *Karl Barth-Eduard Thurneysen Briefwechsel.* Vol. 2, *1921–1930.* Ed. E. Thurneysen. Gesamtausgabe 5. Zürich: Theologischer Verlag.

———. 1975a. *Anselm, Fides quaerens intellectum: Anselm's Proof of the Existence of God in the Context of His Theological Scheme.* Trans. I. W. Robertson. Pittsburgh Reprint Series 2. 2nd ed. Pittsburgh: Pickwick Press.

———. 1975b. *Church Dogmatics.* Trans. G. W. Bromiley. 2nd ed. Vol. I/1. Edinburgh: T&T Clark.

———. 1976a. *Das christliche Leben: Die kirchliche Dogmatik IV/4, Fragmente aus dem Nachlaß, Vorlesungen 1959–1961.* Ed. H. A. Drewes and E. Jüngel. Gesamtausgabe 2/7. Zürich: Theologischer Verlag.

———. 1976b. *Erklärung des Johannes-Evangeliums (Kapitel 1–8): Vorlesung Münster, Wintersemester 1925/1926, wiederholt in Bonn, Sommersemester 1933.* Ed. W. Fürst. Zürich: Theologischer Verlag.

———. 1991. *The Göttingen Dogmatics: Instruction in the Christian Religion.* Trans. G. W. Bromiley. Ed. H. Reiffen. Vol. 1. Grand Rapids: Eerdmans.

Barthélemy, Dominique. 1978. "L'Ancien Testament a mûri à Alexandrie." In *Études d'histoire du texte de l'Ancien Testament*, 127–39. Orbis Biblicus et Orientalis 21. Fribourg: Éditions Universitaires; Göttingen: Vandenhoeck & Ruprecht.

Bauckham, Richard. 1998a. "The Scrupulous Priest and the Good Samaritan: Jesus' Parabolic Interpretation of the Law of Moses." *New Testament Studies* 44: 475–89.

———, ed. 1998b. *The Gospels for All Christians: Rethinking the Gospel Audiences*. Grand Rapids: Eerdmans.

———. 2006. *Jesus and the Eyewitnesses: The Gospels as Eyewitness Testimony*. Grand Rapids: Eerdmans.

Bauer, W., et al. 1999. *Greek-English Lexicon of the New Testament and Other Early Christian Literature*. 3rd ed. Chicago: University of Chicago Press.

Beretta, Francesco. 1999. "De l'inerrance absolue à la vérité salvifique de l'Écriture." *Freiburger Zeitschrift für Philosophie und Theologie* 46: 461–501.

Berkhof, Hendrikus. 1990. *Christian Faith: An Introduction to the Study of the Faith*. Trans. S. Woudstra. Rev. ed. Grand Rapids: Eerdmans.

Bertram, G. 1961. "Septuaginta-Frömmigkeit." *Die Religion in Geschichte und Gegenwart* 5: 1707–9.

Bieringer, Raimund. 2006. "Annoncer la vie éternelle: L'interprétation de la Bible dans les textes officiels de l'Église catholique romaine." *Revue théologique de Louvain* 37: 489–512.

Bockmuehl, Markus. 2001. "Resurrection." In *The Cambridge Companion to Jesus*, ed. M. Bockmuehl, 102–18. Cambridge: Cambridge University Press.

———. 2003. *Jewish Law in Gentile Churches: Halakhah and the Beginning of Christian Public Ethics*. Grand Rapids: Baker Academic.

———. 2006. *Seeing the Word: Refocusing New Testament Study*. Studies in Theological Interpretation. Grand Rapids: Baker Academic.

Bockmuehl, Markus, and Michael B. Thompson, eds. 1997. *A Vision for the Church: Studies in Early Christian Ecclesiology in Honour of J. P. M. Sweet*. Edinburgh: T&T Clark.

Boyd-Taylor, Cameron. 2006. "In a Mirror Dimly—Reading the Septuagint as a Document of Its Times." In *Septuagint Research: Issues and Challenges in the Study of the Greek Jewish Scriptures*, ed. W. Kraus and R. G. Wooden, 15–31. Society of Biblical Literature Septuagint and Cognate Studies 53. Atlanta: Society of Biblical Literature.

Braaten, Carl E., and Robert W. Jenson, eds. 2003. *In One Body through the Cross: The Princeton Proposal for Christian Unity; A Call to the Churches From an Ecumenical Study Group*. Grand Rapids: Eerdmans.

Braybrooke, Marcus. 1990. *Time to Meet: Towards a Deeper Relationship between Jews and Christians*. London: SCM Press; Philadelphia: Trinity Press International.

Brown, Raymond E. 1963. "Unity and Diversity in New Testament Ecclesiology." *Novum Testamentum* 6: 298–308.

———. 1984. *The Churches the Apostles Left Behind.* New York: Paulist Press.

Bultmann, Rudolf. 1971. *The Gospel of John: A Commentary.* Trans. G. R. Beasley-Murray. Philadelphia: Westminster.

Chadwick, Henry. 1967. "Lessing, Gotthold Ephraim." In *Encyclopaedia of Philosophy*, ed. P. Edwards, vol. 4, 443–46. New York: Macmillan.

Chapman, Stephen B. 2006. "Reclaiming Inspiration for the Bible." In *Canon and Biblical Interpretation*, ed. C. G. Bartholomew et al., 167–206. The Scripture and Hermeneutics Series 7. Grand Rapids: Zondervan.

Childs, Brevard S. 1979. *Introduction to the Old Testament as Scripture.* Philadelphia: Fortress.

———. 1985. *The New Testament as Canon: An Introduction.* Philadelphia: Fortress.

———. 1992. *Biblical Theology of the Old and New Testaments: Theological Reflection on the Christian Bible.* Minneapolis: Fortress.

———. 2004. *The Struggle to Understand Isaiah as Christian Scripture.* Grand Rapids: Eerdmans.

———. 2005. "Speech-Act Theory and Biblical Interpretation." *Scottish Journal of Theology* 58: 375–92.

Claussen, Johann Hinrich. 1997. *Die Jesus-Deutung von Ernst Troeltsch im Kontext der liberalen Theologie.* Beiträge zur historischen Theologie 99. Tübingen: Mohr Siebeck.

Coady, C. A. J. 1992. *Testimony: A Philosophical Study.* Oxford: Clarendon Press; New York: Oxford University Press.

Congar, Yves. 1966. *Tradition and Traditions: An Historical and a Theological Essay.* Trans. M. Naseby and T. Rainborough. London: Burns & Oates.

Cullmann, Oscar. 1956. "The Tradition." In *The Early Church*, ed. A. J. B. Higgins, 55–99. Philadelphia: Westminster.

Culpepper, R. Alan. 2005. "Designs for the Church in the Gospel Accounts of Jesus' Death." *New Testament Studies* 51: 376–92.

Dalferth, Ingolf U. 1994. *Der auferweckte Gekreuzigte: Zur Grammatik der Christologie.* Tübingen: Mohr Siebeck.

Daniélou, Jean. 1953. "Réponse à Oscar Cullmann." *Dieu Vivant* 24: 105–16.

Davies, W. D., and E. P. Sanders. 1999. "Jesus: From the Jewish Point of View." In *The Cambridge History of Judaism*, ed. W. Horbury et al. Vol. 3, *The Early Roman Period*, 618–77. Cambridge: Cambridge University Press.

Davis, Ellen F., and Richard B. Hays, eds. 2003. *The Art of Reading Scripture.* Grand Rapids: Eerdmans.

de Jonge, Marinus. 1988. *Christology in Context: The Earliest Christian Response to Jesus.* Philadelphia: Westminster.

de la Potterie, Ignace. 1988. "Interpretation of Holy Scripture in the Spirit in Which It Was Written." In *Vatican II: Assessment and Perspectives*, ed. R. Latourelle, 220–66. New York: Paulist Press.

Dias, Patrick V. 1968. *Vielfalt der Kirche in der Vielfalt der Jünger, Zeugen und Diener.* Ökumenische Forschungen 1/2. Freiburg: Herder.

———. 1974. *Kirche in der Schrift und im 2. Jahrhundert.* Handbuch der Dogmengeschichte. Freiburg: Herder.

Dodd, C. H. 1936a. *The Apostolic Preaching and Its Developments: Three Lectures with an Appendix on Eschatology and History.* London: Hodder & Stoughton.

———. 1936b. *The Present Task in New Testament Studies: An Inaugural Lecture Delivered in the Divinity School on Tuesday, 2 June, 1936.* Cambridge: Cambridge University Press.

Dreyfus, François. 1985. "Divine Condescendence (*synkatabasis*) as a Hermeneutic Principle of the Old Testament in Jewish and Christian Tradition." *Immanuel* 19: 74–86.

Dunn, James D. G. 1988. *Romans.* 2 vols. Word Biblical Commentary 38A, 38B. Dallas: Word.

———. 1989. *Christology in the Making: A New Testament Inquiry into the Origins of the Doctrine of the Incarnation.* 2nd ed. London: SCM Press.

———. 2006. *Unity and Diversity in the New Testament: An Inquiry into the Character of Earliest Christianity.* 3rd ed. London: SCM Press.

Evans, C. Stephen. 1999. "Methodological Naturalism in Historical Biblical Scholarship." In *Jesus and the Restoration of Israel: A Critical Assessment of N. T. Wright's Jesus and the Victory of God*, ed. C. C. Newman, 180–205. Downers Grove, IL: InterVarsity Press.

Fernández Marcos, Natalio. 2001. *The Septuagint in Context: Introduction to the Greek Version of the Bible.* Trans. W. G. E. Watson. Leiden: Brill.

Fitzmyer, Joseph A. 1979. "The Semitic Background of the New Testament Kyrios-Title." In *A Wandering Aramean: Collected Aramaic Essays*, 115–42. Society of Biblical Literature Monograph Series 25. Missoula, MT: Scholars Press.

———. 1982. *A Christological Catechism: New Testament Answers.* New York: Paulist Press.

Florovsky, Georges. 1962. "The Concept of Creation in Athanasius." *Studia Patristica* 6: 36–57.

Ford, David F. 1979. "Barth's Interpretation of the Bible." In *Karl Barth: Studies of His Theological Methods*, ed. S. W. Sykes, 55–87. Oxford: Clarendon Press.

Frey, Clemens. 1993. *Christliche Weltverantwortung bei Albert Schweitzer, mit Vergleichen zu Dietrich Bonhoeffer.* Albert Schweitzer Studien 4. Bern: Paul Haupt.

Frymer-Kensky, Tikva, et al. 2002. "Controversy: Jewish-Christian Dialogue: Jon D. Levenson & Critics." *Commentary* 113, no. 4: 8–21.

Geiselmann, Josef Rupert. 1962. *Die Heilige Schrift und die Tradition: Zu den neueren Kontroversen über das Verhältnis der Heiligen Schrift zu den nichtgeschriebenen Traditionen.* Quaestiones Disputatae 18. Freiburg: Herder.

Gilbert, Maurice. 2002. "Textes bibliques dont l'Église a défini le sens." In *L'autorité de l'Écriture*, ed. J.-M. Poffet, 71–94. Lectio Divina. Paris: Cerf.

Gilbertson, Michael. 2003. *God and History in the Book of Revelation: New Testament Studies in Dialogue with Pannenberg and Moltmann.* Society for New Testament Studies Monograph Series 124. Cambridge: Cambridge University Press.

Grässer, Erich. 1979. *Albert Schweitzer als Theologe.* Beiträge zur historischen Theologie 60. Tübingen: Mohr Siebeck.

———. 1984. "Albert Schweitzer und Rudolf Bultmann: Ein Beitrag zur historischen Jesusfrage." In *Rudolf Bultmanns Werk und Wirkung*, ed. B. Jaspert, 53–69. Darmstadt: Wissenschaftliche Buchgesellschaft.

———. 2003. "Das Paulusbild Albert Schweitzers." *Zeitschrift für Theologie und Kirche* 100: 187–98.

Griffiths, Paul J. 2003. "On *Dominus Iesus*: Complementarity Can Be Claimed." In *Learning from Other Faiths*, ed. H. Häring, J. M. Soskice, and F. Wilfred, 22–24. Concilium. London: SCM Press.

Guinot, Jean-Noël, ed. 1980. *Commentaire sur Isaïe.* By Theodoret, Bishop of Cyrrhus. Vol. 1. Sources chrétiennes 276. Paris: Cerf.

Guitton, Jean. 1992. *Portrait du Père Lagrange.* Paris: Robert Laffont.

Gundry, Robert H. 2005. "Hermeneutic Liberty, Theological Diversity, and Historical Occasionalism." In *The Old Is Better: New Testament Essays in Support of Traditional Interpretations*, 1–17. Wissenschaftliche Untersuchungen zum Neuen Testament 178. Tübingen: Mohr Siebeck.

Gunkel, Hermann. 2006. *Creation and Chaos in the Primeval Era and the Eschaton: A Religio-Historical Study of Genesis 1 and Revelation 12.* Trans. K. W. Whitney Jr. Biblical Resource Series. Grand Rapids: Eerdmans.

Günzler, Claus. 1996. *Albert Schweitzer: Einführung in sein Denken.* Munich: C. H. Beck.

Gzella, Holger. 2002. *Lebenszeit und Ewigkeit: Studien zur Eschatologie und Anthropologie des Septuaginta-Psalters.* Bonner biblische Beiträge 134. Berlin: Philo.

Hanhart, Robert. 1984. "Die Bedeutung der Septuaginta in neutestamentlicher Zeit." *Zeitschrift für Theologie und Kirche* 81: 395–416.

———. 1999. *Studien zur Septuaginta und zum hellenistischen Judentum.* Ed. R. G. Kratz. Forschungen zum Alten Testament 24. Tübingen: Mohr Siebeck.

———. 2002. "Introduction: Problems in the History of the LXX Text from Its Beginnings to Origen." In *The Septuagint as Christian Scripture: Its Prehistory and the Problem of Its Canon*, ed. M. Hengel, trans. M. E. Biddle, 1–17. Edinburgh: T&T Clark.

Harl, Marguerite, ed. 1986–. *La Bible d'Alexandrie.* Paris: Cerf.

Harnack, Adolf von. 1908. *The Mission and Expansion of Christianity in the First Three Centuries.* Trans. J. Moffatt. Rev. ed. 2 vols. London: Williams & Norgate; New York: G. P. Putnam's Sons.

Harrington, Daniel J. 1982. *The Light of All Nations: Essays on the Church in New Testament Research.* Good News Studies 3. Wilmington, DE: Glazier.

Harris, Harriet A., and Christopher J. Insole. 2005. "Verdicts on Analytical Philosophy of Religion." In *Faith and Philosophical Analysis: The Impact of Analytical Philosophy on the Philosophy of Religion*, ed. H. A. Harris and C. J. Insole, 1–20. Aldershot: Ashgate.

Hauerwas, Stanley, and L. Gregory Jones. 1989. "Introduction: Why Narrative?" In *Why Narrative? Readings in Narrative Theology*, ed. S. Hauerwas and L. G. Jones, 1–18. Grand Rapids: Eerdmans.

Hays, Richard B. 1989. *Echoes of Scripture in the Letters of Paul.* New Haven: Yale University Press.

———. 1996. *The Moral Vision of the New Testament: Community, Cross, New Creation; A Contemporary Introduction to New Testament Ethics.* San Francisco: HarperSanFrancisco.

Hengel, Martin, ed. 2002. *The Septuagint as Christian Scripture: Its Prehistory and the Problem of Its Canon.* Trans. M. E. Biddle. Edinburgh: T&T Clark.

Henry, Carl F. H. 1990. "Canonical Theology: An Evangelical Appraisal." *Scottish Bulletin of Evangelical Theology* 8: 76–108.

Heron, Alasdair I. C. 1981. "Homoousios with the Father." In *The Incarnation*, ed. T. F. Torrance. Edinburgh: Handsel Press.

Hick, John, ed. 1977. *The Myth of God Incarnate.* Philadelphia: Westminster.

Horbury, William. 1997. "Septuagintal and New Testament Conceptions of the Church." In *A Vision for the Church: Studies in Early Christian Ecclesiology in Honour of J. P. M. Sweet*, ed. M. Bockmuehl and M. B. Thompson, 1–17. Edinburgh: T&T Clark.

———. 2003. *Messianism among Jews and Christians: Twelve Biblical and Historical Studies*. London: T&T Clark.

Hossfeld, Frank-Lothar, and Erich Zenger. 2005. *Psalms 2: A Commentary*. Trans. L. M. Maloney. Hermeneia. Minneapolis: Fortress.

Howell, Wilbur S. 1961. *Logic and Rhetoric in England, 1500–1700*. New York: Russell & Russell.

Hübner, Hans. 1990. *Biblische Theologie des Neuen Testaments*. 3 vols. Göttingen: Vandenhoeck & Ruprecht.

Hume, David. 1962. *A Treatise of Human Nature: Being an Attempt to Introduce the Experimental Method of Reasoning into Moral Subjects*. Ed. D. G. C. Macnabb. London: Collins.

Jenson, Robert W. 2006. "On the Doctrine of Atonement." *CTI Reflections* 9: 1–13.

Jeremias, Joachim. 1969. *Jerusalem in the Time of Jesus*. Trans. F. H. Cave and C. H. Cave. 3rd ed. London: SCM Press.

Jobes, Karen H. 2006. "The Septuagint Textual Tradition in 1 Peter." In *Septuagint Research: Issues and Challenges in the Study of the Greek Jewish Scriptures*, ed. W. Kraus and R. G. Wooden, 299–322. Society of Biblical Literature Septuagint and Cognate Studies 53. Atlanta: Society of Biblical Literature.

Jobes, Karen H., and Moisés Silva. 2000. *Invitation to the Septuagint*. Grand Rapids: Baker Academic; Carlisle: Paternoster.

Jüngel, Eberhard. 1989. "Response to Josef Blank." In *Paradigm Change in Theology: A Symposium for the Future*, ed. H. Küng and D. Tracy, 297–304. New York: Crossroad.

Käsemann, Ernst. 1951. "Begründet der neutestamentliche Kanon die Einheit der Kirche?" *Evangelische Theologie* 11: 13–21.

———. 1960. "Amt und Gemeinde im Neuen Testament." In *Exegetische Versuche und Besinnungen*, vol. 1, 109–34. Göttingen: Vandenhoeck & Ruprecht.

———. 1964. "The Canon of the New Testament and the Unity of the Church." In *Essays on New Testament Themes*, 95–107. Trans. W. J. Montague. Studies in Biblical Theology 41. London: SCM Press.

———. 1968. *The Testament of Jesus: A Study of the Gospel of John in the Light of Chapter 17*. Trans. G. Krodel. New Testament Library. London: SCM Press; Philadelphia: Fortress.

———. 1969. "Unity and Multiplicity in the New Testament Doctrine of the Church." In *New Testament Questions of Today*, 252–59. Trans. W. J. Montague. New Testament Library. London: SCM Press.

————, ed. 1970. *Das Neue Testament als Kanon: Dokumentation und kritische Analyse zur gegenwärtigen Diskussion.* Göttingen: Vandenhoeck & Ruprecht.

————. 1980. *Commentary on Romans.* Trans. G. W. Bromiley. London: SCM Press.

————. 1982. *Kirchliche Konflikte.* Vol. 1. Göttingen: Vandenhoeck & Ruprecht.

————. 1998. "Theologischer Rückblick bei der akademischen Feier in der Aula der Universität Tübingen am 12. Juli 1996 aus Anlaß seines 90. Geburtstages." *Transparent* 52: 8–14.

Kasper, Walter. 1976. *Jesus the Christ.* Trans. V. Green. London: Burns & Oates; New York: Paulist Press.

————. 2006. "Mission of Bishops in the Mystery of the Church: Reflections on the Question of Ordaining Women to Episcopal Office in the Church of England." Address to the Church of England Bishops' Meeting, 5 June 2006. http://www.cofe.anglican.org/news/pr6006b.html.

Kelly, J. N. D. 1978. *Early Christian Doctrines.* Rev. ed. San Francisco: Harper & Row.

————. 2006. *Early Christian Creeds.* 3rd ed. London: Continuum.

Kelsey, David H. 1999. *Proving Doctrine: The Uses of Scripture in Modern Theology.* Harrisburg, PA: Trinity Press International.

Kierkegaard, Søren. 1985. *Philosophical Fragments, Johannes Climacus.* Ed. H. V. Hong and E. H. Hong. Kierkegaard's Writings 7. Princeton, NJ: Princeton University Press.

Kinzer, Mark. 2005. *Postmissionary Messianic Judaism: Redefining Christian Engagement with the Jewish People.* Grand Rapids: Brazos Press.

Kirchschläger, W. 1995. "Die Entwicklung von Kirche und Kirchenstruktur zur neutestamentlichen Zeit." *Aufstieg und Niedergang der römischen Welt* II.26.2: 1277–1356.

Koch, Dietrich-Alex. 1986. *Die Schrift als Zeuge des Evangeliums: Untersuchungen zur Verwendung und zum Verständnis der Schrift bei Paulus.* Beiträge zur historischen Theologie 69. Tübingen: Mohr Siebeck.

Kraus, Wolfgang. 1995. *Das Volk Gottes: Zur Grundlegung der Ekklesiologie bei Paulus.* Wissenschaftliche Untersuchungen zum Neuen Testament 85. Tübingen: Mohr Siebeck.

Kraus, Wolfgang, and Martin Karrer, eds. Forthcoming. *Septuaginta Deutsch.* Stuttgart: Deutsche Bibelgesellschaft.

Küenzlen, Heiner. 2005. "Der Heilige Geist ist ein Polemiker! Ernst Käsemann." *Offene Kirche (Württemberg)* 4, no. 1: 9. http://www.offene-kirche.de/?select=2&sub=5.

Kuhn, Thomas S. 1970. *The Structure of Scientific Revolutions*. 2nd ed. Chicago: University of Chicago Press.

Küng, Hans. 1962. "Der Frühkatholizismus im Neuen Testament als kontroverstheologisches Problem." *Theologische Quartalschrift* 142: 385–424.

———. 1964. "Der Frühkatholizismus im Neuen Testament als kontroverstheologisches Problem." In *Kirche im Konzil*, 125–55. 2nd ed. Herderbücherei 140. Freiburg: Herder.

Kuyper, Abraham. 1954. *Principles of Sacred Theology*. Grand Rapids: Eerdmans.

Lannert, Berthold. 1989. *Die Wiederentdeckung der neutestamentlichen Eschatologie durch Johannes Weiss*. Texte und Arbeiten zum neutestamentlichen Zeitalter 2. Tübingen: Francke.

Lanser, Susan Snaider. 1981. *The Narrative Act: Point of View in Prose Fiction*. Princeton: Princeton University Press.

Lash, Nicholas. 1986. "Performing the Scriptures." In *Theology on the Way to Emmaus*, 37–46. London: SCM Press.

Leibniz, Gottfried Wilhelm. 1989. "On Contingency." In *Philosophical Essays*, ed. R. Ariew and D. Garber, 28–30. Indianapolis: Hackett.

Lessing, Gotthold Ephraim. 1956. *Lessing's Theological Writings: Selections in Translation*. Ed. H. Chadwick. Library of Modern Religious Thought. London: A&C Black.

Levenson, Jon D. 1993. *The Hebrew Bible, the Old Testament, and Historical Criticism: Jews and Christians in Biblical Studies*. Louisville: Westminster/John Knox.

———. 2001. "How Not to Conduct Jewish-Christian Dialogue." *Commentary* 112, no. 12: 31–37.

———. 2004. "The Agenda of *Dabru Emet*." *Review of Rabbinic Judaism* 7: 1–26.

Lienhard, Joseph T. 1995. *The Bible, the Church, and Authority: The Canon of the Christian Bible in History and Theology*. Collegeville, MN: Liturgical Press.

Lindbeck, George A. 1984. *The Nature of Doctrine: Religion and Theology in a Postliberal Age*. Philadelphia: Westminster.

———. 2003. "The Church as Israel: Ecclesiology and Ecumenism." In *Jews and Christians: People of God*, ed. C. E. Braaten and R. W. Jenson, 78–94. Grand Rapids: Eerdmans.

Lohfink, Gerhard. 1999. *Does God Need the Church? Toward a Theology of the People of God*. Trans. L. M. Maloney. Collegeville, MN: Liturgical Press.

Loisy, Alfred. 1908. *The Gospel and the Church*. Trans. C. Home. London: Pitman.

Lowe, Malcolm. 2000. "The Critical and the Skeptical Methods in New Testament Research." *Gregorianum* 81: 692–721.

MacIntyre, Alasdair C. 1981. *After Virtue: A Study in Moral Theory*. Notre Dame, IN: University of Notre Dame Press.

———. 1988. *Whose Justice? Which Rationality?* Notre Dame, IN: University of Notre Dame Press.

Malcher, Ingo. 2003. "Folterknecht mit Hang zur heiligen Messe: Pedro Durán Sáenz soll während Argentiniens Diktatur die deutsche Studentin Elisabeth Käsemann umgebracht haben." *Die Tageszeitung*, 9 October 2003, 13. http://www.taz.de/index.php?id=archivseite&ressort=me&dig=2003/10/09/a0156.

Marshall, Bruce D. 2001. "Israel: Do Christians Worship the God of Israel?" In *Knowing the Triune God: The Work of the Spirit in the Practices of the Church*, ed. J. J. Buckley and D. S. Yeago, 231–64. Grand Rapids: Eerdmans.

Marshall, I. Howard, Kevin J. Vanhoozer, and Stanley E. Porter. 2004. *Beyond the Bible: Moving from Scripture to Theology*. Acadia Studies in Bible and Theology. Grand Rapids: Baker Academic; Milton Keynes: Paternoster.

Martens, Elmer A. 2005. "Moving from Scripture to Doctrine." *Bulletin for Biblical Research* 15: 77–103.

Matlock, R. Barry. 1996. *Unveiling the Apocalyptic Paul: Paul's Interpreters and the Rhetoric of Criticism*. Journal for the Study of the New Testament: Supplement Series 127. Sheffield: Sheffield Academic Press.

McClendon, James W., and James M. Smith. 1975. *Understanding Religious Convictions*. Notre Dame, IN: University of Notre Dame Press.

McCormack, Bruce L. 1995. *Karl Barth's Critically Realistic Dialectical Theology: Its Genesis and Development, 1909–1936*. Oxford: Clarendon Press; New York: Oxford University Press.

McDonald, James I. H. 1980. *Kerygma and Didache: The Articulation and Structure of the Earliest Christian Message*. Society for New Testament Studies Monograph Series 37. Cambridge: Cambridge University Press.

McDonald, Lee Martin, and James A. Sanders. 2002. *The Canon Debate: On the Origins and Formation of the Bible*. Peabody, MA: Hendrickson.

McGovern, Thomas J. 1999. "The Interpretation of Scripture 'in the Spirit.'" *Irish Theological Quarterly* 64: 245–60.

Meeks, Wayne A. 1972. "The Man from Heaven in Johannine Sectarianism." *Journal of Biblical Literature* 91: 44–72.

Meier, John P. 2001. "Jesus, the Twelve, and the Restoration of Israel." In *Restoration: Old Testament, Jewish, and Christian Perspectives*, ed. J. M. Scott, 365–404. Journal for the Study of Judaism: Supplement Series 72. Leiden: Brill.

Menken, Maarten J. J. 1988. "Die Form des Zitates aus Jes 6,10 in Joh 12,40: Ein Beitrag zum Schriftgebrauch des vierten Evangelisten." *Biblische Zeitschrift* 32: 189–209.

———. 2004. *Matthew's Bible: The Old Testament Text of the Evangelist.* Bibliotheca Ephemeridum Theologicarum Lovaniensium 173. Leuven: Leuven University Press.

Metzger, Bruce M. 1981. *Manuscripts of the Greek Bible: An Introduction to Greek Palaeography.* New York: Oxford University Press.

Mildenberger, Friedrich. 1991–1993. *Biblische Dogmatik: Eine biblische Theologie in dogmatischer Perspektive.* 3 vols. Stuttgart: Kohlhammer.

Millhauser, Steven. 1997. *Martin Dressler: The Tale of an American Dreamer.* New York: Vintage Books.

Minear, Paul S. 1960. *Images of the Church in the New Testament.* Philadelphia: Westminster.

Moberly, R. W. L. 2006. *Prophecy and Discernment.* Cambridge Studies in Christian Doctrine. Cambridge: Cambridge University Press.

Montagnes, Bernard. 2006. *The Story of Father Marie-Joseph Lagrange: Founder of Modern Catholic Bible Study.* Trans. B. Viviano. American ed. New York: Paulist Press.

Moule, C. F. D. 1959. *An Idiom Book of New Testament Greek.* 2nd ed. Cambridge: Cambridge University Press.

Muis, Jan. 1999. "Spricht Gott in der heiligen Schrift? Dogmatische Analyse der dreifachen Gestalt des Wortes Gottes." *Zeitschrift für dialektische Theologie* 15: 131–54.

———. 2000. "Die Rede von Gott und das Reden Gottes: Eine Würdigung der Lehre der dreifachen Gestalt des Wortes Gottes." *Zeitschrift für dialektische Theologie* 16: 59–70.

Müller, Mogens. 1996. *The First Bible of the Church: A Plea for the Septuagint.* Journal for the Study of the Old Testament: Supplement Series 206. Sheffield: Sheffield Academic Press.

Neuhaus, Richard John, ed. 1989. *Biblical Interpretation in Crisis: The Ratzinger Conference on Bible and Church.* Grand Rapids: Eerdmans.

Newman, John Henry. 1903. "Private Judgment on Scripture." In *Selected Treatises of St. Athanasius in Controversy with the Arians*, vol. 2, 247–49. London: Longmans, Green.

Noll, Mark A., and Carolyn Nystrom. 2005. *Is the Reformation Over? An Evangelical Assessment of Contemporary Roman Catholicism.* Grand Rapids: Baker Academic.

O'Donovan, Oliver. 2005. *The Ways of Judgment: The Bampton Lectures, 2003.* Grand Rapids: Eerdmans.

O'Keefe, John J., and Russell R. Reno. 2005. *Sanctified Vision: An Introduction to Early Christian Interpretation of the Bible*. Baltimore: Johns Hopkins University Press.

Ollenburger, Ben C. 2006. "Pursuing the Truth of Scripture: Reflections on Wolterstorff's *Divine Discourse*." In *But Is It All True? The Bible and the Question of Truth*, ed. A. G. Padgett and P. R. Keifert, 44–65. Grand Rapids: Eerdmans.

Pannenberg, Wolfhart. 1977. *Jesus, God and Man*. Trans. L. L. Wilkins and D. A. Priebe. 2nd ed. Philadelphia: Westminster.

Pao, David W. 2002. *Acts and the Isaianic New Exodus*. Grand Rapids: Baker Academic.

Parris, Matthew. 2007. "Shout Your Doubt Out Loud, My Fellow Unbelievers." *The Times*, 21 April 2007, 19.

Pelikan, Jaroslav. 1971. *The Christian Tradition: A History of the Development of Doctrine*. Vol. 1, *The Emergence of the Catholic Tradition (100–600)*. Chicago: University of Chicago Press.

Peterson, Eugene H. 2005. *Christ Plays in Ten Thousand Places: A Conversation in Spiritual Theology*. Grand Rapids: Eerdmans.

Pietersma, Albert. 2006. "Exegesis in the Septuagint: Possibilities and Limits (The Psalter as a Case in Point)." In *Septuagint Research: Issues and Challenges in the Study of the Greek Jewish Scriptures*, ed. W. Kraus and R. G. Wooden, 33–45. Society of Biblical Literature Septuagint and Cognate Studies 53. Atlanta: Society of Biblical Literature.

Pietersma, Albert, and Benjamin G. Wright, eds. 2007. *A New English Translation of the Septuagint*. New York: Oxford University Press.

Pincoffs, Edmund L. 1986. *Quandaries and Virtues: Against Reductivism in Ethics*. Lawrence: University Press of Kansas.

Plantinga, Alvin. 2000. *Warranted Christian Belief*. New York: Oxford University Press.

Pleitner, Henning. 1992. *Das Ende der liberalen Hermeneutik am Beispiel Albert Schweitzers*. Texte und Arbeiten zum neutestamentlichen Zeitalter 5. Tübingen: Francke.

Pontifical Biblical Commission. 2001. *L'interpretazione della Bibbia nella Chiesa: Atti del Simposio promosso dalla Congregazione per la dottrina della fede; Roma, settembre 1999*. Atti e documenti 11. Vatican City: Libreria editrice vaticana.

———. 2002. *The Jewish People and Their Sacred Scriptures in the Christian Bible*. Vatican Documents. Vatican City: Libreria editrice vaticana.

Pratt, Mary Louise. 1977. *Toward a Speech Act Theory of Literary Discourse*. Bloomington: Indiana University Press.

Radner, Ephraim. 2004. *Hope among the Fragments: The Broken Church and Its Engagement of Scripture.* Grand Rapids: Brazos Press.

Rae, Murray. 1997. *Kierkegaard's Vision of the Incarnation: By Faith Transformed.* Oxford: Clarendon Press; New York: Oxford University Press.

———. 2007. "Texts in Context: Scripture and the Divine Economy." *Journal of Theological Interpretation* 1: 1–21.

Rahner, Karl, and Joseph Ratzinger [Benedict XVI]. 1966. *Revelation and Tradition.* Trans. W. J. O'Hara. Quaestiones disputatae 17. New York: Herder and Herder.

Räisänen, Heikki. 1990. *Beyond New Testament Theology: A Story and a Programme.* London: SCM Press; Philadelphia: Trinity Press International.

———. 2000. *Beyond New Testament Theology: A Story and a Programme.* 2nd ed. London: SCM Press.

Ratzinger, Joseph [Benedict XVI]. 1998. *Milestones: Memoirs, 1927–1977.* Trans. E. Leiva-Merikakis. San Francisco: Ignatius Press.

Rausch, Thomas P. 1988. "Unity and Diversity in New Testament Ecclesiology: Twenty-Five Years after Käsemann and Brown." *Irish Theological Quarterly* 54: 131–39.

Reicke, Bo Ivar. 1946. *The Jewish "Damascus Documents" and the New Testament.* Symbolae Biblicae Upsalienses 6. Uppsala: Wretmans.

Reno, Russell R. 2002. *In the Ruins of the Church: Sustaining Faith in an Age of Diminished Christianity.* Grand Rapids: Brazos Press.

Ricœur, Paul. 1974. *The Conflict of Interpretations.* Northwestern University Studies in Phenomenology & Existential Philosophy. Evanston, IL: Northwestern University Press.

———. 1976. *Interpretation Theory: Discourse and the Surplus of Meaning.* Fort Worth: Texas Christian University Press.

———. 1977. "Toward a Hermeneutic of the Idea of Revelation." *Harvard Theological Review* 70: 1–37.

———. 1980. *Essays on Biblical Interpretation.* Ed. L. S. Mudge. Philadelphia: Fortress.

———. 1995. *Figuring the Sacred: Religion, Narrative, and Imagination.* Ed. M. I. Wallace. Trans. D. Pellauer. Minneapolis: Augsburg Fortress.

Rodger, Patrick Campbell, and Lucas Vischer, eds. 1964. *The Fourth World Conference on Faith and Order: Montreal 1963.* Faith and Order Paper 42. London: SCM Press.

Rösel, Martin. 2006. "Towards a 'Theology of the Septuagint.'" In *Septuagint Research: Issues and Challenges in the Study of the Greek Jewish Scriptures,* ed. W. Kraus and R. G. Wooden, 239–52. Society of Biblical Literature Septuagint and Cognate Studies 53. Atlanta: Society of Biblical Literature.

Rössler, Andreas. 1990. "Albert Schweitzer und das freie Christentum." In *Albert Schweitzer heute: Brennpunkte seines Denkens*, ed. C. Günzler, 227–64. Beiträge zur Albert-Schweitzer-Forschung 1. Tübingen: Katzmann.

Ryken, Leland. 2005. "Literary Criticism." In *Dictionary for Theological Interpretation of the Bible*, ed. Kevin J. Vanhoozer, 457–60. London: SPCK; Grand Rapids: Baker Academic.

Ryle, Gilbert. 1949. *The Concept of Mind*. London: Hutchinson.

Sanders, James A. 1972. *Torah and Canon*. Philadelphia: Fortress.

———. 1984. *Canon and Community: A Guide to Canonical Criticism*. Guides to Biblical Scholarship. Philadelphia: Fortress.

———. 1987. *From Sacred Story to Sacred Text: Canon as Paradigm*. Philadelphia: Fortress.

Schaper, Joachim. 1995. *Eschatology in the Greek Psalter*. Wissenschaftliche Untersuchungen zum Neuen Testament 2/76. Tübingen: Mohr Siebeck.

———. 2006. "Messianic Intertextuality in the Greek Bible." In *The Septuagint and Messianism*, ed. M. A. Knibb, 371–80. Bibliotheca Ephemeridum Theologicarum Lovaniensium 195. Leuven: Leuven University Press.

Schenker, Adrian, ed. 2003. *The Earliest Text of the Hebrew Bible: The Relationship between the Masoretic Text and the Hebrew Base of the Septuagint Reconsidered*. Society of Biblical Literature Septuagint and Cognate Studies 52. Atlanta: Society of Biblical Literature.

Schnackenburg, Rudolf. 1961. *Die Kirche im Neuen Testament: Ihre Wirklichkeit und theologische Deutung, ihr Wesen und Geheimnis*. Quaestiones disputatae 14. Freiburg: Herder.

———. 1965. *The Church in the New Testament*. Trans. W. J. O'Hara. New York: Herder and Herder.

Schulik, Ulrich. 1990. "Zwischen Eschatologie und Ethik: Aspekte der Reich-Gottes-Vorstellung Albert Schweitzers." In *Albert Schweitzer heute: Brennpunkte seines Denkens*, ed. C. Günzler, 265–78. Beiträge zur Albert-Schweitzer-Forschung 1. Tübingen: Katzmann.

Schunack, G. 1992. "δοκιμάζω." *Exegetisches Wörterbuch zum Neuen Testament* 1: 825–29.

Schweitzer, Albert. 1901. *Das Messianitäts- und Leidensgeheimnis: Eine Skizze des Lebens Jesu*. Tübingen: Mohr.

———. 1906. *Von Reimarus zu Wrede: Eine Geschichte der Leben-Jesu-Forschung*. Tübingen: Mohr.

———. 1913. *Geschichte der Leben-Jesu-Forschung: Zweite, neu bearbeitete und vermehrte Auflage des Werkes "Von Reimarus zu Wrede."* Tübingen: Mohr.

———. 1914. *The Mystery of the Kingdom of God: The Secret of Jesus' Messiahship and Passion*. Trans. W. Lowrie. London: A&C Black.

———. 1930. *Die Mystik des Apostels Paulus*. Tübingen: Mohr.

———. 1933. *Out of My Life and Thought: An Autobiography*. Trans. C. T. Campion. New York: Holt.

———. 1951. *Christianity and the Religions of the World: Lectures Delivered at the Selly Oak Colleges, Birmingham, February 1922*. Trans. J. Powers. New York: Macmillan.

———. 1955. *The Mysticism of Paul the Apostle*. Trans. W. Montgomery. New York: Macmillan.

———. 1973. *Ausgewählte Werke in fünf Bänden*. Ed. R. Grabs. 2nd ed. 5 vols. Berlin: Union-Verlag.

———. 1987. *Leben, Werk und Denken, 1905–1965: Mitgeteilt in seinen Briefen*. Ed. H. W. Bähr. Heidelberg: L. Schneider.

———. 1988. *Gespräche über das Neue Testament*. Ed. W. Döbertin. Munich: Bechtle.

———. 1995. *Reich Gottes und Christentum*. Ed. U. Luz, U. Neuenschwander, and J. Zürcher. Werke aus dem Nachlaß. Munich: C. H. Beck.

———. 2000. *The Quest of the Historical Jesus*. Ed. J. Bowden. Trans. W. Montgomery et al. 1st complete ed. London: SCM Press.

———. 2001. *Predigten, 1898–1948*. Ed. R. Brüllmann and E. Grässer. Werke aus dem Nachlaß. Munich: C. H. Beck.

———. 2003. *Vorträge, Vorlesungen, Aufsätze*. Ed. C. Günzler, U. Luz, and J. Zürcher. Werke aus dem Nachlaß. Munich: C. H. Beck.

Schweitzer, Albert, and Helene Bresslau. 1992. *Die Jahre vor Lambarene: Briefe 1902–1912*. Ed. R. Schweitzer Miller and G. Woytt. Munich: C. H. Beck.

Seitz, Christopher R. 2001. "Two Testaments and the Failure of One Tradition History." In *Figured Out: Typology and Providence in Christian Scripture*, 35–47. Louisville: Westminster/John Knox.

———. 2006. "The Canonical Approach and Theological Interpretation." In *Canon and Biblical Interpretation*, ed. C. G. Bartholomew, 58–110. Scripture and Hermeneutics Series 7. Grand Rapids: Zondervan.

Shapland, C. R. B., ed. 1951. *The Letters of Saint Athanasius Concerning the Holy Spirit*. New York: Philosophical Library.

Silva, Moisés. 2001. "The Greek Psalter in Paul's Letters: A Textual Study." In *The Old Greek Psalter: Studies in Honour of Albert Pietersma*, ed. R. J. V. Hiebert, C. E. Cox, and P. J. Gentry, 277–88. Journal for the Study of the Old Testament: Supplement Series 332. Sheffield: Sheffield Academic Press.

Smith, D. Moody. 1999. *John*. Abingdon New Testament Commentaries. Nashville: Abingdon.

Söding, Thomas. 2006. "Der biblische Kanon." *Zeitschrift für katholische Theologie* 128: 407–30.

Soulen, R. Kendall. 2003. "Hallowed Be Thy Name! The Tetragrammaton and the Name of the Trinity." In *Jews and Christians: People of God*, ed. C. E. Braaten and R. W. Jenson, 14–40. Grand Rapids: Eerdmans.

Sternberg, Meir. 1985. *The Poetics of Biblical Narrative: Ideological Literature and the Drama of Reading.* Bloomington: Indiana University Press.

Sutherland, Stewart R. 1989. "The Concept of Revelation." In *Religion, Reason and the Self: Essays in Honour of Hywel D. Lewis*, ed. S. R. Sutherland and T. A. Roberts, 35–45. Cardiff, UK: University of Wales Press.

Swete, Henry Barclay. 1900. *An Introduction to the Old Testament in Greek.* Cambridge: Cambridge University Press.

Swetnam, James. 1981. "Jesus as Logos in Heb 4:12–13." *Biblica* 62: 214–24.

Sykes, Stephen W. 1979. "Barth on the Centre of Theology." In *Karl Barth: Studies of His Theological Methods*, ed. S. W. Sykes, 17–54. Oxford: Clarendon Press.

Thiering, Barbara. 1981. "*Mebaqqer* and *Episkopos* in the Light of the Temple Scroll." *Journal of Biblical Literature* 100: 59–74.

Thiselton, Anthony C. 1980. *The Two Horizons: New Testament Hermeneutics and Philosophical Description with Special Reference to Heidegger, Bultmann, Gadamer, and Wittgenstein.* Grand Rapids: Eerdmans.

Tilley, Terrence W. 2000. *The Evils of Theodicy.* Eugene, OR: Wipf & Stock.

Torrance, T. F. 1975. "Athanasius: A Study in the Foundations of Classical Theology." In *Theology in Reconciliation: Essays Towards Evangelical and Catholic Unity in East and West*, 215–66. London: Chapman.

Tov, Emanuel. 2005. "The Evaluation of the Greek Scripture Translations in Rabbinic Sources." In *Interpreting Translation: Studies on the LXX and Ezekiel in Honour of Johan Lust*, ed. F. García Martínez and M. Vervenne, 385–99. Bibliotheca Ephemeridum Theologicarum Lovaniensium 192. Leuven: Leuven University Press.

Treier, Daniel J. 2006. *Virtue and the Voice of God: Toward Theology as Wisdom.* Grand Rapids: Eerdmans.

Tuckett, Christopher M. 2007. Review of *Moving Beyond New Testament Theology? Essays in Conversation with Heikki Räisänen*, ed. T. Penner and C. Vander Stichele. *Review of Biblical Literature* 01. http://bookreviews.org/pdf/5287_5567.pdf.

Ulrich, Eugene C. 1992. "The Canonical Process, Textual Criticism, and Latter Stages in the Composition of the Bible." In *Sha'arei Talmon: Studies in the Bible, Qumran, and the Ancient Near East Presented to Shemaryahu Talmon*, ed. M. Fishbane and E. Tov, 267–91. Winona Lake, IN: Eisenbrauns.

————. 1999. *The Dead Sea Scrolls and the Origins of the Bible*. Studies in the Dead Sea Scrolls and Related Literature. Grand Rapids: Eerdmans; Leiden: Brill.

Ulrichs, Karl Friedrich. 2001. "Käsemann, Ernst." *Biographisch-Bibliographisches Kirchenlexikon* 18: 775–78. http://bbkl.de/k/kaesemann_e.shtml.

van der Kooij, Arie. 1997. "Zur Theologie des Jesajabuches in der Septuaginta." In *Theologische Probleme der Septuaginta und der hellenistischen Hermeneutik*, ed. H. G. Reventlow, 9–25. Veröffentlichungen der Wissenschaftlichen Gesellschaft für Theologie 11. Gütersloh: Chr. Kaiser, Gütersloher Verlagshaus.

Vanhoozer, Kevin J. 2002. *First Theology: God, Scripture and Hermeneutics*. Downers Grove, IL: InterVarsity Press; Leicester: Apollos.

————, ed. 2005a. *Dictionary for Theological Interpretation of the Bible*. London: SPCK; Grand Rapids: Baker Academic.

————. 2005b. *The Drama of Doctrine: A Canonical-Linguistic Approach to Christian Theology*. Louisville: Westminster/John Knox.

Viviano, Benedict T. 2007. *Matthew and His World: The Gospel of the Open Jewish Christians; Studies in Biblical Theology*. Novum Testamentum et Orbis Antiquus 61. Fribourg: Academic Press; Göttingen: Vandenhoeck & Ruprecht.

von Balthasar, Hans Urs. 1986. *Prayer*. Trans. G. Harrison. San Francisco: Ignatius Press.

Wagner, J. Ross. 2002. *Heralds of the Good News: Isaiah and Paul "in Concert" in the Letter to the Romans*. Supplements to Novum Testamentum 101. Leiden: Brill.

————. 2007. "Identifying 'Updated' Prophecies in Old Greek (OG) Isaiah: Isaiah 8:11–16 as a Test Case." *Journal of Biblical Literature* 126: 251–69.

Wannenwetsch, Bernd. 1998. "'Intrinsically Evil Acts'; or: Why Euthanasia and Abortion Cannot Be Justified." In *Ecumenical Ventures in Ethics: Protestants Engage Pope John Paul II's Moral Encyclicals*, ed. R. Hütter and T. Dieter, 185–215. Grand Rapids: Eerdmans.

————. 2000. "Plurale Sinnlichkeit: Glaubenswahrnehmung im Zeitalter virtueller Realität." *Neue Zeitschrift für systematische Theologie und Religionsphilosophie* 42: 299–315.

————. 2002. "Members of One Another: Charis, Ministry and Representation; A Politico-Ecclesial Reading of Romans 12." In *A Royal Priesthood? The Use of the Bible Ethically and Politically; A Dialogue with Oliver O'Donovan*, ed. C. G. Bartholomew et al. 196–220. Scripture and Hermeneutics Series 3. Grand Rapids: Zondervan.

————. 2004. *Political Worship: Ethics for Christian Citizens*. Oxford Studies in Theological Ethics. Oxford: Oxford University Press.

———. 2005. "'Responsible Living' or 'Responsible Self'? Bonhoefferian Reflections on a Vexed Moral Notion." *Studies in Christian Ethics* 18: 125–40.

———. Forthcoming. "Die ethische Dimension der Liturgie." In *Neues Handbuch der Liturgiewissenschaft*. Ed. R. Messner et al. Regensburg: Pustet.

Watson, Francis. 1997. *Text and Truth: Redefining Biblical Theology*. Grand Rapids: Eerdmans.

———. 2006. "Authors, Readers, Hermeneutics." In *Reading Scripture with the Church: Toward a Hermeneutic for Theological Interpretation*, ed. A. K. M. Adam et al., 119–24. Grand Rapids: Baker Academic.

Weaver, Walter P. 1999. *The Historical Jesus in the Twentieth Century: 1900–1950*. Harrisburg, PA: Trinity Press International.

Webb, William J. 2001. *Slaves, Women & Homosexuals: Exploring the Hermeneutics of Cultural Analysis*. Downers Grove, IL: InterVarsity Press.

Webster, John. 2001. "The Dogmatic Location of the Canon." In *Word and Church: Essays in Christian Dogmatics*, 9–46. Edinburgh: T&T Clark.

———. 2003. *Holy Scripture: A Dogmatic Sketch*. Current Issues in Theology 1. Cambridge: Cambridge University Press.

———. 2007. "Resurrection and Scripture." In *Christology and Scripture: Interdisciplinary Perspectives*, ed. A. T. Lincoln and A. Paddison, 138–55. Library of New Testament Studies 348. London: T&T Clark.

Werner, Martin. 1941. *Die Entstehung des christlichen Dogmas: Problemgeschichtlich dargestellt*. Bern and Leipzig: Paul Haupt.

———. 1957. *The Formation of Christian Dogma: An Historical Study of Its Problem*. Trans. S. G. F. Brandon. London: A&C Black.

Westcott, Brooke Foss. 1895. *An Introduction to the Study of the Gospels*. 8th ed. London and New York: Macmillan.

Wigoder, Geoffrey, ed. 1988. *Jewish-Christian Relations Since the Second World War*. Sherman Studies of Judaism in Modern Times. Manchester, UK: Manchester University Press.

Wilk, Florian. 1998. *Die Bedeutung des Jesajabuches für Paulus*. Forschungen zur Religion und Literatur des Alten und Neuen Testaments 179. Göttingen: Vandenhoeck & Ruprecht.

———. 2006. "The Letters of Paul as Witnesses to and for the Septuagint Text." In *Septuagint Research: Issues and Challenges in the Study of the Greek Jewish Scriptures*, ed. W. Kraus and R. G. Wooden, 253–71. Society of Biblical Literature Septuagint and Cognate Studies 53. Atlanta: Society of Biblical Literature.

Wilken, Robert L. 1997. "In Dominico Eloquio: Learning the Lord's Style of Language." *Communio* 24: 846–66.

Williams, Rowan. 1979a. "Barth on the Triune God." In *Karl Barth: Studies of His Theological Methods*, ed. S. W. Sykes, 147–93. Oxford: Clarendon Press.

———. 1979b. *The Wound of Knowledge: Christian Spirituality from the New Testament to St. John of the Cross*. London: Darton, Longman & Todd.

———. 1980. "The Via Negativa and the Foundations of Theology: An Introduction to the Thought of V. N. Lossky." In *New Studies in Theology 1*, ed. S. W. Sykes and D. Holmes, 95–118. London: Duckworth.

———. 1982. *Resurrection: Interpreting the Easter Gospel*. London: Darton, Longman & Todd.

———. 1983. "What Is Catholic Orthodoxy?" In *Essays Catholic and Radical: A Jubilee Group Symposium for the 150th Anniversary of the Beginning of the Oxford Movement 1833–1983*, ed. R. Williams and K. Leech, 11–25. London: Bowerdean Press.

———. 1987. *Arius: Heresy and Tradition*. London: Darton, Longman & Todd.

———. 1988. "The Suspicion of Suspicion: Wittgenstein and Bonhoeffer." In *The Grammar of the Heart: New Essays in Moral Philosophy and Theology*, ed. R. H. Bell, 36–53. San Francisco: Harper & Row.

———. 1989a. "Does It Make Sense to Speak of Pre-Nicene Orthodoxy?" In *The Making of Orthodoxy: Essays in Honour of Henry Chadwick*, ed. R. Williams, 1–23. Cambridge: Cambridge University Press.

———. 1989b. "Language, Reality and Desire in Augustine's *De Doctrina*." *Literature and Theology* 3: 138–50.

———. 1991. "The Literal Sense of Scripture." *Modern Theology* 7: 121–34.

———. 1993. "Doctrinal Criticism: Some Questions." In *The Making and Remaking of Christian Doctrine: Essays in Honour of Maurice Wiles*, ed. S. Coakley and D. A. Pailin, 239–64. Oxford: Clarendon Press.

———. 1995a. "Reading the Bible." In *A Ray of Darkness: Sermons and Reflections*, 134–37. Cambridge: Cowley Publications.

———. 1995b. "Theology and the Churches." In *Michael Ramsey as Theologian*, ed. R. Gill and L. Kendall, 9–28. London: Darton, Longman & Todd.

———. 2000a. "Beginning with the Incarnation." In *On Christian Theology*, 79–92. Challenges in Contemporary Theology. Oxford: Blackwell.

———. 2000b. "Between the Cherubim: The Empty Tomb and the Empty Throne." In *On Christian Theology*, 183–96. Challenges in Contemporary Theology. Oxford: Blackwell.

———. 2000c. "The Discipline of Scripture." In *On Christian Theology*, 44–58. Challenges in Contemporary Theology. Oxford: Blackwell.

————. 2000d. "The Judgement of the World." In *On Christian Theology*, 29–43. Challenges in Contemporary Theology. Oxford: Blackwell.

————. 2000e. *Lost Icons: Reflections on Cultural Bereavement*. Edinburgh: T&T Clark.

————. 2000f. "The Nature of a Sacrament." In *On Christian Theology*, 197–208. Challenges in Contemporary Theology. Oxford: Blackwell.

————. 2000g. *On Christian Theology*. Challenges in Contemporary Theology. Oxford: Blackwell.

————. 2000h. "Theological Integrity." In *On Christian Theology*, 3–15. Challenges in Contemporary Theology. Oxford: Blackwell.

————. 2000i. "Trinity and Pluralism." In *On Christian Theology*, 167–80. Challenges in Contemporary Theology. Oxford: Blackwell.

————. 2000j. "Trinity and Revelation." In *On Christian Theology*, 131–47. Challenges in Contemporary Theology. Oxford: Blackwell.

————. 2000k. "The Unity of Christian Truth." In *On Christian Theology*, 16–28. Challenges in Contemporary Theology. Oxford: Blackwell.

————. 2000l. "Word and Spirit." In *On Christian Theology*, 107–27. Challenges in Contemporary Theology. Oxford: Blackwell.

————. 2001a. "A History of Faith in Jesus." In *The Cambridge Companion to Jesus*, ed. M. Bockmuehl, 220–36. Cambridge: Cambridge University Press.

————. 2001b. "The Unity of the Church and the Unity of the Bible: An Analogy." *Internationale kirchliche Zeitschrift* 91: 5–21.

————. 2003a. *The Dwelling of the Light: Praying with Icons of Christ*. Norwich: Canterbury Press.

————. 2003b. "Historical Criticism and Sacred Text." In *Reading Texts, Seeking Wisdom: Scripture and Theology*, ed. G. Stanton and D. F. Ford, 216–28. London: SCM Press.

————. 2004. *Anglican Identities*. London: Darton, Longman & Todd.

————. 2005a. *Grace and Necessity: Reflections on Art and Love*. Clark Lectures 2005. Harrisburg, PA: Morehouse.

————. 2005b. *Why Study the Past? The Quest for the Historical Church*. Grand Rapids: Eerdmans; London: Darton, Longman & Todd.

————. 2007. "The Bible Today: Reading and Hearing." Archbishop's Larkin Stuart Lecture, Toronto, 16 April 2007. http://www.archbishopofcanterbury.org/sermons_speeches/070416.htm.

Willitts, Joel. 2007a. *Matthew's Messianic Shepherd-King: In Search of "The Lost Sheep of the House of Israel."* Beihefte zur Zeitschrift für die neutestamentliche Wissenschaft 147. Berlin: de Gruyter.

———. 2007b. "Matthew's Messianic Shepherd-King: In Search of 'the Lost Sheep of the House of Israel.'" *HTS Theological Studies* 63: 365–82.

Wittgenstein, Ludwig. 1974. *Philosophical Investigations*. Trans. G. E. M. Anscombe. Oxford: Blackwell.

———. 2001. *On Certainty*. Ed. G. E. M. Anscombe and G. H. von Wright. San Francisco and London: HarperCollins.

Wolterstorff, Nicholas. 2004. "The Unity Behind the Canon." In *One Scripture or Many? Canon from Biblical, Theological and Philosophical Perspectives*, ed. C. Helmer and C. Landmesser, 217–32. Oxford: Oxford University Press.

———. 2006. "True Words." In *But Is It All True? The Bible and the Question of Truth*, ed. A. G. Padgett and P. R. Keifert, 34–43. Grand Rapids: Eerdmans.

Wright, N. T. 2005. *Scripture and the Authority of God*. London: SPCK.

Wytzes, Jelle. 1957. "The Twofold Way I: Platonic Influences in the Work of Clement of Alexandria." *Vigiliae Christianae* 11: 226–45.

———. 1960. "The Twofold Way II: Platonic Influences in the Work of Clement of Alexandria." *Vigiliae Christianae* 14: 129–53.

Young, Frances M. 1990. *The Art of Performance: Towards a Theology of Holy Scripture*. London: Darton, Longman & Todd.

Ziegler, Joseph, ed. 1975. *Eusebius Werke IX: Der Jesajakommentar*. Berlin: Akademie-Verlag.

Zizioulas, Ioannis. 2001. "Uniformity, Diversity and the Unity of the Church." *Internationale Kirchliche Zeitschrift* 91: 44–59.

Scripture Index

Subject Index

Abraham, 70, 169–70
accountability, 179, 187–88, 190
Adam, 171
Aejmelaeus, Anneli, 21
agnōsis, 151–52
Amadeus (Shaffer), 60
analogy, and Scripture, 119
Anglican Identities, 112
Anglicanism, 30, 110, 112
anti-Semitism, 57, 139
Apocrypha, 132, 139
apophasis, 108–9
apostles, 42, 196–97. *See also* discourse: apostolic
apostolicity, 34, 41–43
Apostolic Preaching and Its Developments, The (Dodd), 192
Aquila, 20
Arians, 131, 151
Aristotle, 137, 178, 181, 183n8
art, 114
Athanasius, 11, 150–54, 157, 161–63
atonement, doctrine of, 62–64, 66, 70
Augustine, 18n3, 28, 123
Austen, Jane, 201
authority
  of Christ, 166
  of the church, 166–67
  as from God, 165
  of Scripture, 166–67, 174–75

Balthasar, Hans Urs von, 159–60
baptism, Paul on, 190
Barmen Declaration, 97
Barnes, Michael, 58
Barr, James, 23, 148
Barsam, Ara Paul, 88
Barthélemy, Dominique, 22n30
Barth, Karl, 75, 82, 89, 157–58, 159n46, 163, 198n29, 203
  on command, 11, 169, 171–72
  on Scripture, 10, 92–103, 135, 197, 200
Bauckham, Richard, 196
Bauer, Walter, 38
Baur, F. C., 135
Bea, Augustin, 126
Benedict, 136
Berkhof, Hendrikus, 92n1, 101n29
Bible. See Scripture
Biblical Commission, Pontifical, 11, 135–39
Biblical Theology of the Old and New Testaments (Childs), 23
Biblische Dogmatik (Mildenberger), 95
Billot, Louis, 128–29

Bockmuehl, Markus, 8, 121, 146, 158–59, 199
Boegner, Alfred, 78
Bousset, W., 85
Braybrooke, Marcus, 47–48
Bresslau, Helene, 78
Brown, Raymond, 8, 31, 33–34, 38–39, 41
Bultmann, Rudolf, 51n16, 82, 85n45, 86, 134, 157, 161, 192, 200

canon, 35, 38–39, 49, 121, 135, 145
  development of the, 22–25, 28, 60–61, 130, 167, 203
Cappadocians, 107
Catherine of Siena, 136
Catholic theology, normativity of Scripture in, 10–11, 125–40
Chapman, Stephen, 196n19, 197n25
Childs, Brevard, 8, 17–18, 23–25, 27, 119, 195n17, 197, 203
chōrismos, 151, 153–54
Christ. *See* Jesus
Christ-mysticism, 82, 86–87, 89
Christology in the Making (Dunn), 146
Chrysostom, John, 127

236